Introduction to Civil Litigation

Introduction to Civil Litigation

CILEX | Education

Disclaimer

ISBN: 978-1-911713-20-3
E-ISBN: 978-1-911713-21-0

First paperback edition 2024

Layout by codemantra U.S. LLC

British Library Cataloguing in Publications Data
A catalogue record for this book is available from the British Library

Printed by CILEX Education in the United Kingdom.
CILEX Education
2nd Floor,
The Pinnacle,
Midsummer Boulevard,
Milton Keynes,
MK9 1BP

Cover image: CHUNYIP WONG/iStock

www.cilex.org.uk

CILEX titles are printed by Mimeo, who are very proud to be a part of the Woodland Trust's Woodland Carbon Capture Scheme via Premier Paper. Mimeo partner with Woodland Carbon because 100% of the money they give is spent on planting deciduous trees in the UK. Papers are from sustainable sources and waste is recycled. Mimeo continue to use only Forest Stewardship Council accredited paper in their printed items.

Guide to the Book

This course book contains a range of features which have been developed to help support your learning and reinforce your understanding. The guided tour below explains how to use these features to get the most from your study.

Activity

If you are working within a law firm, do some research into the different methods of communication used within your firm. If some methods mentioned in this chapter are not used in your firm, do some further research into those methods and think about the benefits and risks associated with these methods.

If you are not currently working within a law firm, or your firm already uses all of these methods, choose a couple of communication methods to do further research into and think about the benefits and risks associated with these methods.

Activities

In some chapters you are presented with activities which engage you with the content and help you to develop research skills, explore topics in more depth and consolidate your knowledge.

1.9 Summary

(1) The concept of a contract requires that the parties be in agreement, with a valid offer and acceptance. In addition, something of value must have been contributed, known as consideration. The parties must intend to create a legal relationship.

(2) An agreement requires that there be an offer by the offeror accepted by the offeree.

(3) Offers must be distinguished from invitations to treat which are simply invitations to someone else to make an offer.

(4) The offeror can withdraw the offer at any time before acceptance.

(5) Acceptance must normally be communicated by the offeror to the offeree, although this is not required for unilateral offers. Under the postal rule offers are accepted at the time they are posted.

(6) There are two types of consideration. Executed consideration is where performance of consideration is at the time the agreement is made. Executory consideration is a promise to do something in the future.

(7) Consideration must normally not be past, unless the doctrine of implied *assumpsit* applies. It need not be adequate but must be sufficient, that is, it must have at least some economic value.

(8) An intention to create legal relations will be presumed by the courts in commercial or business agreement. The courts will presume that there is no such intention in family or social agreements. Both presumptions can be rebutted.

(9) To be a valid express term, the other party must have had actual or reasonable notice of its content. The term may be oral, in writing or by way of a notice.

(10) An implied term may be read into a contract by way of a statute, for example the **Consumer Rights Act 2015**, implied by custom or implied by the courts.

Chapter Summaries

At the end of each chapter the key points are summarised, allowing you to reinforce your understanding before moving on to study the next topic. The summaries can also be used for quick revision.

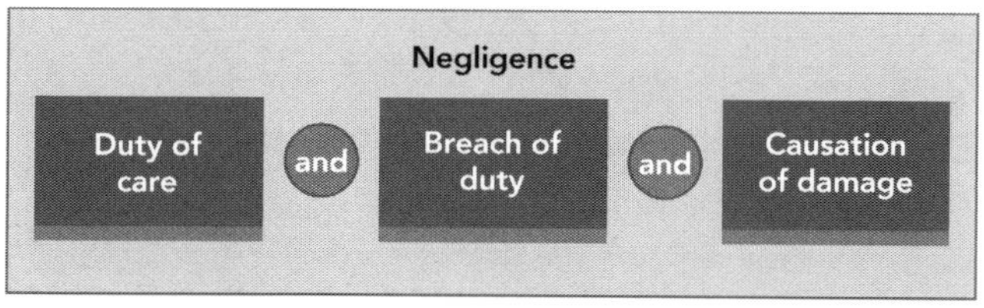

Figures

Figures have been designed to help define complex issues and clearly illustrate key concepts.

Scenario

Northern Security Services Ltd (NSS) issues proceedings against Music Events Ltd (MEL). The claim form and the particulars of claim are deemed served on Wednesday 4 May 2022, so MEL has 14 days (i.e. until close of business on Wednesday 18 May) to file either an acknowledgment of service or a defence.

- If MEL does nothing, NSS may apply for judgment in default on Thursday 19 May.
- If MEL files an acknowledgement of service form within this period, it has a further 14 days in which to file its defence, that is, until Wednesday 1 June. However, if it fails to do so by that date, NSS may apply for judgment in default on Thursday 2 June.

Scenarios

Fictional scenarios run through some chapters, helping to provide context to the material.

Contracts for the sale of goods		
Implied term:	**Business-to-consumer contracts:**	**Business-to-business contracts:**
Satisfactory quality	**s9 CRA 2015**	**s14(2) SGA 1979**
Fitness for purpose	**s10 CRA 2015**	**s14(3) SGA 1979**
Description	**s11 CRA 2015**	**s13 SGA 1979**
Contracts for the supply of services		
Implied term:	**Business-to-consumer contracts:**	**Business-to-business contracts:**
Reasonable care and skill	**s49 CRA 2015**	**s13 SGSA 1982**
Reasonable charge	**s51 CRA 2015**	**s15 SGSA 1982**
Reasonable time	**s52 CRA 2015**	**s14 SGSA 1982**

Tables

Tables have been designed to present information clearly.

Reflective question

Can you think of any other internal clients that exist within your own legal environment and how their role contributes to the overall service delivery?

Reflective Questions

All course books contain reflective questions, positioned at key points throughout the text. These allow you to take time to reflect on what you have learnt, ensure that you have understood the concepts, and contextualise your learning.

Example

In ***Collins v Secretary of State for Business, Innovation and Skills [2014]*** the claimant was diagnosed with lung cancer in 2002 and successfully treated. He attributed the illness to exposure to asbestos between 1947 and 1967 but only instructed solicitors to pursue a claim in 2012, aged 90, after seeing a newspaper advertisement.

The court considered that a reasonable person would have enquired about the possible causes of the cancer by mid-2003. This meant that limitation had expired in 2006, three years later. The proceedings issued in 2012 were six years out of time. In this instance, the court refused to exercise its discretion to extend the primary limitation period as the claim had low value and the litigation costs would be disproportionately high.

Examples

Examples provide you with an opportunity to contextualise what you have learnt and explore legal concepts in a real world setting.

Contents

Table of Cases

Table of Statutes

Table of Secondary Legislation

UK Statutory Instruments

Non-statutory material

Section

CHAPTER 1

Introduction to Contract Law

1.1 Introduction

The foundations of contract law have been established by the common law. Many of the cases are very old, but the principles established are still relevant today. The main aim of contract law, from the 19th century to the present day, is to ensure consistency and certainty, particularly in business transactions.

In this chapter we will introduce you to the following:

- the concept of contract;
- the requirement of agreement, including offer and acceptance;
- the requirement of consideration in a contract;
- the intention to create legal relations;
- the contents of a contract, including express, implied terms, conditions, warranties and innominate terms;
- the methods by which a contract can be discharged including performance and breach;
- the remedies for breach of contract: damages and equitable remedies.

1.2 The concept of contract

A contract is an agreement that gives rise to obligations and which is enforceable and recognised by law. Contracts arise in a range of situations, but all must contain the essentials of a valid contract in order to be recognised by the courts.

The basic essentials of a valid contract are:

- the parties must be in **agreement**, which traditionally means that one of them has made an offer which the other has accepted;
- the parties must have each contributed something of value to the bargain, known as **consideration**; and
- the parties must intend to create a legal relationship.

1.3 Agreement

A contract cannot exist unless the parties are in **agreement**. Although this is the usual starting point to establish that a contract exists, agreement alone is not proof of the existence of a valid contract; consideration and intention to create legal relations must also be found.

1.3.1 The fact of agreement

In order to determine whether there is an agreement, the courts focus on whether there has been an **offer** from one party which is **accepted** by the other (***Gibson v Manchester City Council [1979]***). Together, offer and acceptance are usually referred to as the **factual indicators** of an **agreement**.

1.3.2 Offer

An offer is an expression of willingness to contract on certain terms on which the **offeror** (person making the offer) is prepared to be legally bound following acceptance.

Offers must be **certain** or the whole contract could fail (***Scammell and Nephew Ltd v Ouston [1941]***).

(1) **Offers in unilateral and bilateral contracts**

Offers can arise as part of unilateral or bilateral contracts. A **unilateral** contract results from a unilateral offer, for example, a poster offering a reward for return of a lost cat, which is one-sided; the offeror does not know if it will be taken up.

A **bilateral** contract is one where the parties exchange promises and both have obligations.

(2) **Making an offer**

Offers can be made **orally**, **in writing** or even **by conduct**. They can be made to one person, a group or the "world in general" (***Carlill v Carbolic Smoke Ball Co Ltd [1893]***).

To be a valid offer, the **offeree** (person to whom the offer is made) must have **knowledge** of the offer, which means that the offer must have been **communicated** (***Taylor v Laird [1856]***).

(3) **Offer distinguished from invitation to treat**

An invitation to treat is not an offer and cannot be accepted; it is merely a request to others to make an offer. The display of goods for sale on supermarket shelves is an example of an invitation to treat – see ***Pharmaceutical Society of Great Britain v Boots Cash Chemists [1953]***.

(4) **Terminating the offer**

Once an offer has been made, it can be brought to an end by the following events, as well as by acceptance.

(5) **Revocation**

The offeror can withdraw the offer before it has been accepted (***Payne v Cave [1789]***).

(6) **Rejection**

To reject an offer is to end it. If an offer is answered by another offer, known as a counter-offer, the first offer is automatically terminated (***Hyde v Wrench [1840]***).

(7) **Lapse of time**

An offer lapses at the end of a specified period or, if no period is specified, after a "reasonable time" (***Ramsgate Victoria Hotel v Montefiore [1866]***).

1.3.3 Acceptance

Acceptance is the **final** and **unqualified** (or **unconditional**) assent by the offeree to **all the terms** of the offer: the acceptance must therefore mirror the offer (the "mirror image" rule. Acceptance can be expressed **orally**, **in writing**, or can be inferred from **conduct**.

A response which introduces new terms is not an acceptance but a counter-offer (***Hyde v Wrench [1840]***). Further, an acceptance that is "subject to contract" is not unconditional and does not result in a binding contract being formed.

(1) **Communication of acceptance**

The general rule regarding acceptance is that it must be communicated to the offeror (***Entores v Miles Far East Corporation [1955]***).

(2) **Exceptions to the general rule on communication**

There is no need for communication of acceptance in order to form an agreement in the following situations.

Acceptance by conduct

This can be done, for example, when the offeree supplies or receives goods on terms proposed by the offeror (***Brogden v Metropolitan Railway [1877]***).

Acceptance of unilateral offers

In these cases, there is no need to communicate acceptance to the offeror. Instead, the offeror is deemed to have waived the need for communication of acceptance. Acceptance is instead completed by **performing the requested act** (e.g. returning the lost pet) and then **notifying the offeror** that performance is complete (***Carlill v Carbolic Smoke Ball Co Ltd [1893]***).

Acceptance by post

Under the postal rule, established in ***Adams v Lindsell [1818]*** and applied in ***Household Fire Insurance v Grant [1879]***, acceptance occurs on posting, even if the acceptance is never delivered.

(3) **Acceptance by modern methods of communication**

Whether or not the acceptance was received during office hours appears to be of crucial importance; the development of a body of case law relating to contracts made by email seems to confirm this (***Greenclose v National Westminster Bank [2014]*** and ***Goel and Another v Grant and Another [2017]***).

reg 11 Electronic Commerce (EC Directive) Regulations 2002 confirms that an electronic contract is formed when the customer is able to access the acknowledgement of receipt sent from the supplier/seller. This rule applies to contracts made over the internet, as opposed to by email.

1.4 Consideration

Consideration is an essential element of any contract not made by deed. It is sometimes defined as "the price paid for a person's promise".

There are two types of valid consideration:

- **executed consideration** – performance of the consideration at the time of making the agreement; and
- **executory consideration** – a promise to do something in the future.

1.4.1 The rules governing consideration

Four main rules are used to determine the validity of consideration.

(1) **Consideration must move from the promisee**

This simply means that only a person who has provided consideration can sue on the contract (***Dunlop Pneumatic Tyre Co Ltd v Selfridge & Co Ltd [1915]***).

(2) **Consideration must not be past**

If the act of consideration has already been completed prior to the agreement being entered into, then it is past consideration and not legally enforceable (***Re McArdle [1951]***).

There is an exception to this rule, known as the doctrine of implied *assumpsit* – where there has always been an implication that payment is expected; a later promise or agreement to that effect will be enforceable (***Lampleigh v Braithwait [1615]***).

(3) **Consideration need not be adequate**

To be valid, consideration does not need to be of equal or market value to the thing given in exchange (***Chappell & Co v Nestlé Co Ltd [1960]***).

(4) **Consideration must be sufficient**

Anything which is recognised by law as having some value will be sufficient for consideration (***Thomas v Thomas [1842]***). This includes items of very little, if any, economic value (***Ward v Byham [1956]***).

1.5 Intention to create legal relations

The courts use **rebuttable presumptions** to determine whether parties to an agreement have an intention to be legally bound, due to the practical difficulties in determining a person's actual intention. A rebuttable presumption is an initial assumption that can be overturned by evidence to the contrary.

In **social and domestic agreements**, there is a presumption that there was no intention to be legally bound (***Balfour v Balfour [1919]***).

In **commercial or business agreements**, there is a presumption that the parties did intend their agreement to be legally binding (***Edmonds v Lawson [2000]***).

1.6 The contents of a contract

Examining the contents of a contract helps to establish what the parties are contractually obliged to do.

1.6.1 Basic terminology

It is important to identify the terms of a contract.

A **contractual term** (or **clause**), which is a statement forming part of the contract, must be distinguished from **mere puffs** and **representations**. Mere puffs have no legal effect. Representations, whilst forming no part of the contract, could (if false) give the injured party rights to sue for misrepresentation.

Note that terms of a contract may be **express** or **implied**. An express term is one that has been clearly stated by the parties, either orally or in writing. An implied term is one that has not been stated.

1.6.2 Express terms in contracts

To be a valid express term of a contract, it must be shown that the claimant has had **notice** of that term. Most cases relating to notice concern **exclusion clauses**, which are terms attempting to restrict or remove a party's liability in the event of a contractual breach.

Where the party signs a written contract, they are deemed to be bound by all terms contained in that document, whether or not it has actually been read (***L'Estrange v F Graucob Ltd [1934]***).

Express terms can be incorporated into oral contracts through **actual notice**, which means that the party actually knew about the term at the time of making the contract (***Olley v Marlborough Court Hotel [1949]***).

Where there is no actual notice of the term, **reasonable notice** may be found. This can be established where there is evidence that reasonable steps have been taken to bring the term to the attention of the party (***Parker v South Eastern Railway Company [1877]***).

1.6.3 Implied terms

An **implied term** is read into the contract by statute, by custom or by the courts.

(1) **Terms implied by statute**

Examples of terms implied by statute can be found in the **Consumer Rights Act 2015** (**CRA 2015**).

CRA 2015 applies to all **business-to-consumer contracts** – made between a *"consumer"* and a *"trader"* – including in particular, **goods contracts**, which can be sales contracts, contracts for the transfer of goods, and contracts for hire/hire-purchase. The following terms are implied into all such contracts:

- that goods sold in the course of a business are of satisfactory quality (**s9 CRA 2015**). Satisfactory quality means that goods must be of **the standard that a reasonable person would regard as satisfactory**;
- that goods sold in the course of business are **fit for any particular purpose made known to the seller (s10 CRA 2015)**;
- that the goods will **correspond with any description** given by the seller **(s11(1) CRA 2015)**.

CRA 2015 also implies terms into **services contracts** made in a **business-to-consumer** context. Three of the key terms are that the supplier of the service will:

- use **reasonable care and skill** in carrying out the service (**s49**);
- only request payment of a **reasonable price** for the service, unless a fixed price has been agreed as an express term of the contract (**s51**); and
- perform the service within a **reasonable time**, unless a fixed time for performance has been agreed as an express term of the contract (**s52**).

CRA 2015 has also introduced statutory rights and remedies relating to "digital content". This provides equivalent protection for intangible digital goods (such as downloaded apps, books, films, music and games), whether paid for or supplied free with paid for content (**s33**), as already exists for tangible goods. The relevant sections of the **CRA 2015** are:

- satisfactory quality (**s34**);
- fitness for a particular purpose (**s35**); and
- description (**s36**).

When contracts have been made in a **business-to-business** context, similar implied terms apply under the **Sale of Goods Act 1979** (**SGA 1979**) and the **Supply of Goods and Services Act 1982** as set out below:

Contracts for the sale of goods		
Implied term:	**Business-to-consumer contracts:**	**Business-to-business contracts:**
Satisfactory quality	**s9 CRA 2015**	**s14(2) SGA 1979**
Fitness for purpose	**s10 CRA 2015**	**s14(3) SGA 1979**
Description	**s11 CRA 2015**	**s13 SGA 1979**
Contracts for the supply of services		
Implied term:	**Business-to-consumer contracts:**	**Business-to-business contracts:**
Reasonable care and skill	**s49 CRA 2015**	**s13 SGSA 1982**
Reasonable charge	**s51 CRA 2015**	**s15 SGSA 1982**
Reasonable time	**s52 CRA 2015**	**s14 SGSA 1982**

(2) **Terms implied by custom**

It is rare today for a term to be implied by custom but an example can be found in ***Hutton v Warren [1836]***.

(3) **Terms implied by the courts**

The courts will imply a term into a contract when this has been previously established by case law. These are known as terms **implied by law** (***Liverpool City Council v Irwin [1976]***). They may imply a term into a contract where it is required to make the contract "workable" under the "business efficacy test".

1.6.4 Conditions, warranties and innominate terms

When considering the importance of a contractual term, conditions and warranties need to be distinguished.

(1) A **condition** is a term of the contract that goes to its very root. A breach of a condition will allow the innocent party to **terminate** (or repudiate) the contract and/or sue for **damages**.

(2) A **warranty** is a term of the contract which is less fundamental and does not discharge the contract. A breach of warranty entitles the innocent party **only** to bring an action for **damages**; there is **no** right to terminate the contract.

Terms which are not clearly defined as one or the other are called **innominate terms**. The seriousness of the **effect** of a breach will determine how the courts will treat them (***Hong Kong Fir Shipping Co Ltd v Kawasaki Kisen Kaisha Ltd [1962]***).

1.7 Breach of contract

Breach occurs when one party fails to discharge the contract as agreed. It gives rise to a claim in damages for the injured party and may also permit them to bring the contract to an end.

The available remedy depends upon whether the term breached amounts to a condition or a warranty (see **1.6.4**): compare ***Poussard v Spiers and Pond [1876]*** with ***Bettini v Gye [1876]***.

1.8 Remedies for breach of contract

We will now examine the consequences of a breach of contract. The main remedy in contract law is damages, but other potential remedies may also be available.

1.8.1 Damages

Damages are a money payment made by the party in breach to the other party and are the usual remedy in situations of contractual breach. Damages are a common law remedy, assessed by the courts, and are available to successful claimants as of right.

(1) **The contractual measure of damages**

The aim of damages in contract law is to put the injured party in the position they would have been in had the contract been performed (***Farley v Skinner [2001]***).

Very low amounts of damages may be paid, in different situations. **Nominal** damages are awarded where there has been a breach but no real losses as a result. Where the court considers that, although bringing the case was technically correct, the claimant has been wasting everyone's time, **contemptuous** damages will be awarded.

(2) **Main heads of damages**

Pecuniary damages compensate financial losses. The **loss of bargain/expectation loss** approach to calculating pecuniary damages involves putting the claimant in the position they would have been in had the contract been performed, which means that the court compensates for the cost of **replacement**. In sale of goods cases, the **market price rule** is followed.

The alternative approach for calculating pecuniary damages considers **reliance loss** (sometimes called **consequential loss**) where damages are based on the cost incurred by the claimant as a result of their reliance on the defendant performing their contractual obligations (***Anglia Television Ltd v Reed [1972]***).

Non-pecuniary damages, can be awarded if the object of the contract is to provide pleasure, relaxation, peace of mind or freedom from distress (***Jarvis v Swan Tours [1973]***).

(3) **Claiming damages**

To succeed in a damages claim, the claimant must show four things.

First, they must show that there was a **breach** of contract.

Second, they must show that the breach **caused** the loss complained of.

Third, they must show that the loss was not too **remote** from the breach (***Hadley v Baxendale [1854]***).

This means that the defendant is only liable for damages which:

- a **reasonable person** would have anticipated as being a likely (or **reasonably foreseeable**) result of the breach; or
- the defendant had been **specifically warned** about by the claimant.

Fourth, the claimant must show that they have **mitigated** (minimised) their losses; they will not be compensated for those losses which the court considers that they could have avoided. Importantly, they must show that they have acted reasonably.

1.8.2 Equitable remedies

For situations when the common law remedy of damages is not adequate, several equitable remedies have been developed. Unlike damages, equitable remedies are only available at the discretion of the court.

A decree of **specific performance** is a court order compelling the performance of the contract, for example, to complete the sale of land. It will not be granted where damages would be an adequate remedy. This order will also be refused if it would require constant supervision by the court or it relates to a contract for personal services.

An **injunction** is a court order instructing someone to refrain from an action. It is an equitable remedy which is available only at the discretion of the court.

1.9 Summary

(1) The concept of a contract requires that the parties be in agreement, with a valid offer and acceptance. In addition, something of value must have been contributed, known as consideration. The parties must intend to create a legal relationship.

(2) An agreement requires that there be an offer by the offeror accepted by the offeree.

(3) Offers must be distinguished from invitations to treat which are simply invitations to someone else to make an offer.

(4) The offeror can withdraw the offer at any time before acceptance.

(5) Acceptance must normally be communicated by the offeror to the offeree, although this is not required for unilateral offers. Under the postal rule, offers are accepted at the time they are posted.

(6) There are two types of consideration. Executed consideration is where performance of consideration is at the time the agreement is made. Executory consideration is a promise to do something in the future.

(7) Consideration must normally not be past, unless the doctrine of implied *assumpsit* applies. It need not be adequate but must be sufficient, that is, it must have at least some economic value.

(8) An intention to create legal relations will be presumed by the courts in commercial or business agreement. The courts will presume that there is no such intention in family or social agreements. Both presumptions can be rebutted.

(9) To be a valid express term, the other party must have had actual or reasonable notice of its content. The term may be oral, in writing or by way of a notice.

(10) An implied term may be read into a contract by way of a statute, for example the **Consumer Rights Act 2015**, implied by custom or implied by the courts.

(11) Conditions are terms which go to the heart of the contract allowing the innocent party to terminate the contract and claim damages.

(12) Warranties are less fundamental terms, breach of which allows the innocent party to claim damages only.

(13) Innominate terms allow the courts to decide whether damages are sufficient or whether termination of the contract should apply based on the effect of the breach on the innocent party.

(14) Breach of contract will give the injured party the right to claim damages and, in some cases, terminate the contract. The availability of termination will depend on whether the term was a condition, warranty or innominate term.

(15) Damages are a monetary remedy and are intended to put the claimant in the position they would have been in had the contract been performed.

(16) The claimant must show that the loss was not too remote. In other words, a reasonable person must have anticipated that the damage would be likely in the event of the breach or the defendant must have been specifically warned about the damage by the claimant.

(17) Equitable remedies include specific performance, where the defendant is ordered to carry out some action, and injunctions, where the defendant is ordered to stop carrying out an action.

CHAPTER 2

Introduction to the Law of Tort

2.1 Introduction

A tort is a civil wrong.

English law imposes a duty on everyone to respect the legal rights of others. If this duty is breached, the law of tort allows the injured party to sue the tortfeasor for damages. The person committing the tort is called the "tortfeasor".

In this chapter we will cover:

- capacity to sue and be sued in the tort of negligence;
- the three elements of the tort of negligence;
- the duty of care, including the ***Caparo v Dickman [1990]*** test and the modern "formulation";
- the significance of public policy in relation to the duty of care;
- how psychological/psychiatric harm is dealt with in negligence;
- breach of duty of care, including the reasonable person and the concept of reasonable foreseeability;
- causation in fact and in law;
- damages, including special damages, general damages and damages payable on death.

2.2 Capacity in tort

The general rule is that all natural or legal persons may sue or be sued in the tort of negligence, but it is not normally possible to sue:

- the King;
- judges and witnesses in court;
- mentally incapacitated people; or
- unincorporated associations, except trade unions.

Legal actions on behalf of children must be brought by a **litigation friend**.

2.3 The elements of the tort of negligence

Negligence is a fault-based tort, and three crucial elements must first be proved in order for a claim of negligence to succeed in court. These are summarised in the diagram and explained in the text below.

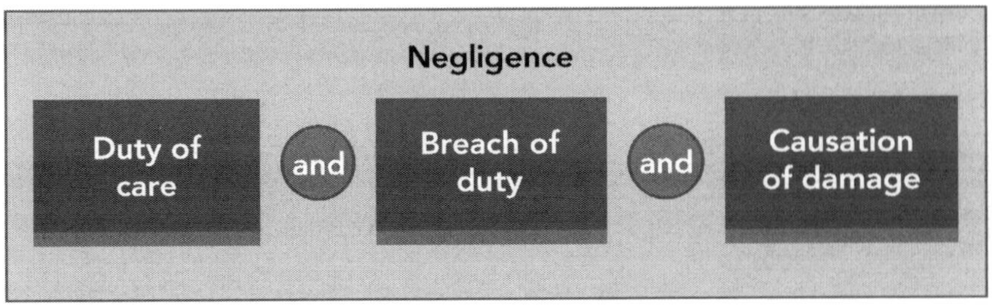

- **Did D owe C a duty of care?**

  In some specific situations, it is established that people owe a duty of care to others, for example, road users and pedestrians. In many circumstances, however, legal rules must be used to decide whether a duty of care is owed.

- **Did D breach the duty of care?**

  A person breaches a duty if they fail to act as a reasonable person in those circumstances would have acted. This is an impersonal, objective standard.

- **Did D's breach of duty cause C to suffer loss or damage?**

  The damage caused must be of a type that the law recognises as being worthy of compensation, such as personal injury or damage to property. The standard of proof, as in all civil matters, is the balance of probabilities.

2.4 The duty of care

The first step in establishing a claim in negligence is determining whether a duty of care exists.

Important cases in this area are:

- ***Donoghue v Stevenson [1932]***, which established the "neighbour" test; and
- ***Caparo Industries plc v Dickman [1990]***, which established what was up until recently called the three-stage test for establishing a duty in a novel situation not covered by precedent. However, the word "test" has now been replaced by the word "formulation" following important decisions by the Supreme Court in ***Michael and Others (FC) (Appellants) v The Chief Constable of South Wales Police and Another (Respondents) [2015]*** and especially ***Robinson v Chief Constable of West Yorkshire Police [2018]***. Both cases make clear that ***Caparo*** was never intended as a test, and that the question of duty always falls to be decided on an incremental basis.

2.4.1 The neighbour test

The definition of "**neighbours**" provided by Lord Atkin in **Donoghue v Stevenson** is: "persons who are so closely and directly affected by my act that I ought reasonably to have them in contemplation as being so affected when I am directing my mind to the acts or omissions which are called in question".

This case was important because it created a new legal relationship between manufacturers and consumers, and because it opened the way for the tort of negligence to be expanded to meet new situations.

2.4.2 Requirements of a duty of care

A duty of care can exist only if there is an existing duty of care in case law or, in a new situation, if three conditions are met.

(1) **Existing situations**

In most circumstances, it will be easy to determine whether there is a duty of care, because the duty will have been established in the existing law – for example, it is well known that road users owe other road users a duty not to cause them injury.

(2) **New situations**

It used to be thought by most lawyers and academics that in the rare circumstances when a claimant is making a claim outside situations covered by existing duties of care, the court would apply the three-stage test from ***Caparo Industries plc v Dickman*** to determine whether a duty of care exists.

Caparo stated that the questions to be asked were:

- Would a reasonable person have foreseen that there was a risk that the claimant might be injured or harmed by the defendant's acts or omissions?
- Was there sufficient proximity between the claimant and the defendant?
- Is it "fair, just and reasonable" on public policy grounds to impose a duty of care?

The Supreme Court has now made clear in ***Michael and Others (FC) (Appellants) v The Chief Constable of South Wales Police and Another (Respondents) [2015]*** and especially ***Robinson v Chief Constable of West Yorkshire Police [2018]*** that for truly novel situations, where there is no precedent (and this is rare), the courts will consider the closest analogies in the existing law. The courts will weigh up the reasons for and against imposing a duty, to decide whether it would be just and reasonable for a duty to be imposed. They may well have the ***Caparo*** "formulation" in mind when doing this, but ***Caparo*** should not be seen as a test in and of itself.

2.4.3 The role of public policy

Public policy is an important consideration in negligence. **s1 Compensation Act 2006** provides that courts should consider the wider policy implications of their decisions to impose liability on someone.

Considerations relating to public policy can be broadly grouped under three headings: statutory authorities, "opening the floodgates" and rescuers.

(1) **Statutory authorities**

The basic position is that the courts are reluctant to impose on public authorities any liability towards individuals, as in ***Hill v Chief Constable of West Yorkshire [1988]***. ***Robinson v Chief Constable of West Yorkshire [2018]*** makes clear that the rules pertaining to statutory authorities are in reality no different from the rules pertaining to private individuals, namely that a duty will generally not be imposed for an omission unless the defendant caused the dangerous situation or assumed responsibility for the claimant.

(2) **"Opening the floodgates"**

The courts have been very reluctant to award damages to claimants in cases where they fear that the case could "open the floodgates" to similar claims. This applies particularly in the area of psychological harm.

(3) **Rescuers**

The general rules in relation to rescuers (that is, where rescuers are the claimants and are injured in the course of their rescue) are that:

- a duty of care may be imposed if a **reasonable person** in the rescuer's position would have **felt obliged to assist**; but
- **no** duty of care will be imposed if the rescuer's intervention is regarded as **unjustifiable and unnecessary interference**.

2.4.4 Psychological/psychiatric harm

Nervous shock

Nervous shock, or psychiatric harm, occurs where C suffers a clinically recognised psychological injury caused by being involved in, or witnessing, a sudden traumatic event caused by D's negligence.

The law has never recognised a duty to a mere bystander (***Bourhill v Young [1942]***), but has accepted that damages should be paid to those whose nervous shock is a reasonably foreseeable consequence of D's negligence (***McLoughlin v O'Brian [1982]***).

The rules relating to a claim for pure psychiatric harm are set out in the following diagram and discussed in the text that follows it.

Pure psychiatric harm

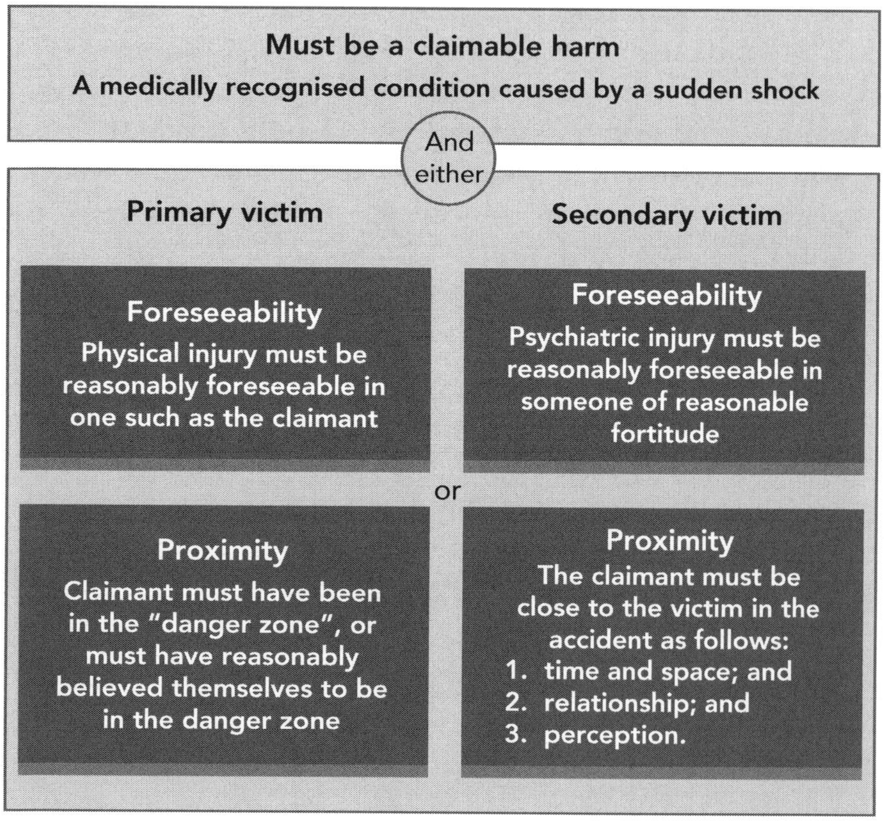

Claimants may be:

- **primary victims**: people within the potential range of physical harm or in the "danger zone". C must show that D could reasonably foresee some kind of "personal injury" – if so, the courts will not distinguish between physical and psychiatric injury, so D will be liable to C for all C's physical and/or psychological injuries;
- **secondary victims**: people outside the potential range of physical harm who suffer medically recognised psychiatric harm brought about by sudden shock through what they see. Such claimants must meet the requirements established in ***Alcock v Chief Constable of South Yorkshire [1992]***:
    - psychiatric harm must be reasonably foreseeable in a person of ordinary fortitude in the claimant's position;
    - there must be a **close relationship of love and affection** between C and the victim;
    - C must be physically close to the accident; and
    - C must actually see or hear the accident or immediate aftermath with their **own senses**.

2.5 Breach of duty of care

The breach of a duty of care is the second major element of the tort of negligence. This is looked at in two parts: first, the court will determine the **standard of care** expected of D. Second, it will look to see whether D has fallen below or breached that standard.

The original test was expressed in ***Blyth v Birmingham Waterworks Co [1856]***: *"Negligence is the omission to do something which a reasonable man, guided upon those considerations which ordinarily regulate the conduct of human affairs, would do, or doing something which a prudent and reasonable man would not do."* Nowadays, the courts will usually judge D's conduct against that of a **reasonable person**.

There are three important things about the test:

- it is **objective**;
- a person can only be **unintentionally** negligent (negligent being legal speak for careless);
- it is **not negligent** to fail to protect against a **very unlikely event**.

2.5.1 The reasonable person

Because the test is objective, no allowance is made for an individual's lack of knowledge or experience. This can lead to hardship for Ds whose expertise is below that of a reasonable person, as occurred with the defendant learner driver in ***Nettleship v Weston [1971]***. The rationale is that the standard attaches to the task or activity and not to the person carrying out that task or activity.

It is accepted that children do not have the same awareness of risk as adults, as shown by ***Orchard v Lee [2009]***, where a 13-year-old boy was not held liable for injuries he caused to a school lunchtime supervisor. In other words, where children are concerned, the court will usually be prepared to consider the standard subjectively and not objectively.

Professional people must achieve *"the standard of the ordinary skilled man exercising and professing to have that special skill"* (***Bolam v Friern Hospital Management Committee [1957]***). The test for medical professionals, such as doctors, is now that they must *"act in accordance with the standards of reasonably competent medical men at the time"* (***Bolam***), provided that the prevailing standard of professional skill is logically supported (***Bolitho v City and Hackney Health Authority [1997]***). This test is applied even if a doctor appears to have made an error of clinical judgment, provided that other reasonable doctors in the same situation might have done the same (***Whitehouse v Jordan [1981]***). In other words, a one-off error might be seen as just that, rather than as negligence.

2.5.2 Reasonable foreseeability of harm

A person is not required to possess expertise beyond that of others in their own profession **at the time of the event**. In ***Roe v Minister of Health [1954]*** D was not liable for a patient's paralysis caused by a then-unknown danger in the usual method of storing spinal anaesthetic.

The more likely the risk of harm, the more foreseeable it is deemed to be, so damage caused by a cricket ball going over a 17-foot-high fence was not worthy of compensation (***Bolton v Stone [1951]***). This assessment of the probability of an event is sometimes called the "magnitude of risk" test.

2.5.3 Other factors in determining breach

There are three other factors that the court may consider when assessing whether D has breached their duty.

(1) **The vulnerability of the claimant**

In circumstances where the risk of serious injury is higher, more caution is required, as in ***Paris v Stepney Borough Council [1951]***, where a one-eyed workman was injured in his remaining eye and went blind.

(2) **The importance of D's objective**

If D is engaged in a socially desirable activity when the tort occurs, it may be justifiable for them to take an abnormal risk: in ***Watt v Hertfordshire County Council [1954]*** a fireman was injured on the way to an accident. This approach is reinforced by the **Social Action, Responsibility and Heroism Act 2015**.

(3) **The cost of avoiding the harm**

It is not necessary for D to go to extreme lengths to protect against a risk. In ***Latimer v AEC [1953]*** the court accepted that it was not necessary to close a factory for a day after an exceptional flood. D merely has to show that they acted as a reasonably competent person carrying out that particular task or activity.

2.5.4 Proof of breach

In order to win their case, C bears the burden of proving, on the **balance of probabilities**, that D breached the duty of care.

s11(1) Civil Evidence Act 1968 permits a criminal conviction to be used as evidence in a negligence case.

2.6 Causation

Even if it is proved that D owed C a duty of care and that D breached that duty, C must still prove that D's breach caused their loss. There must be a **causal link** between the breach and a loss that the law regards as worthy of compensation.

It is necessary to establish causation both **in fact** and **in law**.

Causation in **fact** requires that, on the **balance of probabilities**, the harm would not have occurred "**but for**" the breach; causation in **law** requires that the harm is **not too remote** from the negligent act.

This final requirement for a claim in negligence is summarised in the following diagram.

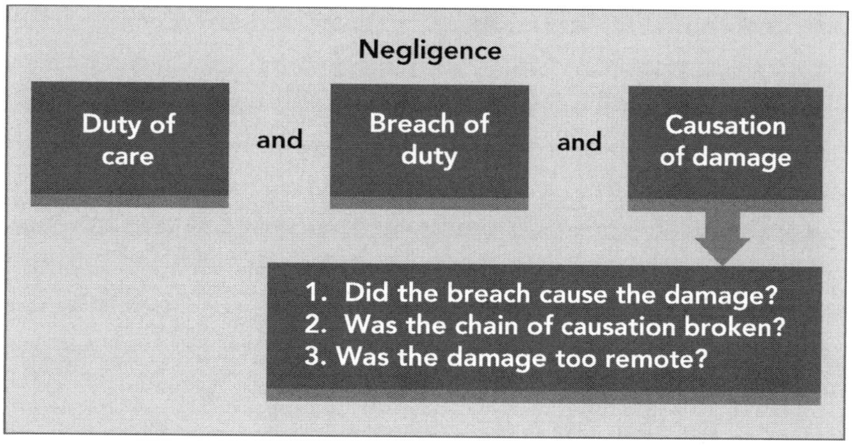

2.6.1 Causation in fact

(1) **The "but for" test**

- **The principle**

To decide whether D's breach caused C's loss as a matter of fact, the normal test is the "**but for**" test: the court has to determine whether the loss or damage would have been suffered but for (that is, had it not been for) D's breach.

In ***Barnett v Chelsea and Kensington Hospital Management Committee [1969]*** a night watchman who died from arsenic poisoning after being negligently sent away by the hospital would have died even if he had been given appropriate medical care, so the breach did not, in fact, cause his death.

- **The "but for" test in practice**

In ***Page v Smith (No. 2) [1996]*** it was held to be more likely than not that the negligently caused car accident had triggered the recurrence of C's chronic fatigue syndrome.

(2) **Multiple potential causes of harm**

The rules on causation can become problematic when there are multiple potential causes of harm. In certain circumstances the "but for" test for causation is deviated from.

- **Where the injury is "indivisible"**

A key issue is whether it is possible to divide the injury into portions, each clearly caused by different events (including different tortfeasors). Under normal circumstances, if it is not possible to divide up an injury, the "but for" test applies.

- **Where the injury is "divisible"**

The situation is more complex when there are multiple causes of harm because the traditional "but for" test would produce unjust results if the defendant's breach has only contributed to (rather than being the sole cause of) the loss suffered by the claimant. The traditional judicial approach was to adapt the test for causation in fact in such circumstances so that a defendant would be liable to a claimant if the defendant's tortious act has made a **material contribution** to the risk that the claimant will suffer harm, or a material contribution to the harm itself.

- **Where it is scientifically impossible to determine who is at fault**

Material increase in risk

Sometimes – and only in the case of some industrial diseases – it is impossible to determine which of a series of possible causes is, in fact, the cause of the damage sustained by the defendant.

In ***McGhee v National Coal Board [1972]*** the claimant cleaned brick kilns and then cycled home. There were no washing facilities at his workplace, and both his work and the cycling caused him to sweat while brick-dust and dirt were on his skin. He suffered from dermatitis (a skin disease) and sued the defendant. Four of the five Law Lords held that, although other factors were also involved, the lack of washing facilities at his workplace had "materially increased the risk of" injury, so the defendant was liable to him. The fifth Law Lord held that the claimant had established, on the balance of probabilities, that the lack of washing facilities had caused the disease.

The practical effect of the material increase in risk test is to remove the requirement that the claimant prove, **on the balance of probabilities**, that the defendant did in fact cause the harm claimed. This is only possible where policy considerations demand it, in the interests of justice.

Mesothelioma cases – special rules apply

Mesothelioma is a fatal lung disease caused by exposure to fibres or dust from asbestos. The disease can take 30 years to develop, and it is thought that the risk of contracting it increases with the level of exposure to asbestos.

It is impossible to quantify which of a number of possible exposures to asbestos causes mesothelioma. As a result, **s3 Compensation Act 2006** provides that any person who **materially increased the risk** of C's exposure to asbestos is **jointly and severally** responsible for the damage, meaning that any one employer can be liable for the **whole of the damages** due to C.

(3) **Successive causes of harm**

There are special rules for situations where there are successive causes of injury: compare the outcomes of ***Baker v Willoughby [1969]*** (where C's second negligently caused injury did not reduce the compensation to which he was entitled as a result of the first negligently caused injury) and ***Jobling v Associated Dairies [1982]*** (where C's subsequent development of a disease reduced D's liability for an injury that had made C incapable of working). In ***Rahman v Arearose [2000]*** Laws LJ said that ***Baker*** and ***Jobling*** can be reconciled by considering the damage for which the tortfeasor "*should justly be held responsible*". This seems to mean that a further deliberate or negligent act does not end the original tortfeasor's liability (***Baker***) whereas a natural disease does end it (***Jobling***).

(4) ***Novus actus interveniens***

It is often the case that a series of linked events ultimately leads to loss or damage. In such cases, the court has to decide whether the later events are sufficient to **break the chain of causation** between D's original negligence and C's loss or damage.

An event which breaks the chain of causation is a ***novus actus interveniens***, which means "new intervening act". There are three types of *novus actus interveniens*.

(a) An act of **nature**, such as storm damage. If such events are reasonably foreseeable, they will not break the chain of causation.

(b) An act of a **third party**. This will not constitute a *novus actus interveniens* if a court considers that it was reasonably foreseeable, or a natural response to D's original negligence.

(c) An act of the **claimant**. The test is whether the claimant acted entirely unreasonably. If so, their actions will break the chain of causation.

2.6.2 Causation in law

Even if causation in fact is established, D's act will not be held to be the legal cause of C's injury if the damage is **too remote** from the negligence.

The decision in ***Overseas Tankship (UK) Ltd v Morts Dock and Engineering Co (The "Wagon Mound") [1961]*** provides the rule governing what sort of damage is recoverable. If the **kind of damage** caused is **reasonably foreseeable** from the acts of D, then D is liable. This may be so even if the **extent of the damage** and the **precise manner of its occurrence** are **not** reasonably foreseeable.

A rule which exists in some tension with the law of remoteness of damage is the "**thin skull**" **rule**. This provides that, whatever C's personal idiosyncrasies and injuries, D must **take his victim as he finds him**. This means that Ds can be liable for much greater harm than would have been expected from a negligent act, although the principle applies **only** if the **type of injury** (but not its extent) was **foreseeable**.

In ***Smith v Leech Brain [1962]*** C's husband died from cancer following a burn that he suffered at work. His predisposition to cancer was not known, but D had to take the victim as D found him, so was liable for his injury, illness and death.

2.7 Damages

Damages are a **sum of money** that D must pay to C if C wins their claim in negligence. The amount of damages is the **quantum**.

If C wins the case, the court **must** award **some** damages. Very low sums can be awarded if:

- no loss has been suffered by C – **nominal** damages;
- C has wasted the court's time by bringing the action – **contemptuous** damages.

In most cases, damages in tort are **compensatory**: their aim is to put C into the **position C would have been in if the tort had not occurred**. This is relatively easy to do if C's losses are **pecuniary** (monetary), and much more difficult if C's losses are **non-pecuniary** – such as personal injury or loss of reputation. Pecuniary damages often include loss of earnings, with the result that well-paid people are awarded higher sums than lower-paid people who have suffered similar injuries.

Damages are calculated under two broad **categories**: **special damages** and **general damages**. Within the latter, there are **heads of damages**.

Every claimant has a duty to **mitigate** (minimise) their losses.

The **Social Security Administration Act 1992** provides that D must repay any benefits that C has received as a result of D's negligence, and these will be deducted from the damages paid to C.

2.7.1 Special damages

Special damages are quantifiable pecuniary losses that can be calculated reasonably accurately. They include:

- transport costs to and from hospital;
- the cost of private medical treatment;

- loss of C's net earnings from the tort to the date of the trial;
- loss of a carer's net earnings;
- the cost of special equipment;
- the cost of repairing or replacing items damaged or destroyed.

2.7.2 General damages

General damages cannot be calculated exactly, because they relate to intangible factors such as pain, and are required to take account of the likelihood of future deterioration in C's health.

The head of **pain, suffering and loss of amenity** covers two distinct things:

- **pain and suffering**, including physical pain, psychological injuries and distress; and
- **loss of amenity**, which includes loss of enjoyment of life – this includes a subjective element that can reflect the importance of the lost enjoyment to a particular claimant.

Another very important head of general damages is **future loss of earnings**, which is calculated using C's net annual income and a multiplier based upon C's age. This is separate from earnings lost before the trial, as these cannot be quantified precisely.

General damages also include the **cost of future care**, as this cannot be known precisely at the date of the trial.

The head of **lost years** is relevant if C's injuries have reduced C's life expectancy. These are calculated by C's predicted lost earnings minus an allowance for living expenses that C would have incurred during those years.

Damages may be paid as a lump sum, under a structured settlement or via a periodical payments order. The last permits the court periodically to reassess C's needs.

2.7.3 Damages payable on death

If C dies as the result of a tort, two kinds of claim can be made: one by C's estate, and one by C's dependants.

The **Law Reform (Miscellaneous Provisions) Act 1934** permits C's personal representatives to claim everything that C would have been able to claim, except lost years, plus C's funeral expenses.

The **Fatal Accidents Act 1976** permits C's dependants to sue for their own financial losses arising from C's death. A surviving spouse, civil partner or parent of a child under 18 may claim a separate sum of £15,120 as bereavement damages. ***Smith v Lancashire Teaching Hospitals [2017]*** extended this to include any cohabitee who has lived with the deceased in the same household for at least two years before the death as husband or wife or civil partner.

2.8 Summary

(1) With a few exceptions, all natural and legal persons may sue and be sued in the tort of negligence, although legal actions on behalf of a child must be brought by a litigation friend.

(2) The three elements of the tort of negligence are duty of care, breach of duty and causation of damages.

(3) A duty of care is owed to a person's "neighbour". Most negligence claims are made in relation to established duties of care.

(4) Where the courts are considering a new type of situation, they will apply the modern three-stage formulation approach in ***Caparo v Dickman [1990]***.

(5) The courts will consider public policy in negligence claims, taking account of the interests of statutory authorities and limiting the risk of opening the "floodgates" to litigation. The interests of rescuers are given priority.

(6) Psychological/psychiatric harm is dealt with in different ways, depending on whether the claimant is a primary victim or a secondary victim who suffers harm as a result of what they see.

(7) When considering whether there has been a breach of duty, the court will first identify the standard of care, taking into account the concept of the "reasonable person" and whether harm was reasonably foreseeable.

(8) The claimant must prove their case on the balance of probabilities.

(9) The claimant must also prove that the defendant's breach caused their loss. Causation in fact is required – this means proving on the balance of probabilities that the harm would not have occurred "but for" the breach.

(10) Where there are several possible defendants, the test for causation in fact is whether a defendant's actions caused a "material increase in risk". Special rules apply in mesothelioma cases.

(11) Causation in law requires that the harm suffered by the claimant must not be too remote. The kind of damage caused must be reasonably foreseeable from the actions of the defendant.

(12) Special damages are quantifiable pecuniary losses that can be calculated accurately. They include transport costs to hospital and loss of earnings.

(13) General damages cover pain, suffering and loss of amenity, future loss of earning and the cost of future care.

(14) Where the claimant dies as a result of a tort, the claimant's personal representatives can claim damages on their behalf on a similar basis. Under the **Fatal Accidents Act 1976** a surviving spouse/civil partner or a parent of a child under 18 years may also claim bereavement damages, currently £15,120.

CHAPTER 3

Civil Litigation and the Courts

3.1 Introduction

Ask someone what they think about "litigation" and you may hear a variety of responses. Several years ago, they would have included tales of "fat cat lawyers", "ambulance chasing" and a "compensation culture". Today, the talk focuses more on "lean times", "access to justice" and "accident victims deprived of compensation". These contrasting views represent the extremes which tend to make headline news; in reality, civil litigation is an area as diverse as the clients whom you may represent.

Litigation is the means by which civil disputes are resolved through the courts. However, many disputes settle before proceedings are issued and only a tiny minority will ever reach a trial. Legal representatives must be able to advise their clients on how to resolve disputes, such as through mediation and negotiation, but also be confident about pushing their client's case through the civil litigation process when this is in the client's best interests.

Despite the negative press, the entire civil justice system is based upon principles designed to encourage fairness, save expense and resolve disputes quickly. To represent your client successfully, you will need to acquire a range of skills to protect their interests and achieve the desired outcome. These include developing effective interviewing and advising, negotiation, drafting, writing and advocacy skills. Your day-to-day working life is unlikely to resemble the glamour of many TV programmes, but it will be varied and demanding.

"Litigation as a last resort" is the mantra underpinning the **Civil Procedure Rules 1998** (**CPR**), which were designed to provide a swift, streamlined system of civil litigation. However, the rules were criticised for failing to reduce the high costs of civil litigation and, as a consequence, further changes to the methods of funding civil claims, the court's approach to managing costs during the litigation process and awarding costs on conclusion of a case were introduced.

Much of the increase in litigation in recent years may have been fuelled by litigants in person becoming more confident (and competent). Nonetheless, clients will continue to need assistance in resolving disputes, particularly the more complex cases. Consider the litigation generated through the development of the new high-speed rail link between London and the Midlands, celebrities' claims for damages arising out of the phone-hacking scandal, and claimants who received huge compensation awards for catastrophic injuries following negligence by doctors and other health professionals. Many of these cases are newsworthy, but just as important is helping a client who has suffered injuries after being knocked off his bicycle on the way home from work.

A litigation lawyer may deal with a variety of disputes. These can range from simple debt collection proceedings and straightforward personal injury claims, through more involved personal injury or contract dispute claims, to highly complex commercial and international disputes.

Because you are at an early stage in your legal career, this course book will concentrate upon the more straightforward personal injury claims and monetary claims.

3.2 Introduction to the civil courts

(1) The civil courts

The main civil courts in England and Wales are the County Court and the High Court of Justice. County Court hearings take place in local court buildings referred to as County Court Hearing Centres. In addition, two County Court Business Centres have been created, one in Salford (which deals with debt claims) and the other in Northampton.

To enable you to identify the appropriate court for the issue, conduct and hearing of particular proceedings, factors such as the case value are important.

(2) **The County Court**

The County Court deals with the more straightforward cases including:

- claims for money only, whether it be for a specific debt or for damages, where the anticipated value of the claim is for £100,000 or less;
- personal injury claims for less than £50,000.

Note that money-only claims are started under **CPR Part 7** and must be issued centrally in the County Court Money Claims Centre (which is part of Salford Business Centre). Contested claims are later transferred to a named County Court hearing centre, primarily to assist the defendant.

(3) **The High Court**

Only the more complex cases are dealt with in the High Court. The main location is at the Royal Courts of Justice in London, but there are District Registries around the country, such as in Birmingham. In general, a claimant can choose the most convenient location for commencing proceedings.

The High Court is divided into three divisions:

- Queen's Bench Division, which covers actions in contract and tort. This is the division we are primarily concerned with in this section of the course;
- Chancery Division, which is used for disputes over, for example, wills and inheritance, company law and bankruptcy;
- Family Division, where family proceedings, including adoption, are considered.

Judicial functions in the High Court sitting in London are shared between:

- Masters, who deal with interim applications and case management matters; and
- High Court Judges, who deal primarily with trials, but also with interim applications and case management as appropriate.

In the District Registries the functions performed by High Court Masters are dealt with by District Judges.

3.2.1 Court personnel

Apart from judges, there are other officials in the courts that you may come into contact with. They include the following.

(1) **The court manager**. This official is the senior civil servant in charge of a court office. Documents sent to the court, particularly statements of case and applications to the court, are addressed to the court manager. They will be supported by various administrative officers including the counter staff whom you will meet when you issue proceedings at court.

(2) **Ushers**. These officials are present when the court is sitting. They sometimes wear legal robes. They perform functions such as noting who is in attendance before hearings, swearing witnesses at trials and ensuring that lists of cases being heard in a single session are dealt with efficiently. When you arrive at court for a hearing you will need to report to the usher.

(3) **Bailiffs and enforcement officers**. Their role includes serving court documents and enforcing court orders and judgments.

3.3 The sources of procedural law

Litigation is essentially divided into three stages:

- the pre-action stage;
- from issue of proceedings through to judgment; and
- steps taken after judgment.

The basic framework of a typical civil claim is set out on the next page. You may find it helpful to refer back to it as you progress through the course book.

During the course of this manual, you will study all aspects of civil litigation. Whilst there are a number of Acts of Parliament that govern legal proceedings, **CPR** are the most important source of information on the procedural law, both in the High Court and the County Court.

CPR are currently divided into 89 Parts, with each Part dealing with one aspect of civil procedure. Most of these Parts are supplemented by Practice Directions, which provide more detailed information on how the rules work – essentially, they put flesh on the bare bones of the rules. They usually bear reference numbers that are the same as the relevant Part of **CPR** so, for example, **Practice Direction 24** (**PD 24**) supplements **Part 24**. **CPR** are regularly updated and details of amendments and updates can be found at www.justice.gov.uk.

Map of the civil action process

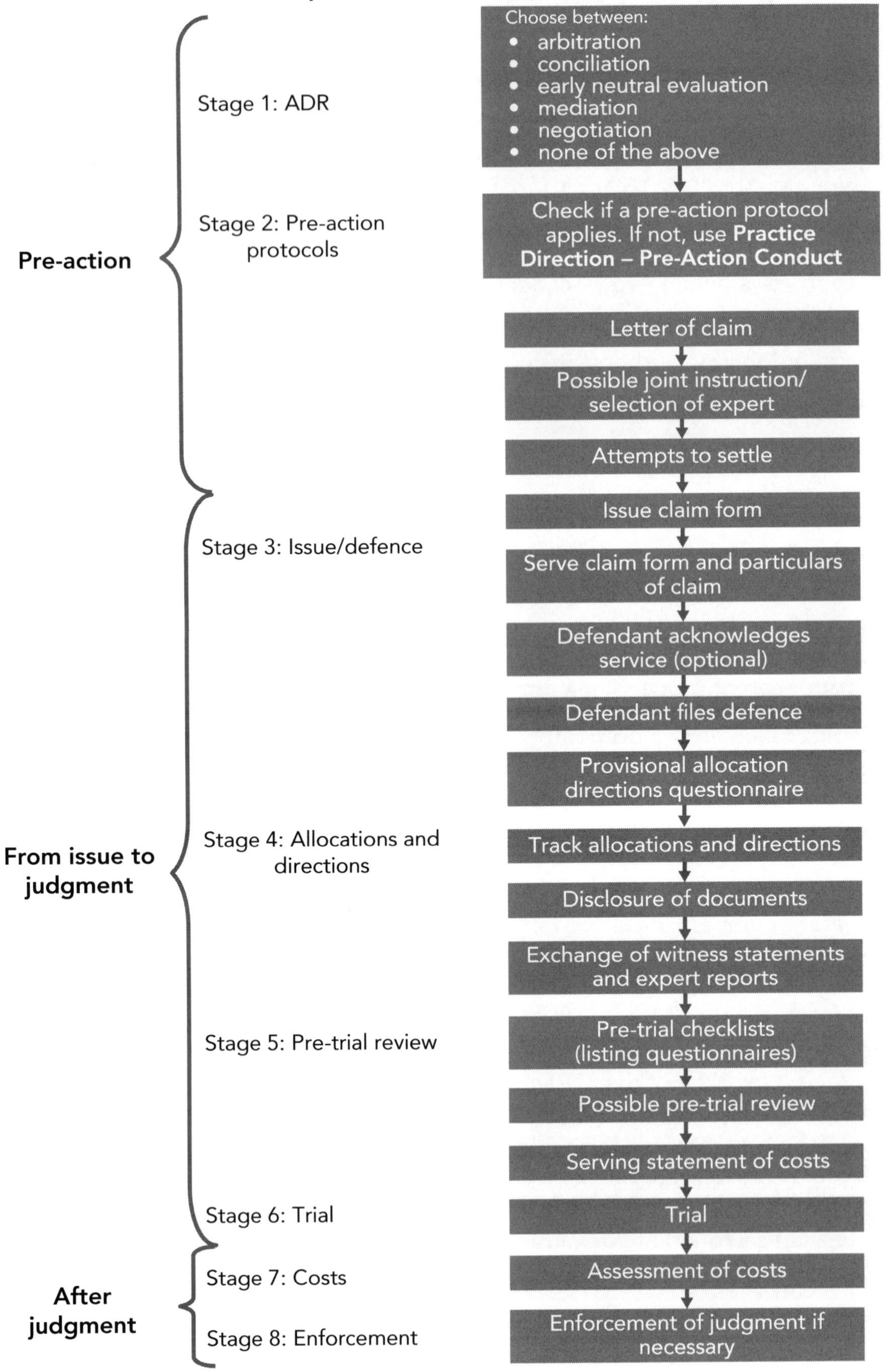

3.4 The overriding objective

The overriding objective of **CPR** is set out in **r1.1**. The aim is **to enable the court to deal with cases justly and at proportionate cost**.

The rule then lists the six objectives the court should seek to achieve when dealing with cases:

- ensuring that the parties are on an equal footing;
- saving expense;
- dealing with the case in ways that are proportionate to:
    - the amount of money involved;
    - the importance of the case;
    - the complexity of the issues; and
    - the financial position of each party;
- ensuring that the case is dealt with expeditiously and fairly;
- allotting to it an appropriate share of the court's resources, while taking into account the need to allot resources to other cases; and
- enforcing compliance with rules, Practice Directions and orders.

Subsequent provisions reinforce the importance of these aims:

- by **CPR r1.2** the court must give effect to the overriding objective when making procedural decisions; and
- **CPR r1.3** requires the parties to assist the court in furthering the overriding objective.

The court, when applying the overriding objective, looks carefully at the facts of each case and the conduct of the parties. This means each case is dealt with individually, ensuring a non-technical, flexible approach, but always in the context of achieving cost-proportionate litigation.

To give practical effect to the overriding objective, the court must take an active role in managing current cases (**CPR r1.4**).

Active case management primarily happens in defended cases. These are the cases where the defendant has been served with proceedings and has filed a defence. It includes:

- encouraging the parties to co-operate with each other in the conduct of the proceedings;
- the court identifying the issues at an early stage, and deciding promptly which issues need to be fully investigated and dealt with at a trial;
- encouraging the parties to use alternative dispute resolution procedures if appropriate (**r1.4(2)(e)**);
- fixing timetables and giving directions to ensure that cases progress quickly and efficiently (**r1.4(2)(g)**); and
- keeping costs under control and taking into account whether the benefits of taking any particular step justify the cost of taking it.

r1.6 refers to **PD1A** which sets out how the overriding objective is to be achieved in relation to vulnerable parties and witnesses. Under **PD1A**, where a witness or party is vulnerable, for example because of a physical or mental disability or their age, the court will consider making directions to enable them to participate fully and give their best evidence.

3.5 Distinction between the civil and criminal courts

The courts of England and Wales are separated into two broad categories: the civil courts and the criminal courts.

The **criminal courts** are the Magistrates' Court and the Crown Court. The Magistrates' Court is where the less serious cases are heard, along with the initial hearings in more serious cases. The Crown Court deals with the most serious offences, such as robbery, murder and rape.

The purpose of criminal jurisdiction is to determine the guilt of people accused before the courts and to decide on punishment if they are found guilty. Effectively, the state is acting to protect the public. Because the consequences are very serious, the court must be sure **beyond reasonable doubt** as to guilt.

The **civil courts**, by contrast, deal with disputes that are generally between individuals or companies, although some cases involve challenging the decisions of government departments or public bodies.

Civil disputes can arise in many different contexts. One is contractual, where a dispute may occur in respect of work, goods or services to be supplied in return for payment, such as building or plumbing work, sales or professional arrangements. Additionally, disputes can arise through the negligence of a party such as road traffic accidents, injuries in the workplace or commercial premises, or malpractice by a professional (doctor or lawyer).

Other areas of law common to civil litigation include family law, landlord and tenant law and employment law, but these are beyond the scope of this manual.

3.6 The purpose and objectives of civil litigation

Cases brought in the civil jurisdiction are usually called "claims". As a result, the person or legal entity (such as a company) bringing the claim, whose rights have been affected, is the **claimant**. The party responding to the case brought against them is the **defendant**.

The process by which a civil case progresses through the system is called litigation, or more specifically in this instance, civil litigation.

The court determines whether the case should succeed and, if so, provides a remedy. The aim is to put the wronged party into the position in which they would have been had there not been a breach of duty or contract.

Since the consequences of the court's decision are less serious than those of the criminal courts as no one is going to lose their liberty, the court needs only to be satisfied on the **balance of probabilities** that a party has proved its case. In other words, it must be more likely than not; or there is a certainty of greater than 50 per cent. This is called the civil standard of proof.

The burden of proof lies with the claimant; they must provide evidence to prove their claim. For example, in a personal injury claim it is up to the claimant to prove that negligence has occurred.

3.7 The scope of civil litigation

Civil litigation, since it deals with the majority of disputes between commercial entities and individuals, has a vast scope. Its main applications are as follows.

Contract disputes:

Types of dispute	Types of claim	Purpose of damages
• Goods and services supplied are defective • Non-payment of sums due • Failure to perform the contract e.g. goods are delivered late or not at all	• Breach of contract • Debt claims • Commercial disputes	• To put the claimant in the position they would have been in had the contract been performed correctly

Claims in tort (civil wrong):

Types of dispute	Types of claim	Purpose of damages
• Road traffic accidents • Trips and slips on the highway or on private property • Accidents at work • Mistakes made by medical or other professionals	• Negligence A duty of care is owed by one party to another, the duty is breached and this causes the other party to suffer loss (financial or otherwise)	To put the claimant in the position they would have been in had the negligent act not occurred
• Noise • Tree roots encroaching • Escape of water onto another's property	• Nuisance Where use or enjoyment of land is repeatedly interfered with by another landowner	To put the claimant in the position they would have been in had the nuisance not occurred

Other areas of law common to civil litigation include family law, landlord and tenant law and employment law, but these are beyond the scope of this manual.

3.8 Digital underpinning

HM Courts and Tribunals Service is responsible for the administration of all courts and tribunals in England and Wales and handles about 4 m cases each year.

Historically the system has been heavily reliant on physical buildings, face to face contact and hearings – and paper! However, this is now changing and a reform programme transforming the use of technology in case management has been introduced.

Digital underpinning involves fundamental changes to the courts' system, such as moving staff to work in new national courts. As stated by the government, the aim is to administer the system more efficiently and provide expert guidance to the public, but also to make the courts more accessible to users, particularly litigants in person.

3.8.1 Civil Money Claims Service

The **Civil Money Claims Service** offers litigation services online. The scheme is available to litigants in person and the claim is made via a public platform, which allows them to issue and respond to claims online. Users can populate text boxes easily and swiftly, establish clear information about what to do next at each stage and check the progress of the online claim with maximum flexibility. Settlement is encouraged and links are provided to mediation services.

3.8.2 Online Court

There is also a further pilot scheme for testing the new Online Court, as recommended by Lord Justice Briggs in his report on the civil courts structure of England and Wales, and this was launched at the end of July 2017.

Although initially invitation only, in future the Online Court will be mandatory for money claims below £25,000. A key aspect of the Online Court is that it involves three stages for running a case:

- an automated "triage" stage where claimants are given access to basic legal advice and assistance in articulating their claim;
- a conciliation stage, which may take a number of forms including telephone, online or face-to-face mediation; and
- a determination stage for cases which have not settled, which may be dealt with by a telephone or video hearing, with the parties all present or by a judicial officer without a hearing.

The rules of the court are simpler than the current **CPR** so that, although lawyers will not be excluded, litigants in person may feel more confident in conducting the case themselves. However, at present, the pilot only deals with claims where the claimant is legally represented.

Appeals are to the County Court and, thereafter, to the Court of Appeal.

HM Courts and Tribunals Service (HMCTS) is changing how certain damages claims must be issued. HMCTS launched the Damages Claims Pilot in May 2021. The pilot was supported by **PD51ZB** and is expected to run until 30 April 2024.

From spring 2022, users wishing to issue a claim that is covered by **PD51ZB** will be required to:

- register with the MyHMCTS platform; and
- issue the claim via the Damages Claims Portal.

3.9 Summary

(1) The three main stages of litigation are: (i) the pre-action stage; (ii) from issue of proceedings to judgment; and (iii) steps taken after judgment.

(2) The main civil courts are the County Court and the High Court.

(3) **CPR** govern the procedure in both the County Court and the High Court. They are subject to regular amendment (updates). **CPR** are divided into **Parts**, each Part having an accompanying **Practice Direction** (**PD**), for example, **Part 7** and **PD 7**.

(4) The overriding objective of **CPR** is to enable the court to deal with cases justly and at proportionate cost.

(5) The civil courts usually deal with disputes between individuals. These generally arise from the breach of a duty or infringement of a right. The court decides whether the claim should succeed and, if so, what the remedy should be. The civil standard of proof is on the balance of probabilities.

(6) The criminal courts deal with determining guilt and punishment of people found guilty of crimes. Since an individual's liberty is at stake, the standard of proof is higher in criminal law, being beyond reasonable doubt.

(7) Civil litigation is vast in scope since it deals with nearly all disputes between individuals, and individuals and companies.

CHAPTER 4

Preliminary Considerations

4.1 Introduction

As a legal representative, it is likely that, at some point, you will handle client money. In a litigation context, this could be:

- money which the client is paying to be held on account of your costs;
- money which the client is paying to you to be held pending payment of damages or a settlement sum;
- money which an opponent is paying to you to be held for your client as damages or a settlement sum.

You have obligations in relation to possible money laundering under the **Money Laundering, Terrorist Financing and Transfer of Funds (Information on the Payer) Regulations 2017** (**MLR 2017**). In this chapter we will outline the steps required under the **MLR 2017** when taking on a new civil litigation client.

Although the public perception is that most cases proceed to a trial, this is far from the reality and many cases fall at the first hurdle. Indeed, if a case has no real prospect of succeeding, a client will not thank their lawyer for pursuing it. Lawyers too must be aware of commercial considerations to ensure the future of their own business. Thus, before commencing an action, certain questions must be answered.

- Can the claim be brought at all?
- Who are the parties and is the defendant worth suing?

- How will the case be funded?

In this chapter, these issues are discussed in turn.

4.2 Money laundering checks

Under the **MLR 2017** law firms must carry out **due diligence**. You will need to verify the identity of each new litigation client. In the case of individual clients, you should check at least one government document verifying their name and address or name and date of birth, normally a passport or photo-card driving licence. In addition, you should also check another supporting document verifying the client's name and address, for example a recent bank statement.

Where the client is a partnership or limited liability partnership (LLP), you should check the above personal documents for each partner, unless the partnership is well established and reputable, in which case verifying its name, address and nature of business will normally be sufficient. Where there is a "beneficial owner" of the partnership with more than 25 per cent of the voting rights/share of capital and profits, you should carry out the personal checks on that individual.

Where the client is a company which is not listed on a regulated market (including a private company), you should complete a companies search – see https://www.gov.uk/get-information-about-a-company. This will enable you to check the company's full name, address and nature of its business, together with details of two directors. You should also check whether there is a beneficial owner with ownership of more than 25 per cent of the shares or voting rights and ensure that personal checks are made on that individual.

In certain circumstances **enhanced due diligence** may require additional checks, for example, where the legal representative has not met the client face to face.

Any issues or queries arising from these checks should be referred to your firm's Money Laundering Reporting Officer (MLRO).

Further information about money laundering requirements for law firms is available at https://www.sra.org.uk/solicitors/resources/money-laundering/.

4.3 Limitation

Before commencing action, the lawyer must check that the case is not "time-barred". In other words, the client has left it too late to bring a claim – a concept known as limitation.

The **Limitation Act 1980** (**LA 1980**) sets down strict time limits relating to the time between the cause of action (e.g. the date the faulty goods were sold in a contract claim) and the commencement of the litigation relating to that event. This is known as the **limitation period**. It prevents a potential defendant from remaining under a constant threat of litigation for events that happened years ago and recognises the difficulties each party may have in bringing or defending a claim once memories of witnesses have faded.

The general rule

Limitation periods operate to provide a defendant with a **technical defence** to a claim that is issued a long time after the events in question took place. The general rule is that actions commenced outside the limitation period will not be allowed to proceed, although extensions may be available in exceptional circumstances.

Allowing a case to be lost on limitation grounds could lead to a professional negligence claim and so it is vital that the lawyer operates an efficient case management system or diary system.

4.4 Calculating limitation periods

The main limitation periods are as follows.

Personal injury claims	3 years
Most other tort claims	6 years
Contract claims	6 years

Time starts to run for limitation purposes when the cause of action occurs, that is, the date on which the claim could have been brought. This is usually:

- in negligence cases, when the claimant suffers damage as a result of the alleged negligent conduct, for example, the date of the road traffic accident;
- for children who suffer personal injuries the time limit does not start to run until they reach their 18th birthday;
- in contract claims, when the contract was breached. Thus, in a claim for damages for late delivery it will be when the goods should have been delivered under the terms of the contract.

Example

A road traffic accident occurred on 6 October and the claimant wishes to sue for personal injuries suffered as a result. The limitation period would start running on 7 October, with the last day for issuing being on 6 October three years later.

4.4.1 Extending limitation

For most types of claim the limitation periods laid down by **LA 1980** are final. In some cases, however, this does not apply.

Personal injury claims

In personal injury claims, the client has three years from the date of the cause of action to bring their claim. However, not everyone will know, at the date of the cause of action, that they even have a claim. Therefore, time may not start running in personal injury cases until a later date known as the "date of knowledge", that is, when the claimant first became aware that their injury was linked to the original accident – perhaps as a result of seeking medical advice. This is particularly relevant in personal injury cases involving exposure to asbestos, where it may be many years later that the claimant discovers they have contracted an asbestos-related disease.

Discretion to extend limitation

If the claimant has failed to meet the limitation date, the court has discretion to extend it, but will rarely do so.

Example

In ***Collins v Secretary of State for Business, Innovation and Skills [2014]*** the claimant was diagnosed with lung cancer in 2002 and successfully treated. He attributed the illness to exposure to asbestos between 1947 and 1967 but only instructed solicitors to pursue a claim in 2012, aged 90, after seeing a newspaper advertisement.

The court considered that a reasonable person would have enquired about the possible causes of the cancer by mid-2003. This meant that limitation had expired in 2006, three years later. The proceedings issued in 2012 were six years out of time. In this instance, the court refused to exercise its discretion to extend the primary limitation period as the claim had low value and the litigation costs would be disproportionately high.

4.4.2 Summary of limitation

What is limitation?	The strict time limit imposed on when a claimant can issue proceedings against a defendant in relation to a cause of action, for example: • the date of the accident in a personal injury claim; and • the date the invoice was due for payment in a debt case.
What is the effect?	Limitation periods provide defendants with a technical defence to a claim where the claimant has issued proceedings after the expiry of the limitation period.
General rule	The court will not allow actions commenced outside the limitation period to proceed.
Reasons?	(1) Protects a potential defendant from an indefinite threat of litigation arising from events which occurred years ago. (2) Recognises the evidential difficulties of bringing a claim when witnesses' memories may have faded.
Limitation periods	• Personal injury claims – three years. • Other tort and contract claims – six years.
Limitation period for children	The time limit is three years, but this does not start until the child reaches the age of 18.
Extending limitation	• Limitation periods are usually final. • The court has discretion to extend the deadline but will rarely do so. • May be extended so that it expires three years after the date of knowledge. • Actual knowledge arises when the claimant knew the injury was caused by the defendant's default. • Constructive knowledge is the date when the claimant ought to have realised they had a claim from facts available to them, for example, from a medical report.

4.5 Viability

Before launching into litigation, it is important to check whether it is worth doing so. In particular:

- **Who is the defendant?** In addition to identifying the correct defendant, you must ensure that they are sued in the correct capacity, whether it be as an individual, a partnership or a limited company.
- **Where is the defendant?** Such information is required to ensure that the proceedings can be served effectively.
- **Will the defendant be able to pay any judgment?** There is little point in suing an individual defendant who is on the verge of bankruptcy or a company which is about to fall into liquidation, as enforcement of the judgment would be impossible. If there is any doubt about a defendant's ability to pay, further enquiries should be made including:
    - a search of Companies House which will reveal important information about the financial state of a company;
    - the use of a credit rating company as this is a relatively cheap way of finding information;
    - a search of the Land Registry;
    - a search of the Register of Judgments;
    - instructing an enquiry agent/private investigator; and
    - asking the client or other sub-contractors if they have any information.

4.6 Financing litigation

Identifying how a case will be financed is vital, both to the lawyer (as the method may influence how much and how quickly the firm will be paid) and to the client. There are a number of alternative ways through which litigation may be financed.

At the outset of the case the lawyer must discuss the issue of costs with the client. They should give the client the best information possible about the likely overall costs and explain the client's potential liability not only for their own costs but also for those of the other party if the client were to lose the case.

General costs rule in civil litigation

Although costs are awarded at the court's discretion, the usual rule in civil litigation is that the unsuccessful party in proceedings is ordered to pay the successful party's costs (**r44.2**). It simply means that the losing party pays the winning party's costs in addition to their own lawyer's costs. This gives rise to the expression that the "loser pays twice".

There are a number of methods of funding a civil litigation claim and these are considered below.

4.6.1 Private funding

Some clients will have no alternative but to fund the case privately or may choose to do so. This is sometimes referred to as "the retainer". Usually, this would be the final option for a client to be taken only when not covered by insurance or where alternative "no win, no fee" arrangements are unavailable.

In this traditional method, the client pays the legal costs of conducting the case at an agreed hourly rate. Charge-out rates are based on the salaries of the staff and fee-earners working at the law firm together with an element representing the firm's profits. A common approach is to fix a single hourly rate for each grade of fee-earner, so the more senior or experienced the lawyer, the higher the figure.

In addition, the client will be expected to pay for **disbursements**. These are sums paid by the firm during the course of litigation in respect of court fees, experts' and counsel's fees, the cost of making copies of photographs and similar expenditure.

The client should be given an estimate of the likely costs and kept informed throughout the case. It is sensible to agree to periodical billing to avoid the client being taken by surprise by a large bill at the end of the case and also to assist with the firm's cash flow.

Unbundling legal services

This is a development which aims to assist those clients who no longer qualify for legal aid but who cannot afford to pay privately. Rather than instructing a solicitor under the traditional full retainer, where the lawyer deals with all matters from initial instructions until the case is concluded, unbundling allows the client to select the occasions when they need legal assistance. It is sometimes referred to as "*à la carte*" legal services.

Unbundling can operate on different levels but may include:

- providing clients with self-help packs;
- providing advice about a specific step or particular issue in a case on one or more occasions;

- checking or drafting documents;
- providing advocacy services.

Small personal injury claims and consumer claims may be suitable for this type of funding (provided there are no other alternatives).

There are some pitfalls in running a case using unbundled legal services as the lawyer may not have sufficient knowledge of the client's situation to advise effectively. It is important to define the scope of the retainer clearly and in writing, but also to record subsequent instructions to avoid future disputes.

Examples of unbundling

In ***Minkin v Landsberg [2015]*** the Court of Appeal ruled that a solicitor employed on a limited retainer to draft a financial consent order had no duty of care to advise on the underlying merits of the agreement. Lady Justice King stated: *"There would be very serious consequences for both the court and litigants in person generally, if . . . a modest and relatively inexpensive drafting exercise of a document . . . may lead to* [solicitors] *having imposed upon them a far broader duty of care."*

However, in ***Sequence Properties Ltd v Patel [2016]*** a harsher approach was adopted towards an individual appealing against a costs order imposed for the late filing of a trial bundle. Judge Asplin refused the application because the applicant had received assistance from a solicitor through "unbundled legal services". The headline for the *Law Society Gazette* article discussing this case was "New judgment 'kills' unbundled legal services". Whilst this may be an over-exaggeration, there is no doubt that the judgment does reinforce the importance of drafting the retainer and specifying exactly what it does not include.

4.6.2 Legal expenses insurance

In many instances, the client can be reassured that their costs will be covered by legal expenses insurance – known as "before the event" (BTE) insurance. This can be taken out as part of a vehicle insurance policy and motorists often do so to give themselves peace of mind. Another source of insurance is household policies. If legal expenses are included, there will be no need for the client to enter into any other funding arrangement as BTE insurance generally covers both sides' costs.

After taking instructions, the lawyer should:

- check the client's insurance policy to determine if it covers legal expenses;
- ensure that the level of cover is sufficient; and

- advise the client as to any excess – this is the initial payment which the client may be required to meet.

4.6.3 Sponsoring organisations

Some clients may find that their legal costs are covered by a sponsoring organisation such as a trade union. This is most likely to apply to employment-related disputes and accidents at work. Often, the sponsoring organisation will insist on a lawyer being instructed from an approved panel.

4.6.4 Conditional fee agreements

(1) **General provisions**

Conditional fee agreements, or CFAs, have become increasingly popular over recent years, particularly as public funding has all but disappeared for litigation. CFAs provide the client with the security of knowing that they will not receive a large costs bill; indeed, such reassurance is often a crucial factor in a potential claimant's decision as to whether to proceed or not.

CFAs are regulated by the **Conditional Fee Agreements Order 2013**. They are often referred to as "no win, no fee" agreements; although not strictly accurate, this is the most common arrangement.

In a CFA, if the client loses, they will not have to pay anything to the law firm acting for them (except disbursements in some cases). However, if the case is won, the client will have to pay their own lawyer's costs but at an enhanced rate. A costs order will usually be sought against the losing party, but the client may be responsible for any shortfall, depending upon the terms under which their lawyer is acting.

In some cases, the client will take out an "after the event" (ATE) insurance policy to cover themselves for the potential liability of paying the opponent's costs and their own disbursements if they were to lose the case, but such policies tend to be expensive as the client is already in a dispute.

(2) **Requirements**

A CFA must be:

- in writing; and
- state the percentage of any success fee.

(3) **The success fee**

If a claim is unsuccessful, the lawyer will not receive their costs, thus the firm will be out of pocket. Law firms must be able to run on a commercial basis and, to make CFAs attractive to the legal profession as well as to clients, the concept of the success fee was introduced.

If a claim is successful, the lawyer receives an enhanced fee to reflect that "success". This will be a percentage increase in the lawyer's normal hourly fee.

Note:

- the percentage of any success fee cannot exceed 100 per cent of the usual charging rate;
- the success fee in personal injury claims is limited to 25 per cent of the damages for pain and suffering.

(4) **Risk assessments**

The lawyer will determine the success fee taking into account factors such as the complexity of the matter, the likelihood of success and the time which the case will involve. This will also assist the lawyer in justifying the level of the success fee to the court should they need to do so.

Example 1

Legal Eagles & Co's usual charging rate for CILEX lawyer, Fiona Ward, is £200 per hour. Fiona is consulted by Hamza Shazad, who wishes to make a claim against Southend Garages Ltd in relation to a car which he purchased. After carrying out a risk assessment, Fiona agrees an uplift of 50 per cent. This means that Fiona's hourly charge-out rate will be £300 per hour if Hamza wins.

Hamza is successful in his claim and he recovers damages of £15,000. Legal Eagles' bill comes to £2,000. However, the success fee would increase this to £3,000.

The base costs of £2,000 and the disbursements would be recoverable from the losing party, Southend Garages Ltd. However, Hamza would be responsible for the success fee of £1,000 and this would be paid from his damages.

Example 2

Stefan has a CFA agreement with Legal Eagles & Co with a 30 per cent success fee. He is awarded £20,000 in damages for pain and suffering arising from a road traffic accident.

Stefan's lawyer's fees are £10,000 and the 30 per cent success fee is £3,000 giving a total of £13,000. The losing party pays the base costs of £10,000 and disbursements, but the entire success fee will be recovered from Stefan's damages as it is less than 25 per cent of those damages.

Alternatively, assume that the success fee is now 80 per cent. Combined with the legal fees of £10,000, the total is £18,000. In this instance, the maximum which Stefan's lawyer may recover towards the success fee is 25 per cent of the damages, that is £5,000. Effectively, there is a cap on the success fee and the total costs the lawyer would receive are £15,000. As a consequence, Stefan's lawyer loses out by £3,000.

4.6.5 Damages-based agreements

These are regulated by the **Damages-Based Agreement Regulations 2013**. Under a damages-based agreement (DBA), the lawyer will not be paid if the case is lost but, if the claim is successful, the lawyer will receive a percentage share of the damages recovered. This is known as a contingency fee and although relatively new in the UK, DBAs are a long-established feature of the US legal system.

However, to ensure that the lawyer does not receive an excessive payment for a limited amount of work:

- the amount which can be recovered is limited to 25 per cent of the damages for personal injury claims and 50 per cent for most other cases; and
- the court will assess the proportionality of that figure under **Part 44** when determining costs.

Costs recoverable under a DBA include the law firm's and counsel's fees. Upfront expenses (such as medical reports) and ATE insurance premiums are not included in the cap.

An example of how this works in practice is provided on the following page.

Example

Components Ltd (CL) enters into a DBA with Legal Eagles & Co which provides for a contingency fee of 20 per cent. The client is successful in its claim against Engineering Services Ltd (ESL) and the defendant is ordered to pay £30,000 in damages for breach of contract.

Under the DBA, CL owes Legal Eagles £6,000.

The court orders ESL to pay £5,000 towards CL's costs. CL will then make up the shortfall of £1,000 from its damages, so that the lawyer receives the agreed amount in costs of £6,000.

CL will actually **receive** £29,000 in damages.

DBAs have not proved very popular amongst both lawyers and clients. As many claims (particularly personal injury claims) are for relatively small amounts of money, a percentage share of the damages would not come close to covering the costs incurred by the lawyer in pursuing the case. At the other end of the spectrum, a client is likely to be most unhappy about their lawyers receiving a significant sum in fees when they are perceived to have done little work before the dispute settled.

Example

In ***Bolt Burdon Solicitors v Tariq and Others [2016]*** the court considered the enforceability of a contingency fee agreement whereby the solicitors would receive 50 per cent of any compensation recovered. The matter involved a claim for compensation against a bank, which was subsequently settled for £821,045. Under the terms of the contingency agreement, the solicitors billed just over £400,000 – the equivalent of approximately £50,000 on an hourly basis. The client appealed on the basis that the DBA was unfair and unreasonable.

This argument was rejected by the judge who stated that the agreement was not unfair as Mr Tariq knew *"exactly what he was agreeing to"*. Mr Justice Spencer also referred to the commercial realities of the situation: *"In truth, the agreement represented a speculative joint business venture in which the solicitors were taking all the risk and the client was exposed to no risk at all"*.

This case is a clear example of a "pure" DBA agreement and the message is that, if such fees are to be awarded, the law firm is likely to be successful if they can justify the percentage.

Comparison of CFAs and DBAs

(1) The additional percentage charged is calculated by reference to an uplift in the solicitor's usual hourly rate in CFAs, but is linked to the damages received in DBAs.

(2) The success fee and the contingency fee are both limited to 25 per cent of the damages in personal injury claims.

(3) In other claims, the success fee is limited to 100 per cent of the usual charging rate in CFAs; but the contingency fee cannot exceed 50 per cent of the damages in DBAs.

(4) In both arrangements, the client does not have to pay their solicitor if the case is lost.

(5) Neither cover the opponent's costs or disbursements, which must be covered separately.

(6) Both must be in writing.

The inherent difficulties of predicting the outcome of litigation affect the availability and terms of funding arrangements.

Qualified one-way costs shifting

You should understand the operation of qualified one-way costs shifting (QOCS). This applies to personal injury claims and modifies the general rule that the losing party pays the successful party's costs. The effect is that:

- an unsuccessful defendant still has to pay the successful claimant's costs; but
- an unsuccessful claimant does not have to pay their opponent's costs.

This avoids the need for the client to take out ATE insurance for their opponent's costs but the claimant should still consider taking out such insurance:

- to cover their own lawyer's disbursements; and
- to protect against the costs risk created by a defendant's **Part 36** offer.

You should be aware of those cases when QOCS does not apply and the defendant can enforce a costs order against the claimant including where:

- the claim has been struck out;
- the claimant has been fundamentally dishonest.

4.5.6 Litigation funding agreements and the voluntary code of funding

A litigation funding agreement is an arrangement whereby a private, commercial third party provides the finance for all or part of a litigant's legal costs in return for an agreed share in the outcome if the case is successful. This share is usually a percentage of damages recovered and thus it is a contingency fee agreement. If the case fails, the claimant will not owe the funder, which will lose its money and financial stake.

Litigation funders can sign up to a voluntary code of conduct and the Association of Litigation Funders aims to promote best practice in litigation funding – see https://associationoflitigationfunders.com/ .

The key aspects of the voluntary code are to:

- require funders to maintain adequate financial resources at all times;
- require that funders behave reasonably and only withdraw from funding in specific circumstances and, if termination is disputed, they must obtain the opinion of an independent and jointly instructed KC;
- prevent the funders from controlling the litigation and jeopardising the acting lawyers' compliance with their professional duties (although funders may be kept informed on the progress of their case).

4.6.6 Legal aid

Public funding, otherwise known as legal aid, is dispensed by the Legal Aid Agency and has a significantly reduced scope in civil litigation claims. Many firms no longer undertake publicly funded work and the scheme itself is fairly complex.

4.6.6.1 Debt and contract cases

In relation to debt or contract cases, legal aid is only available:

- if an individual's home is at immediate risk of sale or repossession (usually by a mortgage lender); or
- if the individual faces eviction from the home, perhaps due to bankruptcy proceedings.

In relation to this limited range of cases, eligible clients may receive advice and assistance by way of **legal help**. Legal help provides help and advice on how the law applies to a particular case and how to proceed, and can be spent on initial work up to a set limit. The client must qualify under a financial eligibility test and there must be sufficient benefit to justify the spending of public money.

Legal help does not cover taking court proceedings. If proceedings are necessary, eligible clients may receive public funding by way of **legal representation**. An application must be made and if this is successful, a lawyer prepares the case and speaks on the party's behalf in court.

The application is determined in accordance with a means test and a merits test, specifically:

- whether the case could be dealt with by, for example, mediation;
- whether the case can be funded in any other way, such as through insurance or a CFA;
- whether the case justifies the spending of public money. This question includes consideration of whether a reasonable person of private means would fund the case.

4.6.6.2 Personal injury

As previously mentioned, most cases involving personal injuries caused by negligence are excluded from public funding. Public funding is currently available for a very limited range of clinical negligence claims which are beyond the scope of this manual.

Example

Assume that Maria Di Tella, a 24-year-old computer technician, is attending an initial interview for the purpose of seeking damages arising out of the installation of a defective central heating system in her home.

As part of the interview, you should consider funding, including **conditional fee agreements and damages-based agreements**. You will need to find out about her financial resources. As she is a computer technician and seeking damages for a breach of contract claim, she will not be eligible for public funding. She is extremely unlikely to be funded through sponsorship such as from a trade union. Maria may have legal expenses insurance through her home insurance policy, but otherwise, private funding or a CFA are the most obvious choices.

4.7 Summary

(1) **LA 1980** sets down strict time limits within which proceedings must be issued. These time limits run from the date of the cause of action.

(2) For most tort claims, this period is **six years**. For personal injury claims, it is **three years**; for contract claims, **six years**.

(3) For personal injury cases, time may not begin to run from the date of the cause of action, but instead from the "date of knowledge".

(4) The court has a discretionary power to extend the limitation period.

(5) CILEX lawyers and solicitors are required to give clients information about costs, including details of how, when and by whom costs will be paid. Public funding is extremely limited and, if the claim is not covered by insurance, alternative methods of funding are now available. These include conditional fee agreements (CFAs), damages-based agreements (DBAs) and unbundled legal services.

(6) CFA success fees are deductible from the claimant's damages. The CFA percentage success fee is calculated by reference to the solicitor's costs and capped at 100 per cent of the lawyer's usual hourly rate and, for personal injury cases only, 25 per cent of the damages.

(7) DBA success fees are calculated as a percentage share of the damages recovered, and capped at 25 per cent in personal injury claims and 50 per cent in other claims.

(8) Some claims may be funded by commercial funders under litigation funding agreements.

(9) Legal aid is rarely available for civil litigation claims.

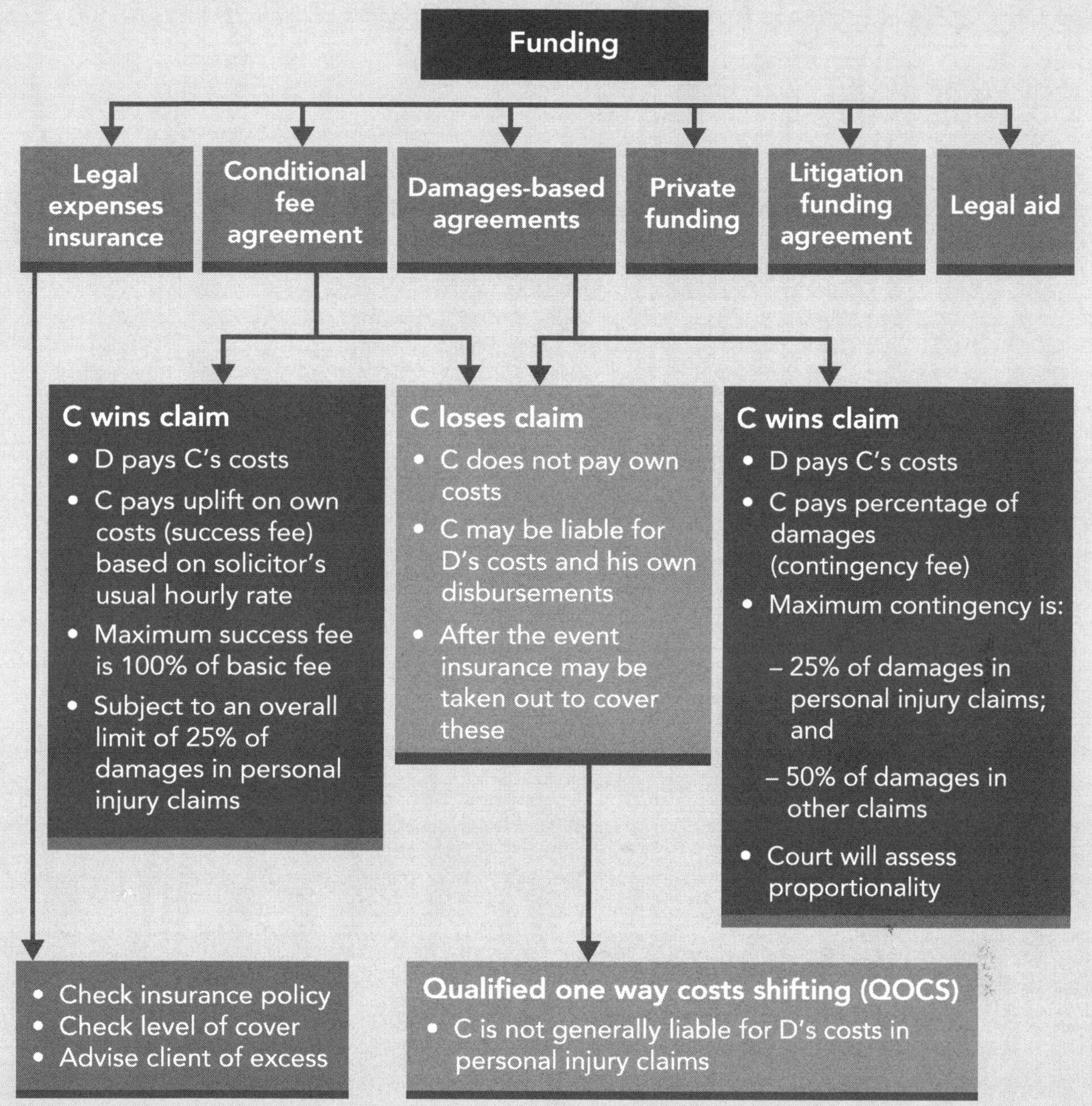
Funding
Legal expenses insurance
Conditional fee agreement
Damages-based agreements
Private funding
Litigation funding agreement
Legal aid
C wins claim
• D pays C's costs
• C pays uplift on own costs (success fee) based on solicitor's usual hourly rate
• Maximum success fee is 100% of basic fee
• Subject to an overall limit of 25% of damages in personal injury claims
C loses claim
• C does not pay own costs
• C may be liable for D's costs and his own disbursements
• After the event insurance may be taken out to cover these
C wins claim
• D pays C's costs
• C pays percentage of damages (contingency fee)
• Maximum contingency is:
– 25% of damages in personal injury claims; and
– 50% of damages in other claims
• Court will assess proportionality
• Check insurance policy
• Check level of cover
• Advise client of excess
Qualified one way costs shifting (QOCS)
• C is not generally liable for D's costs in personal injury claims

CHAPTER 5

Alternative Dispute Resolution

5.1 Introduction

Litigation is considered the last resort and parties should seek to resolve disputes amicably before bringing proceedings against each other.

This can be achieved by the parties attempting alternative dispute resolution (ADR). This is a collective term which covers any means of settling disputes outside of the traditional litigation process. It is referred to specifically in **CPR** and the court must encourage parties to use ADR if the court considers it appropriate (**CPR r1.4(2)(e)**).

Set out below is a summary of the general advantages and disadvantages of ADR over litigation, which you will go on to consider in more detail.

Advantage	Disadvantage
Speed	Enforceability of awards
Flexibility	Limited disclosure
The client can withdraw at any time	Opponent can withdraw at any time
Preserves business relationships	

Advantage	Disadvantage
Privacy	
Cost	

There are a number of methods by which ADR can be achieved: arbitration (of which there are two types – judicial and contractual), negotiation, mediation, conciliation and early neutral evaluation. Many of these involve the use of an independent third party, such as a mediator, to help the parties break the deadlock.

5.2 Negotiation

Negotiation, in which the parties or their lawyers discuss possible solutions to the problem, may occur either face to face or by correspondence. Such discussions can be open, although they rarely are, or "without prejudice". This means that the subject matter of those discussions is not revealed in any subsequent litigation if the discussions are unsuccessful, allowing the parties to negotiate freely.

Advantages of negotiation:

- it can be done at any point in the process, that is, before and/or during the litigation process;
- the parties can walk away at any time;
- it may avoid the need to bring proceedings or attend trial;
- the outcome is usually confidential and private;
- avoiding litigation may preserve the relationship of the parties if it is an ongoing one.

Disadvantages of negotiation:

- there are possible representation (CILEX lawyer/solicitor and counsel) costs in without prejudice meetings;
- the demands of the other side, particularly litigants in person, may be unrealistic, hampering progress.

5.3 Mediation

The popularity of mediation has increased year on year. The parties and an independent mediator gather at a neutral venue. Generally, there is a public room for the parties and mediator to meet in and a number of private rooms. Initially, the parties will outline their dispute to the mediator in the presence of the other side. After this, the parties separate into private rooms and the mediator will speak to each, often repeatedly, to try to reach a solution. If the parties reach agreement, it is written down and will be binding.

Advantages of mediation:

- the parties agree a resolution of their choice, allowing wider scope than that of the courts;
- this tailored "win-win" result compares favourably with the adversarial "win-lose" outcome of litigation and enables the parties to continue their relationship on a positive footing; this is particularly important in a business relationship;
- the parties can walk away at any time;
- the mediator is independent and neutral;
- it is a confidential process;
- it is quicker and cheaper than litigation;
- the parties cannot use information obtained in mediation in court as it is without prejudice.

Disadvantages of mediation:

- hiring a mediator can be costly, even though the parties generally split the costs;
- the parties must pay their own costs of attending;
- the other party may not share the same attitude to mediation as your client so that resolution is not guaranteed;
- mediation is unsuitable if a party wants to set a legal precedent (the benchmark by which similar cases will be dealt with);
- it is unsuitable if a party needs an injunction;
- if a client has an overwhelmingly strong case, they may prefer the court to find in their favour rather than compromise.

Automatic referral to mediation for small claims

Cases issued in the County Court which are allocated to the small claims track will be automatically referred to mediation provided that all parties have indicated their agreement. There are, however, some exceptions such as personal injury claims.

5.4 Arbitration

Arbitration is a substitute for litigation, and an arbitration clause requires the parties to go through arbitration rather than court proceedings. Any relevant dispute will be referred to an independent arbitrator, who is likely to be an expert in the particular area of dispute. Although an arbitration procedure will be adopted, the parties are not required to follow the more formal procedure required in court. Once a decision has been made by the arbitrator, this will be final and binding. However, the arbitrator may reserve the award until it has been paid and, if necessary, it can be enforced through the courts.

There are different types of arbitration and two examples are set out below.

Judicial arbitration is a process in which the parties seek a final and binding decision that deals with the areas of dispute. It can involve expert determination where the parties refer their dispute to a third party who is both neutral and a specialist in the area of the dispute. Alternatively, the parties can choose to go to an arbitration panel hearing, which is like a tribunal (similar to a court). The increasing use of Sharia courts is an example of this.

Contractual arbitration is where the parties are contractually bound to use a particular arbitration process in the event of any dispute instead of pursuing the matter through the litigation process. It is common in certain industries such as shipping and construction, although many holiday contracts also contain an arbitration clause.

Advantages of arbitration:

- there is no need for litigation;
- it is quicker than going to court;
- it is likely to be cheaper, particularly if the arbitration scheme is run by a trade body as any fees associated with the process will usually be less than those required by the court;
- the decision is made by an impartial third party who will have a degree of expertise in the matter;
- it is private and confidential – there is no public decision. This may be of particular importance to commercial clients who wish to preserve any existing business relationship or to keep the terms confidential.

Disadvantages of arbitration:

- an arbitration panel or expert are potentially costly;
- parties often want to be represented by lawyers, which adds significantly to the total cost of arbitration;

- the process can be time-consuming;
- the decision is binding with very limited rights of appeal.

5.5 Conciliation

Conciliation is a similar process to mediation and negotiation with similar advantages and disadvantages. It has been used in complex multi-party disputes such as some employment disputes.

5.6 Early neutral evaluation

Early neutral evaluation (ENE) is a form of ADR in which the parties refer their dispute to a third party (usually an expert in the field) to make a preliminary assessment of the merits of the case. The aim is to determine the likely outcome of the dispute if it proceeds to trial. The neutral third party will hear evidence and discuss the case with each party on a without prejudice basis before making a recommendation.

The court's powers of case management (**Part 3**) specifically include ordering and hearing an ENE, and a party may now be compelled to take part. The reasoning behind this is that parties are more likely to listen to advice from a judge particularly given the ever-increasing numbers of litigants in person, who may have an unrealistic view of their case.

The advantages are that the process is quick and confidential and assists the parties in reaching a reasoned settlement. However, a disadvantage may be that the option is non-binding.

5.7 Overview

The court's role is simply to encourage the use of ADR where it is appropriate and the parties cannot be compelled to take part against their wishes. However, the pre-action protocols stress that litigation should be seen as a last resort. Furthermore, where a party unreasonably refuses a proposal that ADR should be used, the court may take this into account later when it comes to deciding what order to make as to costs.

Set out below is a summary of the most common types of ADR.

Type of ADR	Description	Outcome
Negotiation	Discussions between the parties to seek agreement.	Voluntary agreement

Type of ADR	Description	Outcome
Mediation	A neutral third party discusses the problem and possible solutions with the parties.	Voluntary agreement
Arbitration	The dispute is decided by one or more arbitrators who are usually experts chosen from a particular field or professional body.	The decision of the arbitrator is binding on the parties and enforceable in the courts.
Conciliation	The conciliator plays a proactive role in trying to resolve the dispute.	Voluntary agreement
Early neutral evaluation	A third party makes a preliminary assessment of the case at an early stage in the dispute and makes a recommendation.	Voluntary agreement

5.8 Co-operation

We have seen that, as part of its active case management function, the court encourages the parties to co-operate with each other in the conduct of litigation. On occasion, correspondence between the lawyers involved in the litigation may become relevant to a matter before the court. If, on reading these letters, the judge decides that either party has been obstructive or difficult, costs may be ordered against the law firm deemed to be in the wrong.

5.8.1 Failure to engage with a reasonable request for ADR

As well as the commercial advantages and costs savings which may result from using ADR, there are sanctions if the client refuses to take part. In ***Halsey v Milton Keynes General NHS Trust [2004]*** the Court of Appeal recognised that it would be futile to order an unwilling party to refer their dispute to mediation. However, if a client unreasonably refuses to do so, the court may penalise the offending party in costs, whether the client wins or loses.

The principle has been extended so that failure to respond at all to an invitation to participate in ADR is itself unreasonable, even if there is a good reason for refusing to do so.

Example

In ***Laporte v Commissioner of Police of the Metropolis [2015]*** two protesters failed in their claim for damages after alleging they had been assaulted and falsely imprisoned. The police commissioner refused to engage in ADR because he believed the claim was spurious (a view endorsed by the final outcome), but despite this, the defendant only recovered two-thirds of his costs.

Example

However, the Court of Appeal decision of ***Gore v Naheed and Ahmed [2017]*** highlights that there are exceptions to this general rule. The case involved a dispute about a right of way for vehicle access. Despite Mr Gore refusing to engage in mediation, the judge did not order costs because he considered that mediation had no realistic prospect of succeeding and would only add to the costs and there were complex questions of law which needed to be addressed.

The message is clear that whilst parties can turn down invitations for ADR if they consider it inappropriate and they cannot be compelled to take part, they do need to engage with the idea. As a minimum, a party refusing ADR is advised to respond to their opponent in writing, setting out their reasons for doing so.

5.9 Summary

(1) Alternative dispute resolution and co-operation are important aspects of resolving civil disputes.

(2) The methods by which ADR may be achieved are arbitration, negotiation, mediation, early neutral evaluation and conciliation.

(3) If the court considers that a successful party unreasonably refused to consider ADR, the court may impose costs sanctions on the successful party.

CHAPTER 6

Pre-action Protocols

6.1 Introduction
6.2 Pre-action protocols and the Practice Direction on Pre-Action Conduct and Protocols
6.3 Protocols relevant to personal injury claims
6.4 Information required in a personal injury claim
6.5 Low value personal injury protocol claims
6.6 The Pre-Action Protocol for Low Value Employers' Liability and Public Liability Claims (the EL/PL Protocol)
6.7 Fixed costs fees
6.8 Stages in the RTA Protocol
6.9 No doctrine of mistake in RTA portal
6.10 Claims which leave the protocol/portal
6.11 Pre-Action Protocol for Personal Injury Claims (the Personal Injury Protocol)
6.12 Failure to comply with the pre-action protocols
6.13 Fundamental dishonesty and dismissal provision
6.14 Defendant's insurers and the Motor Insurers' Bureau
6.15 Debt claims
6.16 Pre-Action Protocol for Debt Claims
6.17 Practice Direction on Pre-Action Conduct and Protocols
6.18 Summary

6.1 Introduction

The tasks that a lawyer undertakes on behalf of the client at the outset are particularly important. There is much to do before a claimant's lawyer can issue proceedings. If this initial work is not carried out thoroughly and instructions are not taken fully, at best the lawyer could suffer the embarrassment of having to keep referring back to the client for simple details and information. At worst, the lawyer may have obtained only half of the information required and, if proceedings are issued on this basis, they may be struck out. Remember also that the court will expect the parties, in accordance with the overriding objective, to act reasonably and, in general, to try to avoid proceedings.

It may seem odd, but at the beginning of an action it is important to remind the client that the likelihood of reaching trial is not very high. The vast majority of cases "settle" (a compromise is agreed) before trial, and letters to clients should never be expressed in terms of "when this matter goes to trial . . ." as this is only a small possibility.

In this chapter we will review the pre-action rules which must be followed before issuing court proceedings. These are known as pre-action protocols and they are annexed to https://www.justice.gov.uk/courts/procedure-rules/civil/rules.

6.2 Pre-action protocols and the Practice Direction on Pre-Action Conduct and Protocols

The protocols explain the conduct and set out the steps the court would normally expect the parties to take before commencing proceedings for particular types of civil claims. In particular, they are designed to maximise the exchange of information at the pre-action stage so that the dispute can be settled, thereby saving time and costs, or to enable any subsequent litigation to be streamlined. Pre-action protocols are in force for a number of types of case including:

- debt claims;
- personal injury;
- professional negligence claims;
- certain claims in road traffic accidents.

The protocols are vitally important, and practitioners must understand and make proper use of them where they apply.

The protocols outline a structured approach to the making of claims and their progress before proceedings are issued. This ensures that, if the case cannot be settled, it will proceed to trial more swiftly, since most of the work has been done pre-action.

The general objectives of the pre-action protocols are to:

- encourage the **exchange of early and full information** about a prospective legal claim;
- enable the parties to **avoid litigation** by agreeing a settlement of the claim before commencement of proceedings;
- support the **efficient management of proceedings** where litigation cannot be avoided; and
- to ensure the costs incurred are **proportionate** to the value of the claim and the issues in dispute.

Failure to comply may lead to sanctions later on, such as costs penalties.

In cases not covered by an approved protocol, the court will expect the parties (in accordance with the overriding objective) to adopt a similar approach. Parties must adhere to the relevant provisions in the **Practice Direction – Pre-Action Conduct and Protocols** (**PDPAC**), which contains similar provisions.

NB para 2 Practice Direction on Pre-Action Conduct and Protocols states that: "A person who knowingly makes a false statement in a pre-action protocol letter or other document prepared in anticipation of legal proceedings may be subject to proceedings for contempt of court."

6.3 Protocols relevant to personal injury claims

The protocols relevant to personal injury claims and within the scope of this manual comprise:

- the Pre-Action Protocol for Personal Injury Claims (the **Personal Injury Protocol**);
- the Pre-Action Protocol for Personal Injury Claims Below the Small Claims Limit in Road Traffic Accidents (the **RTA Small Claims Protocol**);
- the Pre-Action Protocol for Low Value Personal Injury Claims in Road Traffic Accidents (the **RTA Protocol**); and
- the Pre-Action Protocol for Low Value (Employers' Liability and Public Liability) Claims (the **EL/PL Protocol**).

The Personal Injury Protocol was introduced in 1998 and was supplemented by the low value protocols, which apply to claims with a value of or below £25,000. These have reduced significantly the application of the original Personal Injury Protocol, which now applies only to higher value claims or where a claim leaves the original protocol, perhaps because liability is disputed.

6.4 Information required in a personal injury claim

During the initial interview with the client, apart from funding, you should obtain sufficient information to advise on the merits of the case. This will include details on the following.

(1) The circumstances of the accident including the date, time, location, who was involved and any witnesses.

(2) Whether the police were called and whether criminal proceedings were brought against either party.

(3) What injuries were suffered and how these were treated, together with details of any continuing effects or treatment.

(4) What financial losses the client suffered including loss of earnings, costs of repairing the car, medical expenses, etc.

(5) Details of any social security benefits claimed.

This will enable you to place an approximate value on the claim to determine which protocol applies. You should then set about gathering the evidence, both documentary and witness, to support your client's claim.

We will now consider the pre-action protocols.

6.5 Low value personal injury protocol claims

The low value personal injury protocol claims were introduced to meet concerns about increasing numbers of road traffic accident (RTA) personal injury claims. They are designed to speed up the processing of claims and make use of fixed costs at different stages.

6.5.1 The Pre-Action Protocol for Personal Injury Claims Below the Small Claims Limit in Road Traffic Accidents (the RTA Small Claims Protocol)

The **RTA Small Claims Protocol** applies where:

- the claim arises from a road traffic accident which occurred in England or Wales on or after 31 May 2021;
- the claim includes a claim for damages for injury; and
- the claimant values the overall claim at no more than £10,000 and the claim for damages for injury at no more than £5,000, save that the value of any **non-protocol vehicle costs** is excluded for the purposes of valuing the **claim**.

This protocol is entirely run through an online portal which is designed to be used by litigants-in-person. See https://www.officialinjuryclaim.org.uk/make-a-claim/.

6.5.2 The Pre-Action Protocol for Low Value Personal Injury Claims in Road Traffic Accidents (the RTA Protocol)

The **RTA Protocol** has the following features.

(1) It sets out a clear and rigid timetable which all the parties must follow to ensure the matter comes to an early conclusion. This prevents cases from drifting, or even grinding to a halt, as occurred in the past. It ensures that defendants, who may benefit from delays in paying out settlements, can no longer do so and keeps the pressure on lawyers to press the case forward.

(2) Fixed costs are a feature of the scheme. This limits the costs which lawyers may charge for each step in the proceedings, and also avoids disputes about those costs.

(3) The whole process is conducted by the claimant and defendant representatives (usually, claimant lawyer and defendant insurer) through a purpose-made electronic portal, which is financed by the insurance industry.

This protocol applies to RTA claims with a value of £25,000 or below where the small claims track would not be the normal track for that claim.

6.5.2.1 The three stages

The protocol sets out a three-stage process. Stages 1 and 2 are pre-litigation, with the court only becoming involved at Stage 3 should the parties fail to reach agreement.

Stage 1 provides for early notification of a claim to the defendant and their insurer. Information is exchanged electronically.

(1) The claimant's representatives must carry out a search on the Claims and Underwritings Exchange Personal Injury (CUE PI) database, which records incidents reported by policy holders to their insurance companies. This requirement is designed to reduce the risk of fraud.

(2) To notify the defendant insurer of the claim the claimant's representative completes the Claim Notification Form (CNF) (form **RTA1**). This provides full information on the circumstances of the accident and any damages claimed for the vehicle and injuries suffered.

(3) RTA1 is sent electronically to the defendant insurer and by first class post to the defendant.

(4) The insurer must send an electronic acknowledgment the next business day after receipt of RTA1 and provide a response to liability within 15 business days.

(5) An admission of liability is required for the claim to remain in the RTA Protocol.

Stage 2 covers obtaining and service of medical evidence, offers to settle and negotiation. Most claims will settle during Stage 2 and the claimant is then paid quickly.

(1) If the insurer admits liability, the amount of the damages will be determined.

(2) The claimant's lawyer will obtain a medical report (form **RTA3**). Note that for soft tissue injury claims, such as whiplash, the claimant's representative must instruct a medical expert from a not-for-profit company, MedCo Registration Solutions (MedCo). This is to ensure the independence of any such reports. The **Whiplash Injury Regulations 2021** set out a tariff of damages payable for pain, suffering and loss of amenity where the claimant has suffered whiplash injuries. The fixed payments are based on a scale calculated on the basis of the period of suffering lasting up to two years. The court has a discretion to increase the tariff payments by up to 20 per cent in exceptional circumstances.

(3) The claimant's lawyer will then complete a Stage 2 settlement pack (form **RTA5**), which will be sent to the insurer. This includes the medical report, a schedule of damages (losses and expenses) and an offer to settle.

(4) The insurer has 15 business days to accept the offer or make a counter-offer.

(5) If a counter-offer is made, there will be 20 business days for negotiation. If agreement is not reached, the claim will move into Stage 3.

Stage 3 arises where compensation cannot be agreed. The court is not involved at all until Stage 3.

(1) The claimant will prepare a Court Proceedings Pack (forms **RTA6** and **RTA7**), which includes the party's final settlement offer.

(2) An application will be made to the court for a hearing. This can either be a paper hearing, in which the judge considers written representations from each party's lawyer; or an oral hearing, where each party attends with a lawyer.

(3) Once agreement has been reached, the damages and fixed costs must be paid within 10 days.

6.6 The Pre-Action Protocol for Low Value Employers' Liability and Public Liability Claims (the EL/PL Protocol)

The **EL/PL Protocol** applies to employers' liability and public liability personal injury claims with an upper limit of £25,000.

Although the stages of the **EL/PL Protocol** contain similar steps to those in the **RTA Protocol**, the timescales which apply in Stage 1 are different. The defendant insurer has 30 days to respond to the liability allegations in an employer liability claim, and 40 days in a public liability claim.

Claims in the **EL/PL Protocol** are subject to a "portal" process similar to that for RTA claims and fixed fees apply.

6.7 Fixed costs fees

Each stage of the low value protocols is subject to fixed fees. Set out below are the costs which apply to the **RTA Protocol** and, as you will see, these are somewhat limited. This is because, although the intention of the protocol is to impose certainty on the parties in relation to costs, the underlying reason is to keep them as low as possible.

The costs payable depend upon the amount of the damages and the stage at which settlement was reached.

RTA Protocol

Claims submitted on or after 31 July 2013	Where the value of the claim for damages is £10,000 or less	Where the value of the claim for damages is £10,000.01–£25,000
Stage 1	£200	£200
Stage 2	£300	£600
Stage 3	£250 paper hearing or £500 oral hearing (to include the advocate's fee)	£250 paper hearing or £500 oral hearing (to include the advocate's fee)

In addition, the claimant will receive their disbursements such as fees paid for medical records and reports and court fees.

EL/PL Protocol

The fixed costs regime is very similar to that of the RTA Protocol, except that they are slightly higher as summarised below:

Accident date on or after 31 July 2013	Where the claim for damages is £10,000 or less	Where the claim for damages is £10,000.01–£25,000
Stage 1	£300	£300
Stage 2	£600	£1,300
Stage 3	£250 paper hearing £500 oral hearing	£250 paper hearing £500 oral hearing

6.8 Stages in the RTA Protocol

The stages of the **RTA Protocol** are summarised in the diagram below.

RTA Protocol

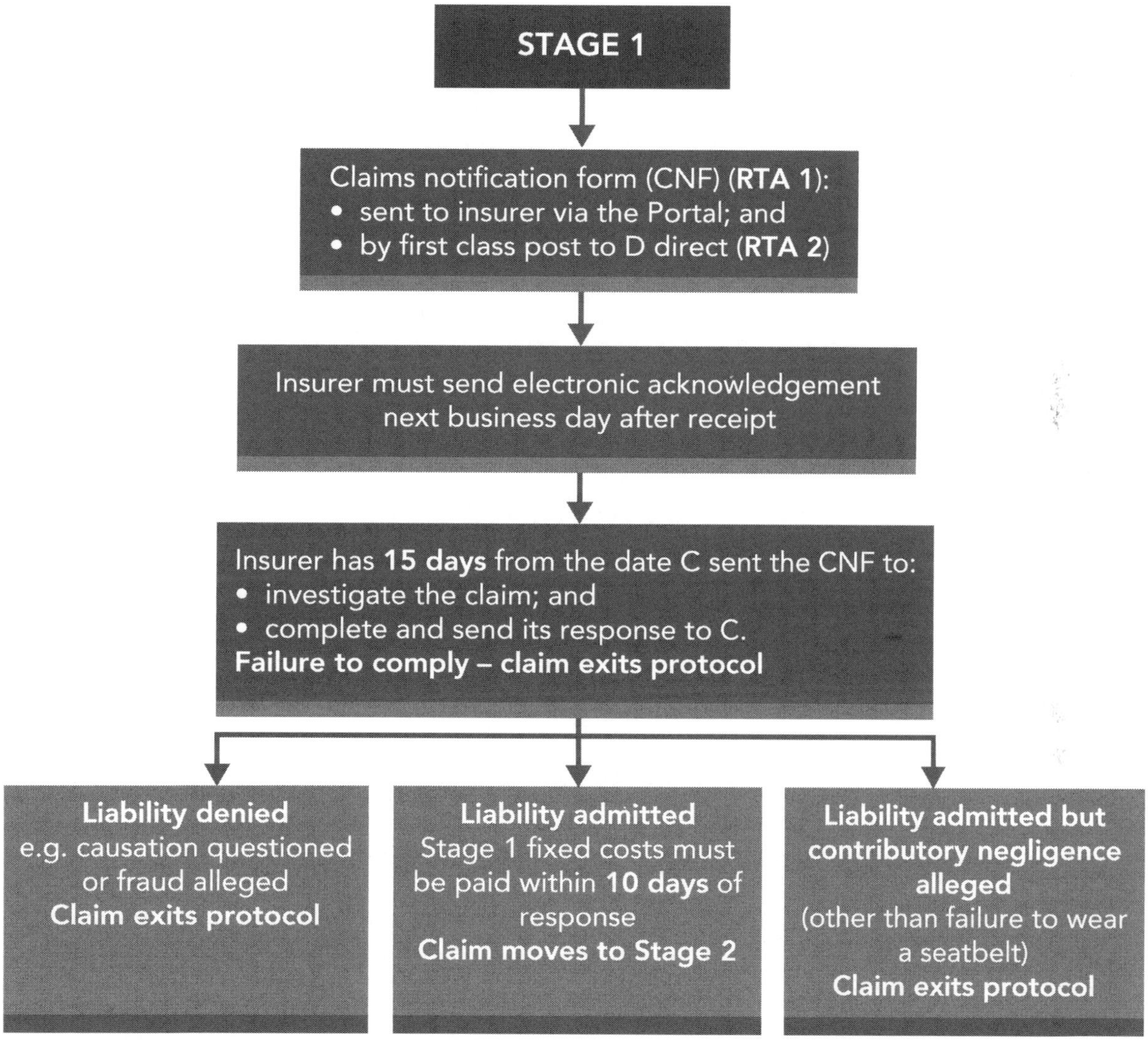

STAGE 2

C provides insurer with Stage 2 settlement pack (**RTA 5**) including:
- medical report
- schedule of damages (losses and expenses)

Insurer has 15 days "initial consideration period"
- to consider Stage 2 settlement pack; and
- accept C's offer: or
- make a counter-offer.

(If necessary) a further 20 days "negotiation period"
to consider counter-offer and negotiate to try to reach agreement.

C's offer or D's counter-offer accepted?
Insurer has 10 days to pay damages and Stage 2 costs

If no settlement is reached **claim moves to Stage 3**

STAGE 3

C sends Court Proceedings Pack (forms **RTA 6** and **RTA 7**) to D to include the parties' final offers

Proceedings issued under CPR Part 8
After five days C submits claim to the court for a hearing to determine final assessment of damages

Paper hearing
- value of claim assessed on papers already submitted
- written judgment given with reasons

Oral hearing
- can be requested by either party
- limited to submissions on existing evidence only

Damages and fixed costs payable within **10 days**

6.9 No doctrine of mistake in RTA portal

If a claims handler inadvertently clicks "yes" and accepts a sum offered in the electronic RTA portal, they cannot rely on the common law doctrine of genuine mistake to avoid the acceptance/agreement. In ***Draper v Newport [2014]*** the court stated that this was to avoid satellite litigation which would risk undermining the certainty, speed and costs of the portal system and, in turn, the ability for the system to deal with cases justly and proportionately.

6.10 Claims which leave the protocol/ portal

As mentioned earlier, most low value personal injury claims begin in the **RTA** or the **EL/PL Protocols**, and the **Personal Injury Protocol** only becomes relevant if the claim leaves the initial low-value protocols.

The main reasons for a claim leaving the **RTA** or the **EL/PL Protocols** are:

- liability is disputed, including an allegation of contributory negligence (unless this relates to failure to wear a seatbelt);
- the value of the claim exceeds £25,000;
- allegation of fraud;
- defendant insurer's failure to respond to the timescales in Stage 1.

On leaving the **RTA Protocol**, the claim would be pursued under the **Personal Injury Protocol** and the CNF is treated as the letter of claim.

6.10.1 Fixed costs after exiting portal

Fixed costs continue to apply where a claim exits the RTA Protocol/portal unless the case is allocated to the multi-track – perhaps because the amount in dispute increases beyond the £25,000 threshold figure. The amount of fees/costs payable depends on the stage when the claim was settled and whether it was disposed of at trial. Details of these fixed costs are in **Part 45**.

6.11 Pre-Action Protocol for Personal Injury Claims (the Personal Injury Protocol)

This protocol is designed for road traffic accidents, tripping, slipping and work accident cases. It provides that, before issuing proceedings, the following matters should be dealt with in the order set out below.

(1) The claimant may choose to send an informal letter to the defendant or their insurer at an early stage to raise awareness of the claim. Doing so will not start the protocol timetable.

(2) Two copies of a **letter of claim** should be sent to the defendant as soon as sufficient information is available to substantiate a realistic claim. One copy is for the defendant and the other for their insurer.

(a) The letter of claim should contain:

- a clear summary of the facts (in other words a description of how the injuries were caused with some indication of how the recipient of the letter is responsible for it);
- the nature of the injuries and details of the financial losses claimed;
- if the injuries are ongoing, the letter should invite the defendant to help meet the claimant's immediate needs by use of rehabilitation.

(b) The letter of claim should indicate which documents should be disclosed by the defendant at this stage.

(3) The defendant must reply within 21 days naming any insurer. A failure to reply within this time justifies the issue of proceedings without further compliance with the protocol. This letter is not a full response to the letter of claim, but an acknowledgment of it. It triggers the three-month investigation period discussed below.

(4) During those three months, the defendant should investigate the claim and state whether liability is denied and, if so, on what grounds. The defendant must also outline their own version of events and enclose any documents relevant to liability.

(5) If contributory negligence is alleged (i.e. the defendant alleges that the claimant caused or contributed to their injuries), the claimant should respond to the allegations raised before proceedings are issued.

(6) The claimant's solicitor must send a schedule of details of losses and expenses, together with supporting documents, as soon as possible.

(7) The next step will be to obtain medical evidence dealing with the client's injuries. The protocol encourages the use of a jointly selected medical expert.

(8) Once these steps have been taken, the parties are encouraged to consider negotiating with each other before starting proceedings.

An example of a letter of claim for personal injury is set out below.

To: Henry Morgan, Defendant

Dear Sir,

Re:	Our client:	Penelope Taylor
	Our client's address:	3 Seaview Villas, Seagull Terrace, Medchester, MD3 4XX
	Our client's employer:	Medchester Medical Practice, 36–42 Gordon Street, Lincoln, LN8 2AB

We are instructed by Penelope Taylor to claim damages in connection with a road traffic accident on 7 May 2022 at the junction of Walmesley Street and Sandford Street, Bury St. Edmunds, Suffolk.

Please confirm the identity of your insurers. Please note that the insurers will need to see this letter as soon as possible; it may affect your insurance cover and/or conduct of any subsequent proceedings if you do not show this letter to them.

The circumstances of the accident were that our client's car, registration number P653 JSD, was travelling along Walmesley Street in the direction of Bury St. Edmunds town centre when you, driving a car, registration number N522 KTY, emerged from the side road known as Sandford Street from the left of our client's car, failed to stop at the stop line at the mouth of the junction, and collided with our client's car.

The reasons why we are alleging fault are that it was negligent to fail to stop at the junction, that you failed to slow down in time, or to see or take account of the presence of our client's car, and collided with her vehicle which was travelling on the major road at the junction.

A description of our client's injuries is as follows:

- whiplash injury to her cervical spine;
- sprain injury to her left ankle; and
- post-traumatic shock.

Our client received treatment at Hanson Memorial Hospital, Medchester. The hospital reference number is XXX.

Our client is still suffering from the effects of the injury. We invite you to participate with us in addressing her immediate needs by use of rehabilitation.

Our client is employed as a medical receptionist by Medchester Medical Practice, 36–42 Gordon Street, Lincoln LN8 2AB, and has had a total of four weeks off work immediately following the accident. Her approximate net weekly income is £350.

We are obtaining a police report and will let you have a copy of the same upon your undertaking to meet half the fee.

At this stage we would expect the documents contained in Section A of the RTA standard disclosure lists to be relevant to this claim. A copy of Section A is attached.

A copy of this letter is attached for you to send to your insurers. Finally, we expect an acknowledgment of this letter within 21 days by yourselves or your insurers.

Yours faithfully

Tompkins & Co.

PRE-ACTION PROTOCOL FOR PERSONAL INJURY CLAIMS
ANNEX B1

To

Defendant

Dear Sirs

Re: **Claimant's full name**

Claimant's full address

Claimant's clock or works number

Claimant's employer (name and address)

We are instructed by the above named to claim damages in connection with an **accident at work/road traffic accident/tripping accident** on **(day)** of

(year) at **(place of accident which must be sufficiently detailed to establish location).**

Please confirm the identity of your insurers. Please note that the insurers will need to see this letter as soon as possible and it may affect your insurance cover and/or the conduct of any subsequent legal proceedings if you do not send this letter to them.

Clear summary of the facts

The circumstances of the accident are:

(brief outline)

Liability

The reason why we are alleging fault is:

(simple explanation e.g. defective machine, broken ground)

We are obtaining a police report and will let you have a copy of the same upon your undertaking to meet half the fee.

Injuries

A description of our clients' injuries is as follows:

(brief outline)

The description should include a non-exhaustive list of the main functional effects on daily living, so that the defendant can begin to assess value/rehabilitation needs.

(In cases of road traffic accidents)

Our client (state hospital reference number) received treatment for the injuries at (name and address of hospital).

Our client is still suffering from the effects of his/her injury. We invite you to participate with us in addressing his/her immediate needs by use of rehabilitation.

Loss of earnings

He/She is employed as (**occupation**) and has had the following time off work **(dates of absence)**. His/Her approximate weekly income is **(insert if known)**.

If you are our client's employers, please provide us with the usual earnings details which will enable us to calculate his/her financial loss.

Other financial losses

We are also aware of the following (likely) financial losses:

Details of the insurer

We have also sent a letter of claim to **(name and address)** and a copy of that letter is attached. We understand their insurers are **(name, address and claims number if known)**.

At this stage of our enquiries we would expect the documents contained in parts **(insert appropriate parts of standard disclosure list)** to be relevant to this action.

A copy of this letter is attached for you to send to your insurers. Finally, we expect an acknowledgment of this letter within 21 days by yourselves or your insurers.

Yours faithfully

6.11.1 Selection of experts under the Personal Injury Protocol

The Personal Injury Protocol regards the joint selection of a single expert to be the norm. Usually this will apply to the medical expert but on occasions also to liability experts, for example, engineers. The protocol encourages the claimant to obtain a medical report, disclosing it to the defendant, who then asks questions and/or agrees it and does not obtain their own report. A medical report must be attached to the particulars of claim when the claim is issued. The parties can seek permission of the court to instruct further experts after proceedings have been issued.

6.12 Failure to comply with the pre-action protocols

Where there is a rational justification for failing to comply with the pre-action protocols, there will be no adverse consequences.

Where a failure to comply arises through slackness or deliberate flouting, the offending party may be penalised in costs.

6.13 Fundamental dishonesty and dismissal provision

s57 Criminal Justice and Courts Act 2015 (**CJCA 2015**) requires the court to dismiss the whole of a personal injury claim where it is satisfied, on the balance of probabilities, that the claimant has been fundamentally dishonest in relation to any element of the claim for personal injury or related claim. Dismissal of the entire claim is mandatory unless the court considers that to do so would cause the claimant to suffer *substantial injustice*.

Examples

The courts are taking a robust approach to the issue of fundamental dishonesty. In ***London Organising Committee for the Olympic and Paralympic Games (in Liquidation) v Sinfield [2018]*** the High Court gave new guidance on its effect. The claimant had wrongly claimed damages for gardening services, but the balance of his claim was legitimate. Despite this, his claim was dismissed in its entirety. Judge Knowles stated that the fact that the greater part of the claim was genuine was "neither here nor there".

However, in a rather different case, ***Ravenscroft v IKEA [2015]***, the judge made it clear that the courts are equally prepared to respond vigorously to defendants who use it as a strategy to persuade claimants to drop or settle their claims.

6.14 Defendant's insurers and the Motor Insurers' Bureau

In personal injury cases where the defendant is a driver, additional points concerning insurance companies should be considered.

(1) **Road Traffic Act 1988**

Under **s143(1) Road Traffic Act 1988** (**RTA 1988**), it is compulsory for drivers to have insurance for personal injury and consequential loss caused to third parties.

However, if a driver has insurance cover on their car but the vehicle is lent to, or borrowed or stolen by, someone who has no insurance, the insurers will still pick up the liability as "insurer concerned". If that uninsured driver has an accident, the victim will be compensated by the insured driver's insurers under **s151 RTA 1988**.

This may seem somewhat unfair on the insurance company as it is obliged to pay out for a driver of whom it has no knowledge, particularly as (under normal circumstances) that driver may have been refused insurance. However, failing to receive compensation would be even more unfair on the victim of the accident and so this legal requirement is in place for public policy reasons.

It is vital to give notice to insurers under **s152 RTA 1988** either before or within seven days of the issue of proceedings. This is because insurers will only be liable to pay out in the situations referred to above if notice of proceedings has been given within this deadline.

(2) **Motor Insurers' Bureau (MIB)**

The MIB came into being as a result of concern that, despite compulsory motor insurance (which, of course, led to a vast amount of business for the insurance industry), there were cases where victims of road accidents could not obtain compensation because some people drive while uninsured, and others fail to stop after accidents and remain untraced. The MIB is effectively a syndicate of insurance companies which meets approximately 25,000 claims each year and it acts as a "safety net" for the innocent victim. To cover these situations two agreements were made between the MIB and the Minister for Transport.

There are two main agreements, these being the **Uninsured Drivers' Agreement 2015** and the **Untraced Drivers' Agreement 2017**.

These cover personal injury and fatal road accident cases and include claims for consequential loss and property damage. Under these agreements, the claimant brings proceedings in the normal way, but the MIB has to pay any judgment obtained provided the formal requirements have been observed.

The **Uninsured Drivers' Agreement 2015** requires the innocent victim to apply to the MIB providing certain information and documentation. If the MIB declines liability, proceedings should be commenced against both the driver and the MIB. If the driver is found liable, the MIB must satisfy the judgment if it remains unpaid after seven days.

There is a supplementary **Uninsured Drivers' Agreement 2017** which amends the **Uninsured Drivers' Agreement 2015** by deleting the exclusion of claims for damage to the claimant's own vehicle, where they knew or ought to have known it was uninsured.

The **Untraced Drivers' Agreement 2017** applies to "hit and run" situations occurring after 1 March 2017, where the driver cannot be traced. Because of this, it is not possible to commence court proceedings and so an application must be made to the MIB on behalf of the innocent victim. However, there are some exclusions, such as where the victim voluntarily allowed themselves to be carried in the vehicle despite knowing it was stolen. The **Untraced Drivers' Agreement 2017** covers personal injury and property damage (but only if coupled with an award for "significant personal injury") with an excess of £400.

The following flowchart summarises the key issues relating to RTA policies.

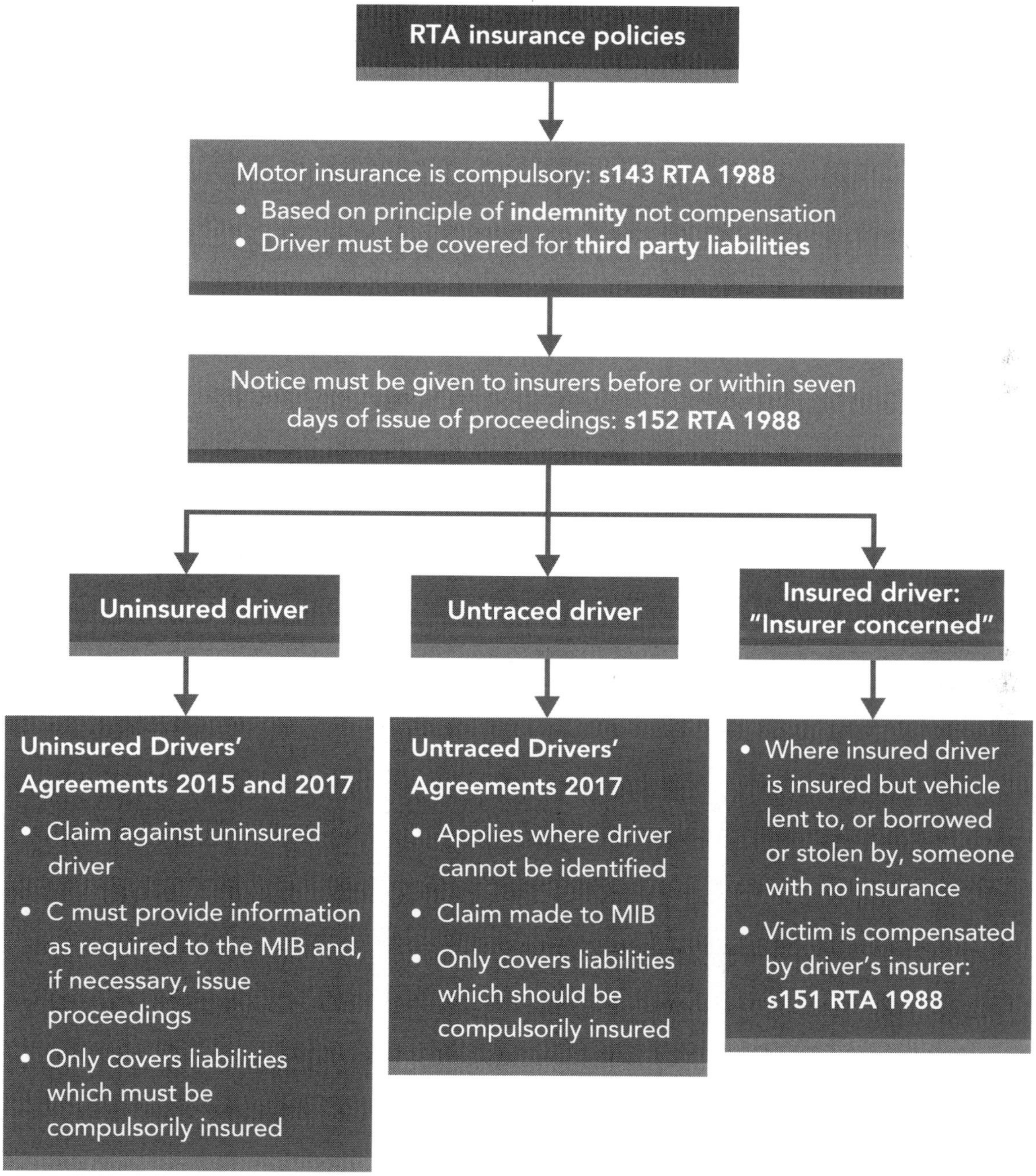

6.15 Debt claims

Debt claims fall into a number of categories. Common ones are:

- unpaid invoices for goods sold and delivered;
- unpaid invoices for services provided such as building works, advertising services, accountants' fees and many more;
- money borrowed and not repaid; and
- hire charges.

Debt claims may be brought against companies or individual debtors. Firms handling large numbers of debt claims will often utilise specialist case management software and adopt standard instructions and reporting procedures. This is because the client will want to recover the debt with as little expense as possible to prevent recovery being uneconomic.

Taking instructions

The following information will be required.

(1) How the debt arose, including the date of the contract and details of the payment obligation. You will need the contract documentation and the invoice (if any) being sued upon. It is often the case that sums due under invoices are payable 14 or 30 days after the invoice.

(2) Precisely how much is owed.

(3) Details of what has happened since the amount fell due. Have reminders been sent? Has the debtor given any reasons for non-payment and do they have any merit? (Possible defence.)

(4) Whether the matter is capable of resolution by means of ADR. This must be considered even though it may be exploited by an unscrupulous debtor to avoid payment and defer the issue of proceedings against them.

Next steps

Having taken instructions:

- remind your client to keep you informed of any further communications or payments from the debtor; and to retain all relevant documents including those that arrive in the future;

- make enquiries about the financial standing of the debtor to avoid "throwing good money after bad":
  - limited liability companies:
    - conduct a search of Companies House to check the most recent filed accounts for the company; and
    - search the Royal Courts of Justice to check another creditor has not already issued winding up proceedings;
  - partnerships and individuals:
    - check whether the client has information on the debtor's assets; and/or
    - seek a status report from a firm of enquiry agents;
  - search at the Land Registry to ascertain if the debtor owns the land and if there are any debts secured against it.

6.16 Pre-Action Protocol for Debt Claims

Debt claims are covered by the **Pre-Action Protocol for Debt Claims (PPDC)**.

PPDC applies to any business including sole traders and public bodies (the "creditor") which brings a claim against a debtor who is either an individual or a sole trader (the "debtor"). It does not apply to business to business debts (unless the debtor is a sole trader).

PPDC has four aims.

(1) To encourage communication between the parties at a very early stage, so that both parties have all the information they need to clarify the issues that are in dispute.

(2) To enable them to achieve settlement without the need for court proceedings, for example, by agreeing repayment plans.

(3) To encourage the parties to act in a reasonable and proportionate manner, having regard to the size of the debt.

(4) To support the efficient management of court proceedings where these prove necessary.

PPDC sets out clear steps which must be followed.

- The creditor must send the debtor a letter of claim including full details of the debt owed, an up-to-date statement of account with details of interest and charges, and how the debt can be paid. The standard Reply Form, Information Sheet and Financial Statement forms which are annexed to the protocol should also be included.
- The debtor should respond using the Reply Form provided within 30 days. They may request documents or include those they believe are relevant.
- If there are still issues in dispute after disclosure has taken place, the parties should consider alternative dispute resolution.
- Court proceedings should only be issued if no response is received within 30 days; alternatively, if agreement cannot be reached. However, the creditor must wait 30 days from the letter of claim before doing so and allow extra time if necessary for the debtor to seek legal or debt advice or in order to pay.

The court will expect the parties to have complied with **PPDC** before commencing proceedings and may take this into account when making directions for the management of the case. Costs sanctions may also be imposed.

PPDC impacts on debt collection in a number of ways. The letter of claim needs to include far more detail, and the creditor may face sanctions for non-compliance if the case does proceed to court. The standard forms provide a more structured response and will assist individuals and sole traders in responding to letters of claim. In particular, the reasons for non-payment are more likely to be identified at an early stage. However, there are concerns that **PPDC** will increase the length of the debt collection process due to the timescales set out in **PPDC**, which could delay the issue of proceedings by around three months.

6.17 Practice Direction on Pre-Action Conduct and Protocols

All other claims which fall outside the protocols will be dealt with under the **Practice Direction on Pre-Action Conduct and Protocols** (**PDPAC**). This includes business to business debts (unless the debtor is a sole trader). The preliminary investigations and steps set out earlier in this chapter will need to be carried out. Thereafter, once you are clear about the nature of the claim, you must proceed in accordance with **PDPAC**.

Pre-action steps

The parties are required to exchange sufficient information so that they understand each other's position, to consider ADR and attempt to settle the dispute without recourse to proceedings.

PDPAC expressly states that only reasonable and proportionate steps should be taken by the parties to seek to resolve the matter and costs incurred should be proportionate.

Complying will require:

- the claimant to write to the defendant with concise details of the claim, including a summary of the facts, the sum due and how the amount is calculated;
- the defendant to provide a response within a reasonable time – 14 days in a straightforward claim and three months maximum in a very complex case – to include:
    - confirmation of whether the claim is accepted; and
    - if not, the reasons why; and
    - details of any counterclaim; and
- the parties disclosing key documents relevant to the issues in dispute.

Expert evidence is only permitted with the court's permission as most disputes can be resolved without this.

A sample letter of claim to a business debtor is set out below.

> Firm's letterhead and reference   Date
>
> Defendant's name and address
>
> Dear Sirs,
>
> Re: Filbert Engineering Limited
>   Invoice G3456
>
> We are instructed on behalf of Filbert Engineering Limited. Pursuant to your order dated 5 April 2020 our client sold and DELIVERED to you a number of machine tools as set out in our client's invoice numbered G3456. The sum due under the invoice is £42,000 plus VAT of £8,400, making a total of £50,400. A copy of the invoice is enclosed with this letter.

We understand that our client has not yet received any payment. In accordance with the Practice Direction on Pre-Action Conduct and Protocols we invite you to consider alternative dispute resolution (ADR) to seek to resolve this matter without recourse to litigation. We suggest mediation would be appropriate.

If you refuse or ignore our invitation to engage with ADR and in the continued absence of payment in full to our client within 14 days from the date of this letter, we reserve the right to issue proceedings to recover payment without further notice.

If this becomes necessary, our instructions are to seek costs and interest in addition to the above-stated sum. Your payment should be sent to this firm.

You may wish to seek legal advice.

Yours faithfully,

If no payment is made, consider ADR and issuing and serving proceedings.

6.18 Summary

(1) Some actions are governed by **pre-action protocols**, for example, personal injury cases and some debt claims. These define the steps which must be taken before proceedings are issued, with the intention of avoiding litigation by agreeing a settlement.

(2) Low value personal injury claims (£25,000 or below in value) will begin using specific protocols such as the RTA Small Claims Protocol, the RTA Protocol and the EL/PL Protocol but will continue under the Personal Injury Protocol if the claim leaves the initial protocol.

(3) There are set stages through which cases must proceed in the RTA and EL/PL Protocols as follows:

- in Stage 1 the parties consider liability; and, if liability is admitted, the claim proceeds to;
- Stage 2, where quantum evidence is obtained and disclosed and settlement offers made and negotiated by both parties;
- if settlement cannot be agreed, the claim proceeds to Stage 3, where the claimant can issue proceedings for the case to be heard either at a paper-only hearing or with each party making representations.

(4) The personal injury pre-action protocol regards the joint selection of a single expert as the norm, although it remains possible for each party to instruct their own expert.

(5) A checklist for the initial interview with a client in a personal injury claim must include **funding** considerations, information to establish the **liability** of the defendant and information to establish the **quantum** (amount) of the damages.

(6) Fixed costs apply to RTA claims with a value up to £25,000 as these claims are subject to the RTA Small Claims Protocol and the RTA Protocol, and similar claims under the EL/PL Protocol. If the claims exit the initial protocol and continue under the Personal Injury Protocol, they remain subject to (different) fixed costs/fees dependent on whether the claims settle or proceed to trial, and whether the damages are agreed between the parties or awarded by the court.

(7) In personal injury cases, **ss151** and **152 RTA 1988**, and the Motor Insurers' Bureau if the defendant is uninsured or untraced, must be considered.

(8) For debt claims, a different approach will apply depending upon whether the debtor is an individual or a business. The **Pre-Action Protocol for Debt Claims** applies where a debt claim is brought against an individual or a sole trader. It sets out steps, timescales and standard forms which a creditor must use when suing for the monies owed.

(9) If the type of case has no pre-action protocol, such as debt claims between businesses, the court will still expect the parties to comply with the **Practice Direction on Pre-Action Conduct and Protocols**.

CHAPTER 7

Issue and Service of Proceedings

7.1 Introduction

The vast majority of claims settle at the pre-action protocol stage. If this does not occur, with your client's agreement you should prepare relevant court documents and issue legal proceedings. This chapter summarises the legal elements and practical steps to initiate such proceedings, including:

- where to sue;
- who to sue;
- issue of proceedings; and
- service of documents.

7.2 Where to sue?

The first question is whether to issue proceedings in the High Court or the County Court.

7.2.1 High Court or County Court?

The general rule is that, for money claims, there is no financial upper limit on the value of claims which can be heard in the County Court. However, **CPR** provide further guidance to assist lawyers in determining the appropriate court. In summary:

- if the value of the claim exceeds £100,000, the client may choose either the High or the County Court;
- claims for £100,000 or less must be started in the County Court;
- there are separate rules which apply to personal injury claims. Only those equal to or in excess of £50,000 may begin in the High Court.

Where the value of the claim provides the claimant with a choice of court, the High Court should only be used if:

- the claim is complex; and/or
- the outcome of the case is important to the general public.

However, the High Court may itself transfer the claim to the County Court.

Example

Midlands Metalwork Ltd (MML) is seeking damages for late delivery of a consignment of steel rods. The claim is for the additional costs of £1,000 incurred in replacing the goods at short notice and £7,500 loss of profits. The total estimated value of £8,500 makes this a claim that must be started in the County Court and as a money-only claim, it should be issued in the County Court Money Claims Centre.

7.2.2 Location of court

The High Court sits in London and in several regional District Registries in England and Wales. Proceedings started in the High Court are issued in a named District Registry, for example, Birmingham District Registry, and are sent to that address.

Although there are also several specialist courts, these are beyond the scope of the course book.

With regard to the County Court:

- money-only claims (whether a debt action or for damages) must be issued by the **County Court Money Claims Centre** (CCMCC) and sent to its address at PO Box 527, M5 0BY. The CCMCC is located in Salford, near Manchester;
- other claims may be started at any of the County Court hearing centres throughout the country.

7.3 Who to sue?

Before commencing proceedings, it is important to check that you are suing the correct party and **CPR** set out the rules in this regard.

7.3.1 Children and protected parties

There are special safeguards for children and mental patients (as defined by the **Mental Capacity Act 2005**) because these individuals are considered in law to be unable to make the decisions required of adult litigants.

Generally, children and protected parties have to be represented in litigation by some responsible person, who is called their litigation friend. For children, this is usually a parent. A litigation friend should be someone who can fairly and competently conduct proceedings on behalf of the child or protected party and who has no adverse interest. For example, if a father's negligent driving caused his child's injury, the father could not be the child's litigation friend as he would also be the defendant to the child's claim.

Settlements by or on behalf of children and protected parties will not be valid without the approval of the court.

7.3.2 Partnerships

Companies, partnerships and sole traders are all business entities and particular court rules apply to them.

Partnerships are arrangements by which businesses are carried on by two or more persons with a view to profit. Many professional businesses, such as solicitors and accountants, operate as partnerships.

A partnership has no legal identity of its own and to avoid having to name and serve all the partners individually, the rules state that the claim can be brought against the partnership name.

7.3.3 Sole traders

Sole traders are simply individuals engaging in business, although they will often use a business name. A sole trader must:

- sue in their own personal name; but
- be sued in either their own name or their business name.

7.3.4 Companies and limited liability partnerships

Limited liability companies (and limited liability partnerships) have a separate legal identity.

In proceedings it is therefore essential that the correct registered name of the company is used. There is no point in suing either the directors or the shareholders.

No company has exactly the same name as another. However, companies often have very similar names and it is quite easy to sue the wrong company if a minor mistake is made. This can be as simple as using "Ltd" rather than "Limited". It is partly for this reason that company searches are often conducted before proceedings are commenced.

7.4 Issue of proceedings

Proceedings are started when the court "issues" the claim form by sealing it with the court seal.

7.4.1 Documents needed for issue

The claimant's lawyer will prepare the relevant documents which need to be sent to the court for issue of proceedings. These comprise:

- N1 claim form;
- particulars of claim – may be included on the N1 claim form or a separate document;
- any documents required to be annexed to the particulars of claim, such as a copy of the contract, as indicated by a relevant Practice Direction; and
- for personal injury claims, the medical report and a schedule of past and future expenses and losses.

In addition, sufficient copies for the parties and the court must be sent together with a covering letter indicating who is to serve proceedings, the court or the lawyer and the court issue fee.

7.4.2 Completion of N1 claim form

Forms such as the N1 claim form can be accessed from the Ministry of Justice website. In this chapter, we shall be concentrating on the form required for general proceedings, such as debt and contested personal injury claims issued under **CPR Part 7**.

The N1 claim form provides a summary of the main aspects of the claim and may be accessed at https://assets.publishing.service.gov.uk/government/uploads/system/uploads/attachment_data/file/688390/n1-eng.pdf.

You will find a completed N1 claim form for issue of proceedings in relation to a simple debt action at **Document 1** of the **Appendix**.

The numbered paragraphs below correspond with the numbered items in the claim form.

The Courts and Tribunals Service publishes guidance notes on completion of the N1 claim form and these may be accessed at https://www.gov.uk/government/publications/form-n1-claim-form-cpr-part-7.

(1) **Identification of court**

County Court

The relevant County Court must be set out in the top right-hand corner of the form. For money only claims, this will be the CCMCC.

High Court

For issue in the High Court the name of the relevant High Court Division and local District Registry should be stated. For example:

In the High Court of Justice

Queen's Bench Division

Birmingham District Registry

(2) **For completion by the court**

(a) The claim number is allocated by the court. It is a unique case reference number which parties must quote on all subsequent court documents and correspondence with the court.

(b) The issue date is also inserted by the court.

(3) **Details of parties**

The full, unabbreviated name and title of each party, their status (i.e. claimant or defendant) and their home or business address. Where an individual carries on a business, the **CPR** requires the business name to be added followed by the words "a Firm". Company names should have the appropriate suffix of "Ltd" or "plc".

The full address must also be provided; otherwise, the court will issue but not serve the proceedings.

(4) **Brief details of claim**

The claim form must contain a concise statement of the nature of the claim and specify the remedy that the claimant is seeking.

(5) **Value**

Where the claim is for money (rather than, for example, an injunction), the claim form must state:

- the precise value for a debt action;
- if the claim is for damages, for example in a breach of contract claim, an approximate value must be given:
  - not more than £10,000;
  - more than £10,000 but not more than £25,000;
  - more than £25,000; or
  - the claimant cannot say how much they expect to recover.

This information assists the court in allocating the claim to one of the court's three procedural "tracks".

The rules in relation to personal injury claims are slightly different. For claims of £10,000 or less, a claimant must also state what they reasonably expect to recover in damages for pain, suffering and loss of amenity. In non-RTA claims, if the amount is not more than £1,500, the claim will stay in the small claims track; if it is more than £1,500, it will be allocated to the fast track. In RTA claims, the amount will be £5,000 (or £1,000 in cases involving children and protected persons).

Note that for a High Court claim, to confirm that the correct court has been used to issue the proceedings, the claimant must state that they expect to recover more than £100,000 for damages claims (such as for breach of contract); and more than £50,000 for a personal injury claim. There is no need to provide any further information on value because these figures are (obviously) more than the £25,000 threshold for the multi-track. Hence, all High Court matters will be allocated to the multi-track.

(6) **Preferred County Court hearing centre**

County Court

If a claim is for money only, the claim form must be sent to the CCMCC. It will remain here unless the claim is defended or a hearing is required, at which point the matter will be transferred to:

- the defendant's home County Court; or to
- the claimant's preferred hearing centre as specified on the claim form.

Therefore, it is important that the claimant includes a named court to avoid future costs and inconvenience.

High Court

For issue of proceedings in the High Court, the claimant must specify in which District Registry they would like the case to be tried. Often, District Registries share the physical premises of the County Court hearing centres.

(7) **Defendant's details for service**

The defendant's name and address must be added to this box or their solicitor's details if they have confirmed that they are instructed to accept service of the court proceedings.

(8) **Financial summary of claim**

(a) Amount claimed: In a specified money claim (e.g. a debt claim) the claimant's representatives should include the sum claimed including interest up to the date of issue of proceedings.

(b) Court fee: The court fee charged for issue of proceedings is dependent on the value of the claim. Details of court fees, which may be as high as

£10,000, can be found at the Court and Tribunal Service website at https://www.gov.uk/court-fees-what-they-are

(c) Legal representative's costs: for a specified money claim, the legal representative's costs are fixed as set out in **CPR Part 45**. For a non-specified money claim, such as a claim for damages, the legal costs are not ascertainable at the outset of the claim and therefore "to be advised" should be inserted.

(d) The total amount should be provided where it is possible to itemise all the costs (i.e. in a specified money claim). This is so that a defendant who admits the claim knows exactly what to pay.

For an unspecified sum (such as a damages or personal injury claim), the total amount cannot be calculated at this stage.

(9) **Vulnerable claimant or claimant's witness**

Details should be given if the claimant or one of their witnesses is vulnerable in any way. This will enable the court to make adjustments and comply with **PD1A**.

(10) **Human rights issues**

The claimant must indicate whether the claim includes any issues under the **Human Rights Act 1998**.

(11) **Particulars of claim**

If the claim is for a simple debt, there is usually sufficient space on the claim form to include the particulars (details) of claim, such as the principal sum due and any interest.

Any relevant contract must be attached. If the claim refers to a verbal contract, the particulars should provide details.

In more complex matters, such as a personal injury claim where the claim is for damages, the particulars of claim are prepared as a separate document. The claim form must state either that the particulars are attached or that they will follow.

(12) **Statement of truth**

CPR Part 22 requires the claim form, and the particulars of claim if in a separate document, to be verified by a statement of truth. This can be signed by the claimant as an individual or by their legal representative.

If the statement is signed by the claimant's legal representative, the legal representative signs to confirm the **client's** belief in the contents of the document, not their own. The legal representative must state their capacity and sign in their own name (not the firm's name) and provide their firm's name if appropriate.

The court will take a legal representative's signature made on behalf of a client as a statement that:

- they have the client's authority to sign the statement of truth;
- they have explained to the client that the legal representative is confirming the client's belief in the truth of the contents of the claim form;
- before signing they explained to the client the possible consequences to the client if it should subsequently appear that the client did not have an honest belief in the truth of those facts (the client may be prosecuted for contempt of court).

Because it is the claimant's belief that is relevant, it is considered best practice for the claimant to sign the statement of truth.

If the claimant is a company, someone in a senior position, such as a director, treasurer, secretary, chief executive or manager, must sign the statement of truth. The signatory to the statement of truth must state the position held.

The wording of the statement of truth for statements of case and application notices is now:

"[I believe] [The party believes] that the facts stated in this [name of the document] are true. I understand that proceedings for contempt may be brought against anyone who makes, or causes to be made, a false statement in a document verified by a statement of truth without an honest belief in its truth."

(13) **Legal representative's details**

The end of the form requires details of the claimant's legal representative's address for service of documents.

There are three other methods of issuing proceedings to be aware of.

7.4.3 Issuing proceedings through Money Claim Online

Money Claim Online (MCOL) is an alternative method of issuing proceedings in the County Court. It was introduced with the aim of making justice more affordable and accessible. It allows claims of up to £100,000 to be issued by individuals and organisations over the internet. The claimant can check the status of the claim online, request judgment and enforce it.

CPR PD 51R has introduced an Online Civil Money Claims (OCMC) pilot for money claims in the County Court that would otherwise be made through the Money Claim Online (MCOL) system, and its purpose is to test an online claims process for money claims in the County Court for use by unrepresented parties (litigants in person). It applies to claims of up to £10,000 (where the claimant and defendant are unrepresented) or up to £25,000 (where the claimant and defendant are both represented).

7.4.4 Issuing proceedings through the Claim Production Centre and the County Court Business Centre

Claims can also be started through the Claim Production Centre (CPC) or the County Court Business Centre (CCBC), both of which are based in Northampton. They allow claims to be issued in bulk and are used by claimants such as credit card companies. The same restrictions as with MCOL apply.

7.4.5 Issuing proceedings under the low-value protocol

Low-value (£25,000 or less) RTA personal injury claims are pursued under a separate system which is set out in the **RTA Small Claims Protocol** and the **RTA Protocol**. Further details are contained in **Chapter 6**.

7.5 Service

Serving a legal document involves sending or taking the document to the defendant – in other words, making the defendant aware of the fact that proceedings now exist against them.

Note that serving is different from "filing"; filing involves sending or taking a document to court.

7.5.1 Service of claim form and particulars of claim

The claim form, once issued, must be served within four months of issue.

If the particulars of claim are contained in a separate document from the claim form, it must be served either with the claim form or within 14 days. Usually these documents are sent together.

7.5.2 Service of other documents

During the life of proceedings, it may be necessary to serve other documents on the parties such as statements of case. Rather confusingly, **CPR** has different rules for service of the claim form from other documents, but these are basically the same in respect of how, who and where to serve. Only the "when" is different and this aspect will be dealt with below.

7.5.3 Address for service of documents

The rules governing service of documents are set out in **CPR Part 6**. If a defendant has authorised their lawyer to accept service, the documents should be sent to the lawyer's office. If not, the table below outlines the place of service for different kinds of party.

Nature of party to be served	Place of service
Individual	Usual or last known residence
Individual being sued in the name of a business	Usual or last known residence of the individual, or principal or last known place of business
Individual being sued in the business name of a partnership	Usual or last known residence of the individual, or principal or last known place of business of the partnership
Limited liability partnership	Principal office of the partnership, or any place of business of the partnership within the jurisdiction which has a real connection with the claim
Company registered in England and Wales	Principal office of the company, or any place of business of the company within the jurisdiction which has a real connection with the claim

The existing rules of service under **CPR r6.3** and **r6.20** allow service (amongst other methods) by fax and other means of electronic communication, in accordance with **PD 6A**; or any method authorised by the court under **CPR r6.15** or **r6.27**. It is now common for the courts to allow service via email, if supported by valid reasons, but defendants could evade service by deleting their email account. To ensure service on evasive defendants, electronic messages on social media via Instagram, Facebook, LinkedIn and so on are likely to be permitted under the category of "electronic communication". However, this will require prior consent in writing from the defendant, or the defendant's lawyer, or a court order permitting future service by this alternative method.

7.5.4 Documents to be served

The documents to be served comprise the sealed claim form, the particulars of claim and a response pack. A copy of the response pack (forms N9, N9A, N9B and N9C) is accessible at https://www.gov.uk/government/publications/form-n1-claim-form-cpr-part-7

The response pack is a bundle of official forms comprising:

- an acknowledgment of service form – this is used if the defendant wants to be given an extra 14 days for filing a defence;
- an admission form – if the defendant does not dispute the claim or wants to make an offer to pay by instalments;
- a defence and counterclaim form – if the defendant denies liability or has a claim of their own against the claimant.

Similar but slightly different forms apply depending upon whether the claim is a specified (debt) claim or an unspecified (damages) claim.

7.5.5 Methods of service

Permissible methods of service are set out in **CPR Part 6** and summarised below:

- personal service;
- first class post or document exchange;
- leaving the document at a specified place; or
- by fax or other means of electronic communication such as email.

Generally, service will be by the court, usually by first class post, but the party may notify the court that they wish to do it themselves.

Using the post and leaving documents at the defendant's home or other address for service do not require further explanation.

7.5.5.1 Personal service

Individuals: Personal service consists of leaving the documents with the defendant. It is often done on behalf of claimants by firms of process servers who will simply hand the documents to the person. If the defendant refuses to take the form, it can be dropped at their feet.

Companies: Personal service on a company means service on a person in a senior position, such as a director, treasurer, secretary or chief executive.

Partnerships: Personal service on partners sued in the name of the partnership is effected by leaving the documents with a partner or a person having the control or management of the partnership business at its principal place of business.

7.5.5.2 Document exchange (DX)

This is a system used by the majority of law firms and a number of other businesses for transporting documents between their offices. It only works between offices which are signed up to the system and, generally, documents put into the DX arrive the next business day. It is a permissible method of service only if the other side's legal representatives are also users of the DX system.

7.5.5.3 Electronic methods of service

As to fax and email, the party or their legal representative must have indicated in writing a willingness for service to be accepted in this way. An email address in a statement of case or response to claim is sufficient.

7.5.6 Deemed date of service – claim forms

To avoid disputes about whether and when documents are served, the **CPR** adopt the concept of deemed service. This means that the document will be taken to have arrived on a given day regardless of whether it actually did. This is important because the time within which the defendant must respond to a claim starts from the deemed date of service.

Unfortunately, as mentioned above, there are different rules for claim forms and other documents.

A claim form is deemed to be served on the second business day after the "step required", that is, putting the document in the post or DX, sending it by fax or email or personally serving it at the correct address. Note that a "business day" is any day except Saturday, Sunday or a bank holiday.

Example:

Day served	Deemed served
Friday	Tuesday
Wednesday	Friday
Tuesday	Thursday
Thursday before the May bank holiday	Tuesday

If service is effected by the claimant, they must file a certificate of service (form N215) within 21 days. This can be accessed at https://www.gov.uk/government/publications/form-n215-certificate-of-service.

7.5.6.1 Deemed date of service – other documents

The deemed date of service of documents other than the claim form varies, depending upon the method of service. In summary, such documents are deemed served:

- on the second day after the day of despatch by **post or DX** provided this is a business day; or, if not, on the next business day after that day;
- if served by **personal service, fax, email or by being left at a specified place**:
  - before 4.30 pm on a business day, the same day; or
  - in any other case, the next business day.

Example:

Method of service	Day served	Deemed served
By post	Monday	Wednesday
By post	Friday	Monday
By email	Wednesday at 2 pm	Wednesday
By email	Wednesday at 5 pm	Thursday

7.6 Summary of the usual steps for issuing and serving proceedings

Steps completed by the lawyer

The lawyer drafts all the relevant court documents. These comprise the N1 claim form, particulars of claim, any required documents, for example, the contract together with the court fee and covering letter requesting that the court issue and serve proceedings.

The lawyer sends sufficient copies of the relevant completed documents to be served on each defendant and a copy for the court file.

Steps taken by the court

(1) The court will issue the claim form by entering the issue date on it, sealing it and allocating a claim number. A court file will be opened.

(2) The court then serves the claim form unless the claimant indicates that they wish to arrange for service of the papers themselves. The court will usually serve the documents by first class post, together with a response pack, which will include the standard forms for admitting or defending the claim or acknowledging service.

(3) In a personal injury case, a medical report and schedule of details of any past and future expenses and losses must also be filed and served at the same time as the particulars of claim.

(4) The court will send the claimant a notice of issue, showing the issue date and the deemed date of service. Alternatively, if the claimant has served the defendant, they must file a certificate of service within 21 days of service of the claim form.

7.7 Summary

(1) The majority of claims are started in the County Court. Only debt and contract claims in excess of £100,000, and personal injury claims of at least £50,000, may be issued in the High Court.

(2) Most claims are issued using form N1 under **CPR Part 7**.

(3) The claim form gives a concise statement of the nature of the claim. The particulars of claim is the formal written statement of the nature of the claimant's case and the remedy sought.

(4) The particulars of claim are usually included on the claim form in a debt claim as they are short; whereas they are usually prepared as a separate document in a claim for damages, such as a commercial claim for breach of contract or a personal injury claim, as they are longer.

(5) In a debt claim, the defendant is served with the claim form, the particulars of claim and a response pack. In a personal injury claim, in addition to these documents, the defendant is also served with a medical report and a schedule of details of any past and future expenses and losses.

(6) The rules provide for a variety of methods of service. Service is usually achieved by the court posting the documents by first class post, the deemed date of service being the second business day after they were posted.

CHAPTER 8
Defendant's Response

8.1 Introduction

Once service of the particulars of claim has been effected, the defendant must decide quickly what to do as they only have 14 days from the date of service of the particulars of claim to respond.

The defendant has a choice of:

- filing an admission (**CPR Part 14**); or
- filing a defence (**Part 15**), which may be combined with making a counterclaim (**Part 20**); or
- filing an acknowledgment of service (**Part 10**).

The Courts and Tribunals Service guidance notes on replying to the claim form may be found at https://www.gov.uk/government/publications/form-n1-claim-form-cpr-part-7.

8.2 Admissions

In a debt action or money claim, the defendant can bring the proceedings to a swift conclusion, thus limiting their liability for costs, by admitting the sum due. Admissions are governed by **CPR Part 14**.

A defendant who admits the claim should complete the admission form included in the response pack. There are two types of admission form, one for claims for specified sums of money (debts) and another for unspecified amounts of money (damages). Copies of these forms can be accessed via the links set out below.

- Form N9A – https://www.gov.uk/government/publications/form-n9a-form-of-admission-specified-amount
- https://www.gov.uk/government/publications/form-n9c-admission-unspecified-amount-and-non-money-claims

The defendant may admit either the whole claim or just part. Thereafter, the claimant has 14 days in which to consider any offers made.

There are a number of options.

(1) **Defendant admits whole claim**

If the whole claim is admitted, the defendant must decide on the method of payment. If the whole sum is paid directly to the claimant within 14 days of service of the claim form, the defendant's liability for the claimant's costs will be limited to certain fixed sums laid down in the rules. This assists the defendant because fixed costs are considerably lower than the sums recoverable in contested litigation.

Alternatively, the defendant may request time to pay and make an offer to pay by instalments. To determine whether the offer is acceptable, the defendant must complete a form setting out their personal and financial circumstances. This is sent to the claimant, who will decide whether to accept it. If yes, judgment will be entered for payment by the instalments offered by the defendant. If not, the rate of payment will be determined by the court.

(2) **Defendant admits part of the claim**

A defendant can also use an admission form to make a partial admission, denying the rest of the claim. If this happens, the claimant is asked whether the partial admission is acceptable. If so, this would be in full and final satisfaction of the **whole** claim and judgment will be entered in that sum. The partial admission may be for immediate payment or payment by instalments.

8.3 Defences

A defendant disputing a claim must file a defence.

One of the forms in the response pack is a form of defence and counterclaim, forms N9B and N9D depending upon the type of claim. Both have spaces where the defendant can set out the reasons why the claim is disputed and for details of any counterclaim. Copies of these forms are accessible via the links below.

- Form N9B – https://www.gov.uk/government/publications/form-n9b-defence-counterclaim-specified-amount
- Form N9D – https://www.gov.uk/government/publications/form-n9d-defence-counterclaim-unspecified-amount-and-non-money-claims

Alternatively, the defendant can draft a defence using ordinary paper. This alternative is often used by lawyers acting for clients, because well-drafted defences tend to set out the facts in some detail and the space on the form is quite limited.

8.4 Counterclaims and set-offs

Counterclaim

A counterclaim is any claim made by a defendant against a claimant. The counterclaim may relate to very different facts and issues from the original claim, and may therefore be tried separately if the court thinks it fit to do so.

Example

Swish Ltd (Swish) purchase a consignment of evening dresses from Hockley Fashions Ltd (Hockley). Payment is due in two instalments. Having paid the first, Swish receive a number of complaints from their customers about the quality of the dresses. Swish issue proceedings against Hockley alleging breach of the implied term of satisfactory quality. Hockley respond with a counterclaim for the remaining money due under the contract.

Set-off

A set-off is a special type of counterclaim and applies where the defendant has a separate and existing claim against the claimant which they can balance against the claim. It provides the defendant with a defence to the claim and so absolves them of responsibility. Depending upon its value, the defendant's claim reduces or extinguishes their liability to the claimant.

The counterclaim is outlined in the part of the statement of case for the counterclaim; the set-off is put in the defence.

Example

European Plumbers Ltd (EPL) sue Marek for £25,000 in relation to a central heating contract. However, EPL owe Marek £8,000 for works which he had previously carried out for them. In this instance, Marek may set off the £8,000 so that he only owes EPL £17,000.

8.5 Acknowledgment of service

Acknowledgments of service are used if the defendant is unable to file a defence within the time limit and form part of the response pack.

Acknowledging service "buys" an extra 14 days, so that the defence need not be served until 28 days after service of the particulars of claim.

Example

On 1 October, Kulvinder is served with the claim form and particulars of claim. He has 14 days (not including the day of service) in which to respond.

- He must either acknowledge service or file a defence by 15 October.
- If he files an acknowledgement of service on any day up to 15 October, he has a further 14 days in which to file his defence (i.e. until 29 October).

8.6 Agreed extensions

The parties may agree to extend the time for serving a defence, but any agreement can be for a maximum of a further 28 days only. Time runs from the original date for filing the defence (this gives a total of 56 days from date of service of the particulars of claim).

8.7 Responding to a claim issued through MCOL

A defendant can only respond to a claim using MCOL if the claim was made electronically in the first place. Response times are the same as those in paper claims. The defendant does not have to use MCOL if they do not want to.

MCOL cannot be used if the defendant admits the claim in full: a paper copy of form N9A must be completed.

8.8 Transfer

Where an individual defends a money claim, the case will automatically be transferred to the defendant's home court. Other cases may be transferred depending upon the financial value of the claim and whether it would be more convenient to try the case in another court.

8.9 Summary

(1) The defendant must respond **within 14 days** of service of the **particulars of claim** by filing an admission, a defence (and possibly a counterclaim) or an acknowledgment of service.

(2) The defendant may admit the whole claim and request time to pay, or admit only part of the claim.

(3) Filing an acknowledgment of service gives the defendant an extra 14 days in which to file the defence, giving the defendant 28 days in total from the date of service of the particulars of claim.

(4) A defendant bringing a counterclaim may be able to argue that this is set off against the value of the claimant's claim. There is sometimes confusion

between a counterclaim and a set-off. It can be helpful to think of the counterclaim as a separate cause of action brought by the defendant against the claimant whereas a set-off is part of the defence to the claimant's action.

(5) Refer to the flowchart below for a summary of the time limits for issuing and serving proceedings and responding to a claim. **NB** The flowchart applies to claims issued under **CPR Part 7** and, therefore, does not apply to proceedings issued under Stage 3 of the RTA Protocol (where proceedings are issued under **Part 8**).

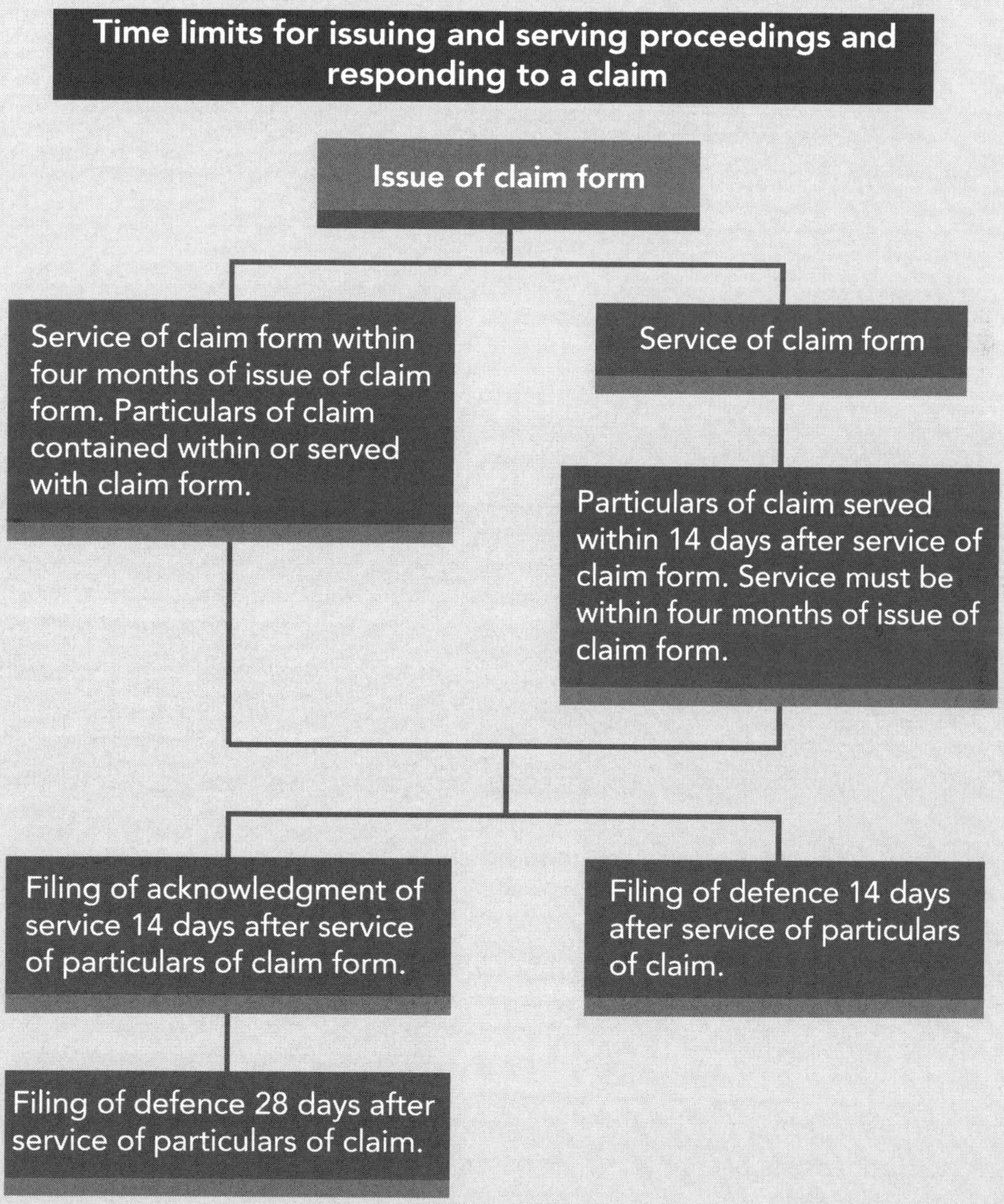

CHAPTER 9

Statements of Case

9.1 Introduction

CPR Part 16 deals with statements of case.

Statements of case are the formal documents used in litigation to define what each party says about the case. They are important because:

- at trial, the court will only decide the issues which have been raised in the statements of case;
- they determine what evidence will be needed; and
- the parties need to know what the allegations are so that they can decide how strong their case is before considering whether to make any offers to settle and on what terms.

Statements of case are usually the first documents that are served between the parties. They are served in sequence, with the claimant serving the claim form and the particulars of claim first, followed by a defence from the defendant, then possibly a reply from the claimant.

The term "statement of case" is defined by the **CPR** to include the following documents:

- the claim form;
- particulars of claim;
- defence;
- counterclaims;
- reply to defence, defence to counterclaim; and
- further information given in relation to the above (**Part 18** requests and responses).

Precedents are a very useful starting point, but it is vital that they are amended to take account of the facts of your own client's case.

Note that the **CPR** have been drafted in plain English and the courts expect statements of case to be drafted in the same style.

Counsel may be instructed for complex statements of case where the claim is complicated or unusual. However, solicitors are expected to draft such documents in straightforward claims to ensure costs are proportionate to the litigation.

9.2 Particulars of claim

The particulars of claim must contain a concise statement of the facts on which the claimant relies.

This means that it must set out the facts giving rise to the dispute and those which demonstrate the required elements of the cause of action on which the case is based.

9.2.1 Breach of contract claims

Where the claimant alleges breach of contract, the particulars of claim should include the following:

Existence of contract

The claimant must establish that a contract exists, although this is rarely disputed in practice. For a claim based on:

- a written contract, the contractual documents must be attached to or served with the particulars of claim;
- an oral agreement, the words used to form the contract must be quoted, together with details of who said them, to whom, and when and where they were spoken.

Terms

Details of any express terms should be included (and these will usually be found in the contract itself) together with any implied terms being relied upon. For example, if the claimant alleges that the goods supplied were not of satisfactory quality.

Breach

The particulars of claim should include information about which terms were breached and how. Examples would be failing to pay the price of the goods, late delivery or poor quality of the items supplied.

Causation and loss

This may be as **straightforward** as the money owed under the contract but could include, for example, a claim for loss of profits or the additional cost of purchasing replacement goods.

9.2.2 Personal injury claims

In other claims, such as personal injury claims, **CPR Part 16** sets out specific details that need to be included in the particulars of claim, for example, the claimant's date of birth.

Details of the remedies being claimed must be provided, specifically, the amount of the damages being claimed and, in a personal injury claim, whether these should be paid by periodical payments or as a lump sum.

9.3 Interest

Full details of any interest claimed, including the rate, period covered and the authority for claiming it, must be included.

Debt claim

In a debt claim, where a specific sum is due, interest may be claimed under one of three different provisions:

- the rate of interest as agreed by the parties in the contract;
- if the contract is silent as to interest and is commercial (between traders/businesses), interest may be claimed under the **Late Payment of Commercial Debts (Interest) Act 1998** at 8 per cent above the Bank of England base rate;
- if the contract is silent as to interest and is non-commercial (between a business/trader and a consumer), interest can be claimed under either **s35A Senior Courts Act 1981** (**SCA 1981**) for claims in the High Court or **s69 County Courts Act 1984** (**CCA 1984**) for claims in the County Court.

Whichever provision applies, the court's decision to award interest is discretionary. However, the claimant should always claim the highest rate available to them and this will usually be found in the contract.

The interest should be calculated, and pleaded as:

- a lump sum for the period between the date on which the cause of action arose up to and including the date of issue; and then
- at a daily rate so that it is easy to provide an updated total.

Example

Let us assume that the claim is for £20,000 and the interest rate is 10 per cent per annum according to the contract.

- To calculate the interest due, you would need to work out the yearly interest rate for the claim. 10 per cent of £20,000 is £2,000.
- Dividing this by 365 gives a daily rate of £5.48.
- If the payment was due on 1 June and the claim was issued on 30 September, the lump sum owed for interest is £668.56. This is worked out by multiplying the number of days (122) by the daily interest rate of £5.48.
- From 1 October until judgment, the claimant would claim the daily rate of £5.48.
- When judgment is awarded, the interest figure would be added to the total sum.

Document 1 of the **Appendix** provides an illustration of this in practice.

Unspecified claim for damages

In a claim for damages (for example, a breach of contract claim for loss of profits or a personal injury claim) where no specific sum is due, the amount of interest cannot be calculated. Interest is pleaded generally under **SCA 1981** for claims in the High Court or **CCA 1984** for claims in the County Court, at such a rate as the court thinks fit. The usual rate of interest is 2 per cent per annum.

Claim for special damages

Where special damages are claimed in personal injury claims, covering expenses such as travel expenses to hospital, interest may be claimed at **half the special account rate** set by the Ministry of Justice. The special account rate varies to reflect changes in the Bank of England base rate.

An example of the wording used is:

"In respect of damages awarded the Claimant claims interest pursuant to s35A of the Senior Courts Act 1981 at such rates and for such period as the Court thinks just."

9.4 Statement of truth

The claim form or particulars of claim must contain a signed statement of truth that its contents are believed to be true (**CPR Part 22**).

Failure to include a statement of truth may result in an application for an unless order. This order provides that unless a particular action is taken, the claim will be struck out.

9.5 Defence

As previously mentioned, where the defendant has instructed a law firm, they will usually draft the defence as a separate document rather than completing an N9 response pack.

9.5.1 Contents of defence

The defence sets out the defendant's answer to the claim. It must state:

- which allegations are denied;
- which allegations are not admitted; and
- which allegations are admitted.

Where a defendant denies an allegation, the defence must state:

- their reasons for doing so; and
- the defence version of events if different from that given by the claimant.

Allegations which are not admitted are those which the defendant wants the claimant to prove. This is usually because the defendant does not know whether it is true or not.

Example 1

Meridian Entertainments plc (Meridian) enter into a contract with Flora Wild, a famous pop star, to entertain their guests at a live concert. Two days before the event, she pulls out. Meridian have to cancel the concert and refund the tickets.

Meridian issues proceedings against Flora for breach of contract and loss of profits. In her defence:

- Flora admits that there was a contract and also the express terms;
- she denies being in breach of the contract stating that the venue was entirely unsuitable for her performance;
- Flora will not admit the losses as she has no knowledge of these. The effect is that Meridian will have to prove them.

Example 2

Hari is involved in a road traffic accident with Petra. He admits the accident took place but denies he was responsible. With regard to the damage to Petra's car, his defence states that this is not admitted. Effectively, he is saying that he does not know how much Petra spent on repairing her car, but regardless, the damage is not his fault.

Once an issue is admitted, it will not need to be proved by the claimant; it is taken to be agreed between the parties. Only the issues that remain disputed will be decided by the court.

Any specific allegation in the particulars of claim that is not dealt with in the defence will be deemed to be admitted (**CPR Part 16**).

Like all other statements of case, a defence must contain a statement of truth.

The defence must be filed at court and served on every other party within 14 days of service of the particulars of claim, or 28 days if the defendant has acknowledged service.

9.5.2 Approach to drafting a simple defence

Because any specific allegation not dealt with in the defence may be taken to be admitted, it is essential to adopt a systematic point-by-point approach to drafting the defence and ensure, as far as possible, that it mirrors the sequence of paragraphs in the particulars of claim. This approach minimises the risk of omitting to respond to a specific allegation.

Document 2 of the **Appendix** provides an example of a defence in a debt claim, prepared as a separate document and in response to the particulars of claim set out in **Document 1**. The numbered paragraphs below correspond to the red numbered items on the defence.

(1) **Name of court**

The defence should mirror the court of issue, namely, the CCMCC.

(2) **Claim number**

This is the unique claim reference number provided by the court on issue of proceedings and stamped at the top of the N1 claim form.

(3) **Details of parties**

The parties' names should be stated in full together with their titles.

(4) **Title of document**

The document should be identified.

(5) **Paragraph numbered (1)**

This mirrors the first paragraph in the particulars of claim (in **Document 1** of the **Appendix**) and deals with the content by admitting that a sales contract existed for the agreed contract price of £42,000. This means that the claimant does not have to prove these points at trial.

Clearly, the defendant would not admit the whole of this paragraph if there was any dispute as to whether a contract was actually made or if there was a dispute about one or more terms of the contract, for example, the contract price. In such circumstances, the defendant would admit the existence of the contract and the date it was made but deny the contract price and submit the defendant's version of the agreed contract price.

(6) **Paragraph numbered (2)**

This mirrors the second paragraph of the particulars of claim and deals with the content. It admits the delivery of the machine tools (the subject of the contract) and an invoice but then alleges breach of contract and provides the defendant's version of events, namely, that the tools did not correspond with the sample. The defence also cites relevant law in support of this allegation (**s15 Sale of Goods Act 1979**).

(7) **Paragraph numbered (3)**

This mirrors the third paragraph of the particulars of claim and deals with the content by denying the claimant's claim for interest on the contract price claimed.

(8) **Statement of truth**

CPR Part 22 requires that the defence (as it is part of the statement of case) be verified by a statement of truth. The same provisions apply as summarised in **7.4**.

9.6 Counterclaim

A counterclaim arises where the defendant says that they have a right of action against the claimant. Another way of putting this is to say that if the defendant had taken action first, they could have commenced an action against the claimant. Counterclaims are governed by **CPR Part 20** and are referred to as **Part 20** claims.

Example

Louis Feng carries out repairs to Daphne MacPherson's roof. Daphne is not satisfied with the quality of the work and refuses to pay.

This refusal will lead Louis to issue proceedings against Daphne claiming the cost of the work and materials provided. Daphne's defence will be that she is not liable to pay Louis for the roof repairs because the work is defective. In the meantime, however, the defective work has caused extensive damage to her home because the roof leaked during a storm. Daphne will want to claim for these losses against Louis and so she will combine with her defence a counterclaim for the damage caused to her house.

A counterclaim will only be relevant if the defendant has actually suffered loss at the hands of the claimant. If the defendant simply has a good reason for not paying a particular debt, but has not incurred loss themselves, they will only file a defence and a counterclaim will not be relevant.

A counterclaim is treated as if it were a claim. The particulars can be set out using one of the forms included in the response pack, or, alternatively, on ordinary paper as the space given on the standard form is very limited.

A counterclaim may be made without permission if filed with the defence. An issue fee based on the full value of the counterclaim is payable.

9.7 Reply to defence and/or defence to counterclaim

Filing a reply is optional. Replies tend to be used to respond to matters raised in the defence not covered by the particulars of claim.

In cases where the defendant serves a defence and counterclaim, the claimant must ensure that they file a defence to the counterclaim to avoid judgment being entered against them for this aspect.

In routine cases the last statement of case is usually the defence.

9.8 False statement of truth

All statements of case require a statement of truth. Proceedings for contempt of court may be brought if a person makes a false statement in a document verified by a statement of truth without an honest belief in its truth.

It is clearly important for lawyers to have statements of case approved by their clients before they are served. Although the rules make provision for a legal representative to sign the statement of truth, it is best practice for the client to do so following clear advice from their lawyer of the consequences of endorsing a statement of truth while knowing that the contents are false.

9.9 Request for further information

Sometimes, a statement of case lacks clarity or fails to set out the case precisely enough. In such cases a request may be made for further information under **CPR Part 18**. Generally, such requests are submitted shortly after the relevant statement of case is served.

Procedure

(1) The party who requires further information should submit a written request on their opponent, giving them a reasonable time in which to respond.

(2) A request should be concise and strictly confined to matters that are reasonably necessary and proportionate to enable the first party to prepare their own case or to understand the case they have to answer.

(3) A request may be made by letter if the request and the likely reply are brief; otherwise, the request should be made in a separate document.

The response must:

- be headed with the name of the court, the title and number of the claim and identify that it is a response to that request;
- repeat the text of each request and set out under each paragraph the response to it.

The response must be served on the parties and filed with the court. It should be verified by a statement of truth.

If a request for further information is not responded to, a **Part 18** application may be made to the court for an order in these terms. However, such an application should only be made where the opponent has failed to respond to a written request for the information.

9.10 Striking out statements of case

CPR Part 3 provides that the court may strike out a statement of case if it appears to the court that it discloses no reasonable grounds for bringing or defending the claim. Examples include those which:

- set out no facts indicating what the claim is about, for example, "Money owed £5,000";
- make no sense;

- contain a coherent set of facts but those facts, even if true, do not disclose a legal claim or do not amount to a defence; and
- in the case of a defence, consists of a bare denial.

Under **CPR** the judge has case management powers to ensure that cases are dealt with expeditiously as required by the overriding objective. Striking out may be used to punish a failure to comply with a rule, Practice Direction or a court order, for example:

"Unless the defendant files a full defence setting out his reasons for denying that the debt is owed within seven days of the date of this order, the defence will be struck out."

The flowchart below gives an overview of striking out claims and defences.

An overview of applications to strike out claim/defence

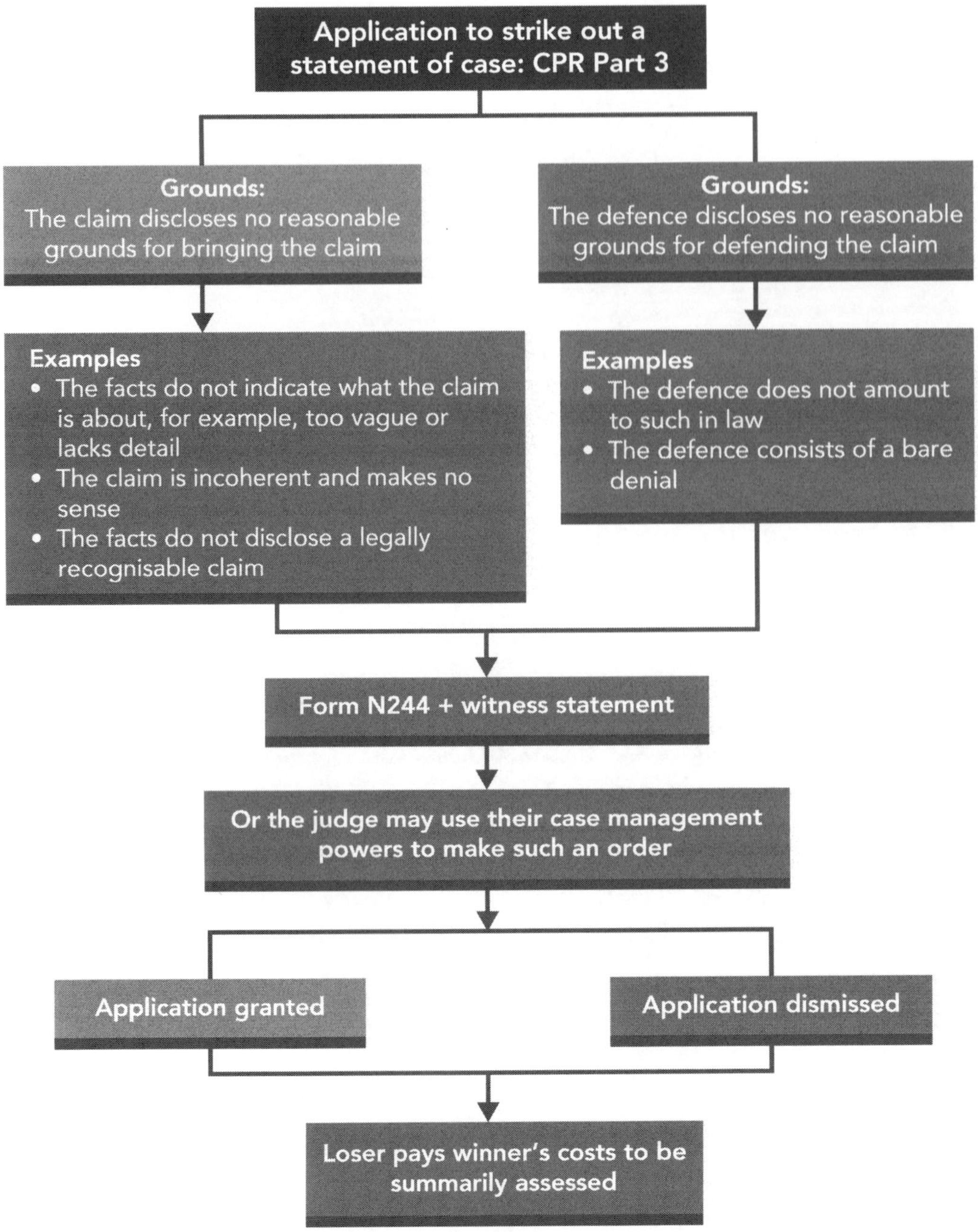

9.11 Summary

(1) **CPR Part 16** deals with statements of case. These are the first formal documents served between the parties. They include the claim form, particulars of claim, defence, **Part 20** claim, reply to defence and further information under **Part 18**.

(2) The particulars of claim must contain a concise statement of the facts on which the claimant relies, details of the remedies sought, details of any interest claimed and a statement of truth.

(3) The defence sets out the defendant's answer to the claim and must state which allegations are denied, those that the claimant must prove (not admitted) and those that are admitted. It must also be verified with a statement of truth.

(4) Counterclaims are claims by the defendant against the claimant and are governed by **CPR Part 20**.

(5) **CPR Part 18** deals with requests for further information, which may be used to seek clarification of, or information on, any matter in dispute.

(6) **CPR Part 3** sets out the court's power to strike out a statement of case and the circumstances when a claim or defence may be struck out.

CHAPTER 10

Default and Summary Judgments

10.1 Introduction

Once proceedings have been issued, the defendant may respond in a number of ways. Obviously, the most favourable outcome for the claimant is that the defendant admits the sum owed and pays in full, but, unfortunately, in many cases this does not occur. The defendant may do nothing at all, they may file an inadequate defence; or, alternatively, they may submit a full defence, in which case the matter will proceed towards trial. In this chapter, we shall consider the options available to the claimant in these circumstances:

- judgment in default – where no defence is filed;
- summary judgment – where the defence is inadequate.

For completeness, the relevant costs orders are included.

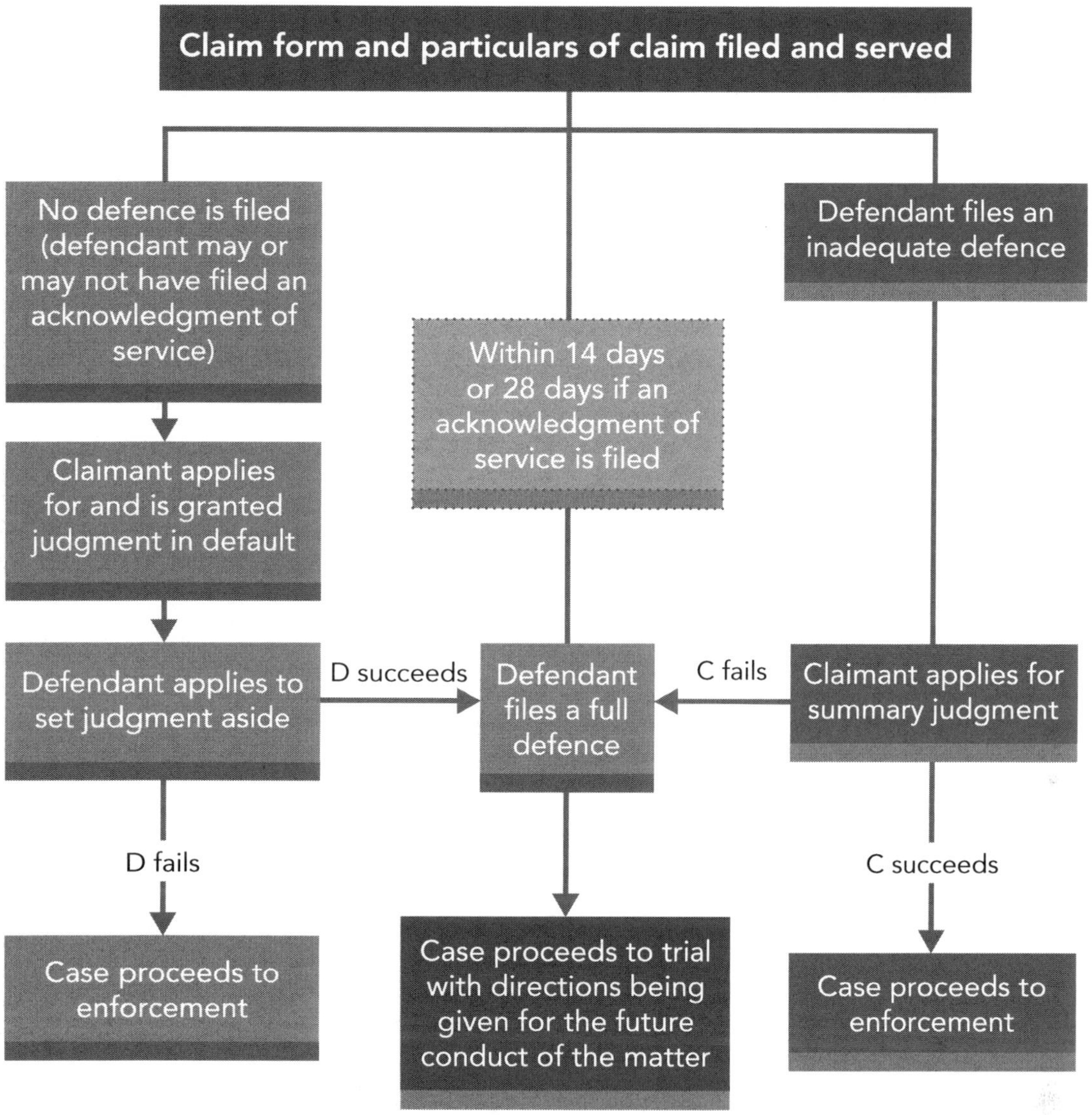

10.2 Judgment in default

If the defendant does nothing, you can reassure your client that **CPR** provides a mechanism to allow the case to proceed, because the alternative would be that the defendant could avoid payment in this way.

Under **CPR Part 12**, if the defendant fails to return the acknowledgement of service, or to file a defence, the claimant can obtain a judgment in default against them. This means that the claimant obtains a judgment without there being a trial of the issues involved in the case. This is a straightforward paper exercise, in which the claimant completes a form requesting the money owed and the judgment will be granted provided that the court is satisfied of the following matters:

- that the particulars of claim have been served on the defendant; and
- the defendant has not filed an acknowledgement of service form or a defence within the relevant time period.

Scenario

Northern Security Services Ltd (NSS) issues proceedings against Music Events Ltd (MEL). The claim form and the particulars of claim are deemed served on Wednesday 4 May 2022, so MEL has 14 days (i.e. until close of business on Wednesday 18 May) to file either an acknowledgment of service or a defence.

- If MEL does nothing, NSS may apply for judgment in default on Thursday 19 May.
- If MEL files an acknowledgement of service form within this period, it has a further 14 days in which to file its defence, that is, until Wednesday 1 June. However, if it fails to do so by that date, NSS may apply for judgment in default on Thursday 2 June.

10.3 Types of default judgment

If the judgment is for a specified amount, that is, a debt, the court will give a final judgment for immediate payment, usually within 14 days. The defendant will also be ordered to pay additional fixed costs under **CPR Part 45**.

However, if the claim is for an unspecified sum such as damages, the court will need to decide the amount of the claim and costs, and further directions will be given to enable these to be assessed.

Example

Continuing with the scenario above, NSS is claiming for the contractual sum due from MEL, but also for loss of profits. If the defendant does not respond to the claim, default judgment will be entered on liability with damages to be decided (assessed) by the court at a later date.

10.4 Setting aside default judgments

Not uncommonly, a lawyer may be instructed by the defendant once enforcement measures have been commenced by the claimant, for example, the arrival of a bailiff at the defendant's premises. At this point, the client may disclose a defence and ask whether the judgment may be set aside under **CPR Part 13**. There are two grounds upon which the defendant may make the application.

10.4.1 The mandatory ground

The judgment will be set aside as of right if it has been entered into wrongly. This would occur if the judgment had been entered into too early, before the time for filing the defence or the acknowledgment had expired, or because the claim had already been paid in full. In such circumstances, the court **must** set the judgment aside and the case will then proceed with directions being given for the future conduct of the case.

10.4.2 The discretionary grounds

Otherwise, the court **may** set aside the judgment on the merits of the case if the defendant:

- has a real prospect of successfully defending the claim; or
- there is some other good reason why the defendant should be allowed to defend the claim. A good reason could include the defendant being on holiday or ill in hospital. It would not include excuses such as pressure of work, the documents being misplaced, etc.

This is usually satisfied by filing evidence in support of the application to set aside, such as a witness statement. Often a draft of the defence is also exhibited.

10.5 Summary judgment

We have considered cases where no defence is filed, but what should the claimant do if the defence received is weak? Although success at trial is likely, a client will want an earlier resolution. **CPR Part 24** provides a solution.

Summary judgment applications may be submitted by either party as follows:

- a claimant against a defendant where the defence filed does not amount to an effective answer to the claim – indeed, it may simply be a delaying tactic;
- a defendant against the claimant where the claimant's case is insubstantial.

An overview of applications for summary judgment

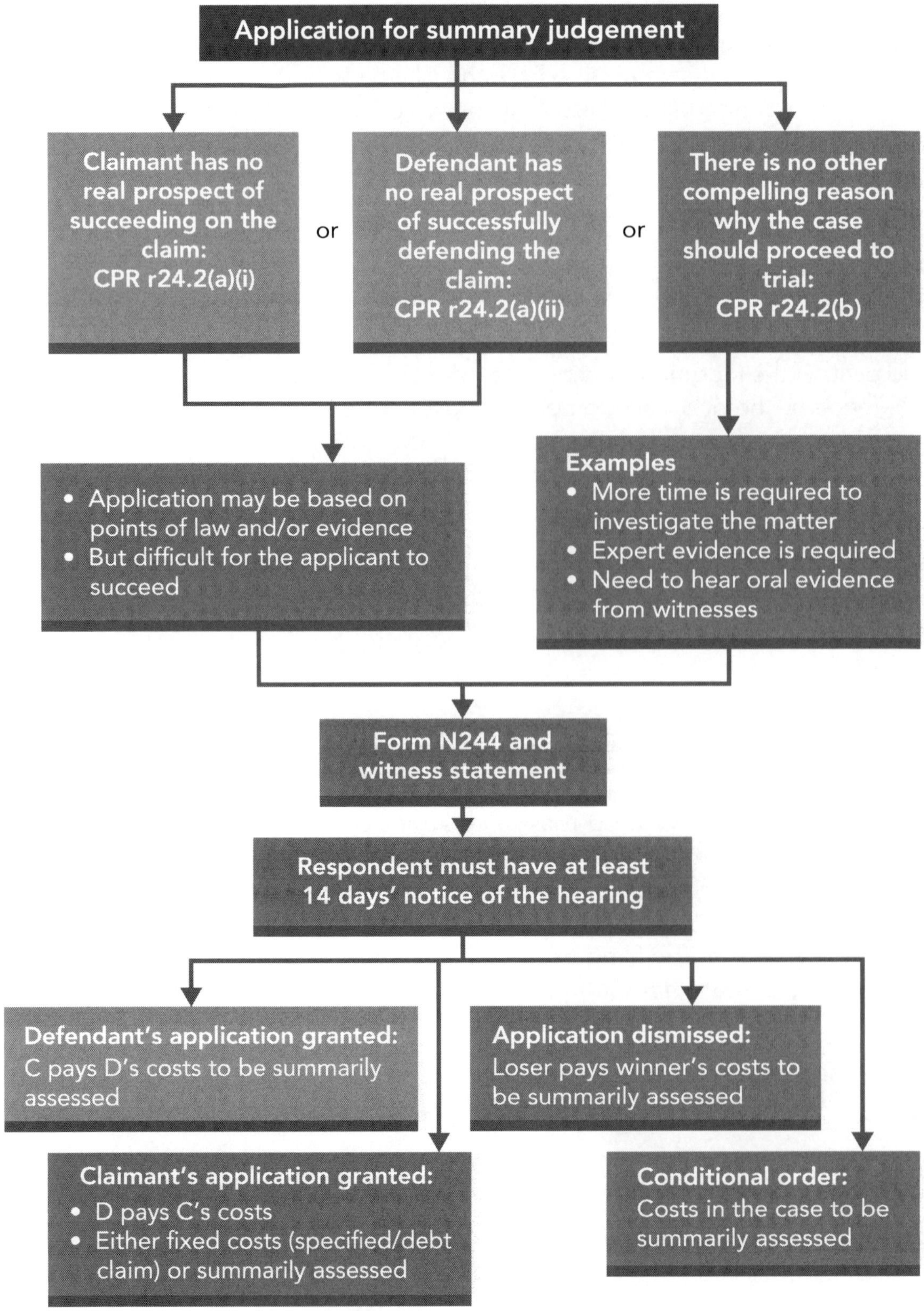

Example

Continuing with the scenario above, let's turn the clock back and assume that the date is Monday 16 May. MEL files a defence which states: "The security guards provided for the concert were inadequate." This is clearly insufficient and whilst the claimant would certainly succeed at trial were this to be the only defence submitted, allowing the case to proceed this far would lead to considerable extra costs being incurred.

To prevent cases trundling along to trial unnecessarily, **Part 24** gives the court the power to award summary judgment if it considers:

- the claimant has no real prospect of succeeding on the claim; or
- the defendant has no real prospect of successfully defending the claim; and
- there is no other compelling reason why the case should proceed to trial.

10.5.1 No real prospect of successfully defending the claim

Whether the parties have a real prospect of succeeding at trial is obviously a matter of evidence and this will vary from case to case. However, the process is designed to weed out those cases which really are somewhat hopeless.

10.5.2 Compelling reason

Such reasons could include:

- the need to allow more time for the matter to be investigated – in particular, if the case is complex or would benefit from expert evidence on technical matters;
- the need to hear from witnesses, particularly if one of the central issues is disputed oral evidence.

10.6 Procedure on a summary judgment application

As with setting aside a default judgment, an application notice will be filed, supported by evidence usually in the form of witness statements.

The applicant's evidence must be served and filed at least 14 clear days before the hearing and the respondent must do likewise at least seven days before the hearing.

Any party who wishes to rely on written evidence in reply may do so provided it is filed at court and then served on the opposing party at least three days prior to the hearing.

10.7 Possible orders

If the claimant has made a **Part 24** application, the court may make a number of orders.

(1) **The application is granted**: judgment is awarded on the claim and the effect is that the case comes to an end other than for enforcement purposes.

(2) **The application is dismissed**: in this instance, the claimant has failed in its attempt to bring the matter to an early conclusion, and will have to pursue the litigation all the way to a trial if necessary.

(3) **A conditional order**: the defendant may continue to defend the case, but only if (in common parlance) they "put their money where their mouth is". The usual condition is that the defendant pays into court the amount of the claim within a set time period, for example, 28 days. This ensures that the defendant is genuine in their desire and ability to defend and is not merely delaying payment. If the defendant fails to meet the condition, the judgment stands and the claimant can enforce it.

If the defendant is the applicant

(4) **The claim may be struck out or dismissed.**

If a claimant of an unspecified sum is awarded summary judgment, there will be another hearing to decide the level of the damages. Costs will also need to be determined.

10.8 Summary

(1) If the defendant has not filed an acknowledgment of service or a defence within 14 days of service of the particulars of claim, the claimant can enter a **judgment in default** under **CPR Part 12**.

(2) Default judgment is entered by the claimant completing and filing a standard form request. In debt (specified) claims, final judgment is entered for the sum owed plus interest and fixed costs. In personal injury and other unspecified claims, judgment is entered on liability, with damages to be assessed by the court at a later hearing.

(3) Default judgments may be set aside or varied under **CPR Part 13**. There are circumstances where the court **must** set aside the default judgment (as of right) and other circumstances where the court **may** set it aside (on the merits).

(4) **Summary judgment** may be applied for by either the claimant or the defendant under **CPR Part 24**. It is available where the court considers that the claimant or defendant has no real prospect of succeeding or successfully defending the claim and there is no other compelling reason why the case should go to trial.

(5) There are **four possible orders** the court may make on an application for summary judgment: judgment on the claim; dismissal of the claim; dismissal of the application for summary judgment; and a conditional order.

(6) When deciding which application is suitable, you should consider carefully the legal definitions for each and ensure that you justify why the particular application is appropriate with a clear explanation which incorporates the facts.

CHAPTER 11
Interim Applications

11.1 Introduction

If a dispute cannot be resolved by negotiation, litigation may be the only way forward. If a case does proceed to trial, there will be a number of steps along the way, some of which will involve making applications to the court. In this chapter, you will consider the different applications that a party to a case can make to resolve issues or, if necessary, to impose sanctions on the other party. These are known as interim applications since they are made in the intervening period before the trial of the case.

There are a number of reasons why a party may wish to apply to the court. However, the underlying aim is to ensure that the case progresses as quickly and efficiently as possible. Below are some examples of situations where a party may seek the court's assistance.

(1) The parties may be unable to comply with a direction, or instruction, from the court. Perhaps the claimant needs more time to serve its list of documents, or a party may wish to apply for a sanction against an opponent who has missed a deadline.

(2) A party may need to throw itself upon the mercy of the court and make an application for relief from a sanction imposed, for example, that the defence be struck out.

(3) The court's involvement may also be required to assist in the preparation of the case for trial, perhaps to force an opponent to respond to a **Part 18** request for further information or to seek disclosure of documents.

(4) On a more mundane note, an interim application may be necessary to deal with procedural matters, such as the amendment of a name of a party, or the substitution or addition of a party.

Before applying to the court, the parties should try to resolve matters amicably between themselves as otherwise there may be costs penalties. This is usually achieved by writing a letter. Only if this fails should an application be made to the court, and the procedure is set out in **Part 23.**

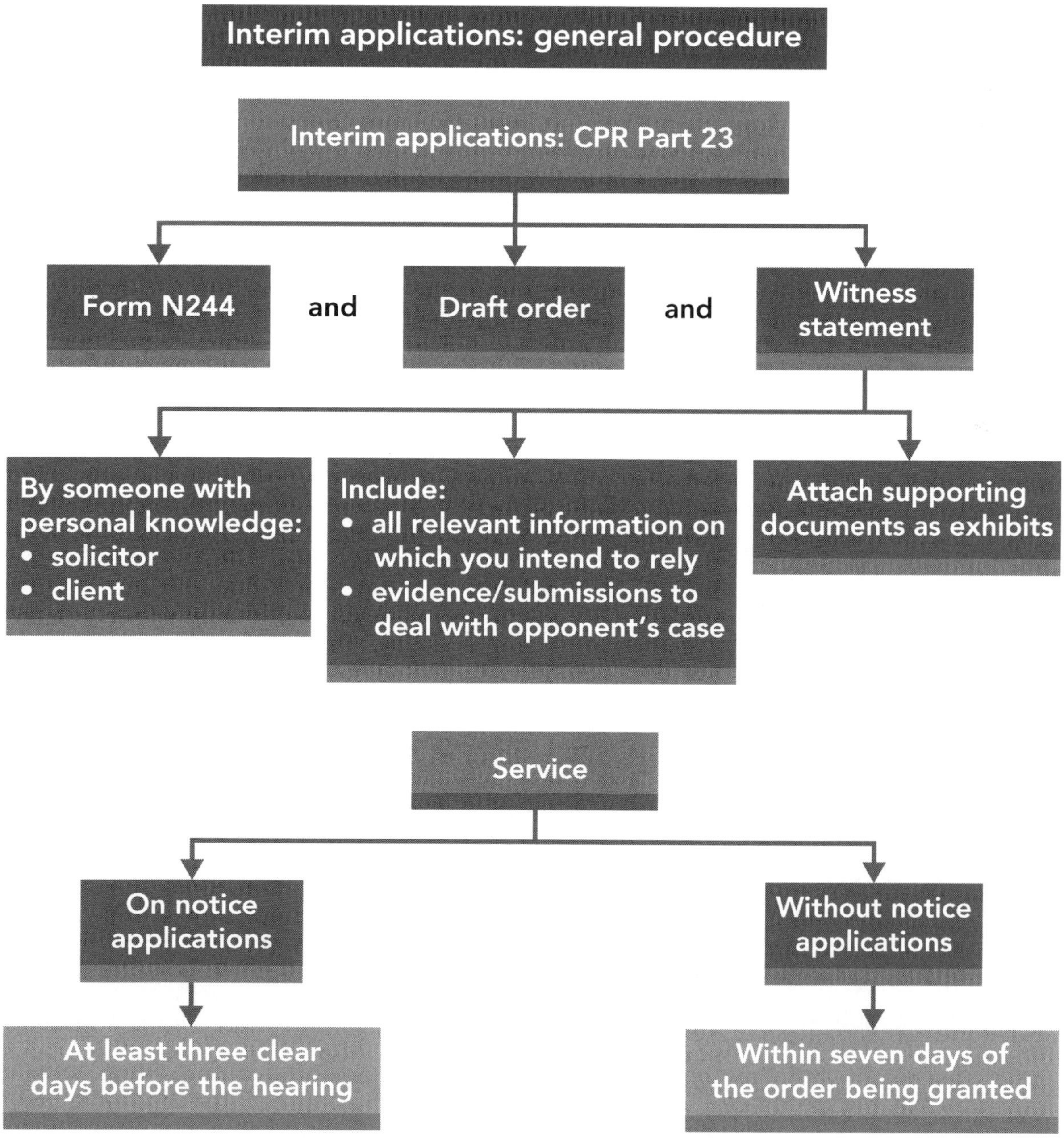

11.2 Applications without notice

The general rule is that all applications must be made on notice to the other parties. This ensures that they are aware of the application so that they can arrange attendance and representation at the hearing.

However, there are exceptions to this rule including where the court is satisfied that there is exceptional urgency or that the overriding objective of **CPR** would be best achieved by so doing. An example would be where the applicant applies to freeze their opponent's financial assets or to search their premises. Clearly, giving notice here could defeat the application. If such an order is made, the respondent may apply to set aside or vary the order within seven days of it being served.

11.3 Applications on notice

Applications must be made by filing an application notice (form N244) a copy of which can be found at https://www.gov.uk/government/publications/form-n244-application-notice.

The application notice must be signed and include the title of the claim, its reference number and the full name of the applicant. It should also state the following.

(1) What order is being sought: note that, except in the most simple of applications, a draft order should be attached to assist the court.

(2) Why the order is being sought: evidence must be provided in support and for a straightforward application this can be outlined on form N244 itself. For more complex applications, a witness statement will be prepared.

The notice must be filed at court with the fee and served on the other party as soon as possible and in any event not less than three days before the hearing.

Three days means clear days (excluding the date of effective service and the date of the hearing). Weekends, bank holidays, Christmas and Good Friday will not be counted.

Example

A hearing is listed for Friday 14 October 2024. The court serves the application notice and evidence in support by first class post. Counting back from the hearing, the three clear days are Thursday 13, Wednesday 12 and Tuesday 11 October.

The documents must therefore arrive with the respondent by Monday 10 October. Given that documents sent in this way are served on the second day after being posted (provided that this is a business day), the latest day on which the documents could be posted is Friday 7 October.

11.4 Where to make the application

The general rule is that an interim application is made to the court where the claim is situated or, if the claim has not yet been issued, to the court where the claim is likely to start.

If the claim is a designated money claim (which must be issued in the County Court Money Claims Centre) the application can be made in any County Court hearing centre.

11.5 Disposal without a hearing

The court may save costs by dealing with cases without the parties attending court if either the judge or the parties agree this would be appropriate. This would apply if the parties have already agreed the terms of the order.

11.6 Hearing by telephone

Active case management in accordance with the overriding objective includes dealing with cases without the parties needing to attend court and by making use of technology. Both may be achieved by dealing with some applications by a telephone conference call and this is becoming increasingly common. However, this will only normally be held if all parties consent.

11.7 Orders made on the court's own initiative

As part of the ethos of active case management, the court can exercise its powers on its own initiative, with the aim being to manage the case and further the overriding objective.

Orders made in this way must include a statement that parties who are affected may apply within seven days (or as the court allows) for the order to be set aside or varied.

11.8 Evidence in support

The general rule is that applications for interim remedies must be supported by evidence. The applicant may do the following.

(1) Set out the factual information in support on the application notice itself and sign the statement of truth.

(2) Rely on a separate witness statement with a statement of truth signed by the witness, which must be served with the application. This should be made by the person who is best placed to address the issues from their own personal knowledge. This may be the lawyer, the client or an appropriate person from the client's business depending upon the substance of the application.

It is important that sufficient detail is included to enable the court to make the correct decision, as there will be no oral evidence or witnesses at the hearing. Although the legal representative will make submissions, the judge will decide the case primarily on the basis of the written evidence.

Following an interim application hearing, the court will normally make a **summary assessment** of costs of the application. This will be unnecessary if the parties have agreed costs.

11.9 Interim payments

One particular application which is commonly made in personal injury matters is for an interim payment. This is an advance payment in respect of likely compensation. The purpose is to give the claimant some money at an early stage in order to avoid the hardship that might otherwise occur through having to wait a long time before obtaining judgment (for example, to enable the claimant to pay for a wheelchair, certain medical treatments or perhaps mortgage arrears, or to reimburse expenses incurred as a result of the accident).

Applications for interim payments are made on notice and must be served at least 14 clear days before the hearing of the application. The evidence in support should set out:

- the amount requested and what the money will be used for;
- the likely damages that will be awarded;

- the reasons for believing a relevant ground (see **11.9.1**) is satisfied;
- in a personal injury claim, details of the damages, both past and future.

All relevant documents in support should be exhibited. In personal injury claims these will include the medical reports.

Respondents must file and serve their witness statements at least seven clear days before the hearing; and the applicant may respond with further evidence at least three clear days before the hearing.

11.9.1 Grounds for obtaining an interim payment

Under **CPR Part 25**, an interim payment may only be ordered if:

- liability has been decided, either by the court, or by the defendant admitting it; or
- the court is satisfied that the claimant has a strong enough case that they will win at trial.

11.9.2 Amount to be ordered

The court is not permitted to order an interim payment of more than a reasonable proportion of the likely amount of any final judgment.

11.10 Costs in interim applications

At the conclusion of the hearing, the judge decides who will pay the costs of the application and how much these will be. This is known as **summary assessment** and avoids the need to revisit costs at a later date. Any such costs are payable within 14 days unless the court orders otherwise. It is sensible for the parties to agree costs in advance of the hearing as this provides the client with certainty. If costs are agreed, the judge is unlikely to reject this figure, unless they consider it disproportionate.

There are some interim applications in which the amount of the costs is fixed under **Part 45** and in these instances the judge has no need to carry out a summary assessment. One such example occurs in summary judgment where the claimant wins and the claim is for a specified sum (a debt).

11.11 Summary

(1) Interim applications are those made between issue of proceedings and trial. They are used to obtain an interim remedy (e.g. an injunction or an interim payment) and also to obtain directions from the court.

(2) **CPR Part 23** contains general rules on applications for court orders. Interim applications may be made on notice or without notice and may be disposed of without a hearing.

(3) An application for an interim remedy must be supported by evidence. Interim remedies are governed by **CPR Part 25**.

(4) **Interim payments** are orders for payment by a defendant on account of any damages or debt which the court may hold the defendant liable to pay.

(5) The evidence in support of an application for an interim payment, and the grounds required for obtaining an interim payment, are stipulated in **CPR Part 25**.

CHAPTER 12
Case Management

12.1 Introduction

In exercising their powers to manage cases, the courts' aim is to comply with the overriding objective of **CPR Part 1** of ensuring that cases are dealt with justly and at proportionate cost. This includes ensuring that they are dealt with expeditiously and fairly, allotting to them an appropriate share of the court's resources and ensuring that cases are dealt with proportionately bearing in mind factors such as the importance and complexities of the issues and the monetary value of the claim.

CPR r1.4(1) provides that the court must further the overriding objective by actively managing cases. **Part 3** contains detailed provisions relating to the court's general case management powers. These are wide-ranging and include powers to make, vary or revoke orders, to strike out a statement of case and to impose sanctions – see **r3.1**. **r3.1A** provides, in addition, that the court must be prepared to adapt its procedures where at least one party is unrepresented in order to ensure that the overriding objective is met.

Courts are expected to be robust, rigorous and interventionist in relation to case management. To this end, **CPR Part 1** includes a provision requiring the courts to enforce compliance with rules, Practice Directions and orders to achieve the overriding objective.

The need for claims to be dealt with at proportionate cost means that costs management is pervasive to all claims brought under **CPR**.

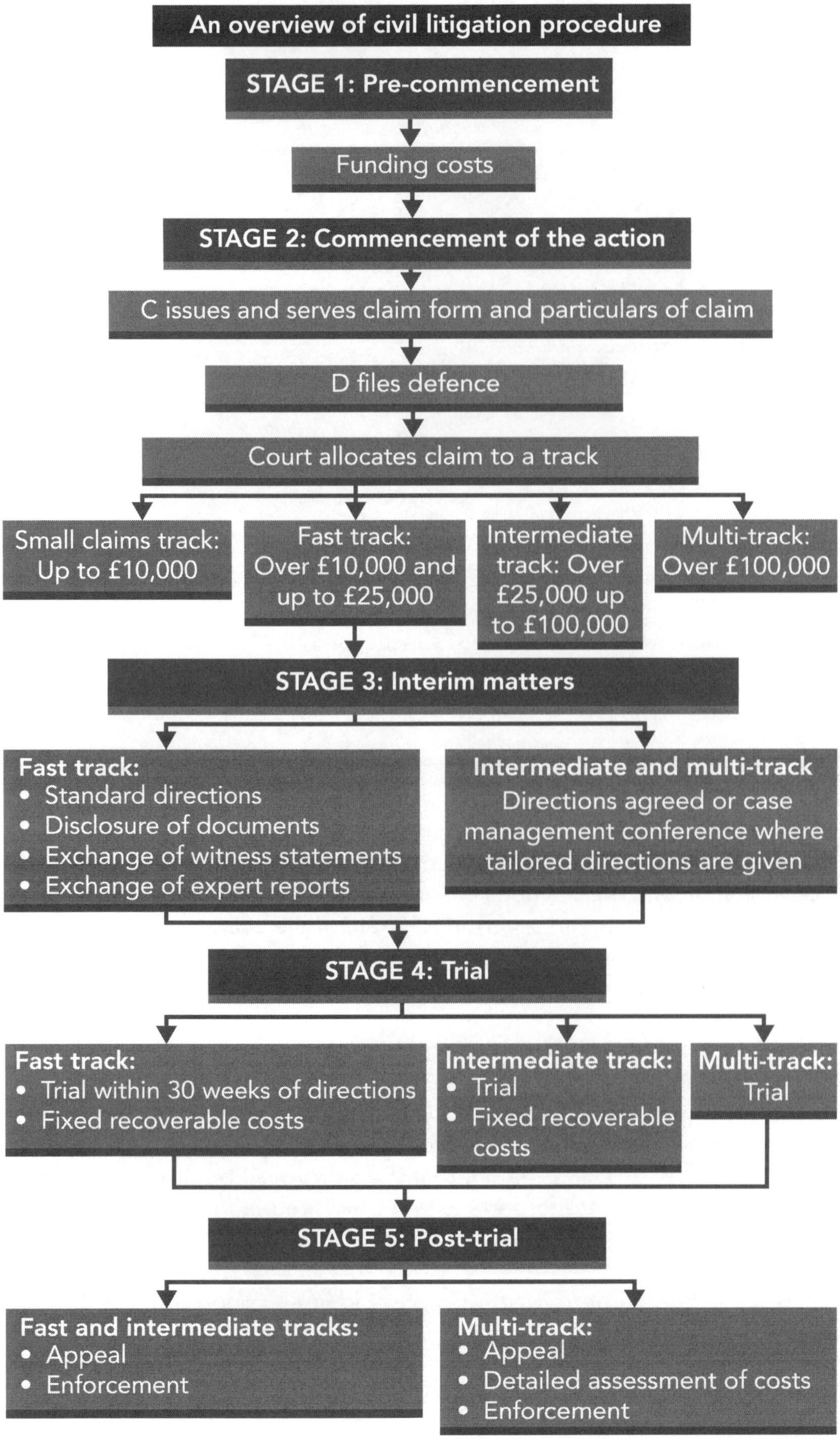
An overview of civil litigation procedure
STAGE 1: Pre-commencement
Funding costs
STAGE 2: Commencement of the action
C issues and serves claim form and particulars of claim
D files defence
Court allocates claim to a track
Small claims track: Up to £10,000
Fast track: Over £10,000 and up to £25,000
Intermediate track: Over £25,000 up to £100,000
Multi-track: Over £100,000
STAGE 3: Interim matters
Fast track:
• Standard directions
• Disclosure of documents
• Exchange of witness statements
• Exchange of expert reports
Intermediate and multi-track
Directions agreed or case management conference where tailored directions are given
STAGE 4: Trial
Fast track:
• Trial within 30 weeks of directions
• Fixed recoverable costs
Intermediate track:
• Trial
• Fixed recoverable costs
Multi-track: Trial
STAGE 5: Post-trial
Fast and intermediate tracks:
• Appeal
• Enforcement
Multi-track:
• Appeal
• Detailed assessment of costs
• Enforcement

Judges will intervene during the early stages of proceedings to ensure that the issues in dispute are narrowed, that cases are prepared economically and speedily and disposed of fairly and without undue delay or expense.

To assist with their progress to trial, defended actions are assigned to one of three case management "tracks".

Different rules apply to the tracks, with the small claims track being run with the least formality. This reflects the fact that these cases are of lower value and, often, the parties represent themselves.

Cases with a monetary value in the range of £10,000.01 to £25,000 will usually be allocated to the fast track. Standard directions are issued and timetables are tight, with the trial taking place within 30 weeks.

Larger and more important cases with a monetary value in excess of £25,000 will be assigned to the multi-track. The courts are given considerable flexibility in the way they manage multi-track cases, with a greater or lesser degree of intervention depending on the importance of the case.

Note that different criteria apply to personal injury claims (see **12.4**).

12.2 Provisional allocation and directions questionnaires

Defended cases will be allocated by the court to an appropriate track.

(1) When the defendant files their defence, a court officer will provisionally decide on the track which appears most suitable for the claim.

(2) The court will serve on the parties a notice of proposed allocation which will require them to file and serve a completed directions questionnaire by a specified date.

The directions questionnaire is used by the court to confirm the track and to determine directions. Parties should agree or propose directions and file and serve these with the questionnaire.

A directions questionnaire (N181) form may be accessed at https://www.gov.uk/government/publications/form-n181-directions-questionnaire-fast-track-and-multi-track.

Summary of N181 questionnaire content

A: Settlement

The parties are asked to confirm whether they require a one-month stay to attempt to settle the matter, either by informal discussion or alternative dispute resolution (ADR); confirmation must be given that you have advised the client of possible costs sanctions if they do not do so.

If there is no wish to attempt to settle the claim before the court hearing, the party has to provide written reasons on the form.

B: Court

You must set out whether there is any reason why the case needs to be heard in a particular County Court hearing centre or High Court and, if so, why.

C: Pre-action protocols

In this section, you are asked if there is a relevant pre-action protocol and, if so, whether you have followed it. If not, you must give reasons.

D: Case management information

This includes:

- whether any applications have been made so far (and details);
- if your proposed directions indicate a track which would not be the normal track for the claim, you must provide reasons for your choice;
- the scope and extent of disclosure of documents, including electronic documents.

E: Experts

In this section, you state whether you consider the case is suitable for a single joint expert, and if not, give details of any experts which you wish to use at the trial, including the cost.

F: Witnesses

This requires the parties to list all the witnesses of fact they intend to call at the trial.

G: Trial or final hearing

Here, the parties must give a realistic estimate of how long the trial will last.

H: Costs

- If the party is legally represented and the case is likely to be allocated to the multi-track, their legal representative must file and serve a costs budget on form **Precedent H**.

The budget will provide a summary of costs, both past and future.

I: Other information

You should include any other information you consider will help the judge to manage the claim, such as applications which the party intends to make. You should also identify any vulnerable witnesses and any needs or adjustments which will need to be met.

J: Directions

The parties must attempt to agree proposed directions. These act as a timetable of the procedural steps which will take the claim all the way to trial. A draft order should accompany the form.

(1) For multi-track claims, proposed directions must be based on the "menu" of specimen directions which can be found on the Ministry of Justice website.

(2) Proposed fast track directions must be based on **CPR Part 28**.

12.3 Failing to file a directions questionnaire

CPR Part 26 sets out the consequences of failing to file a directions questionnaire.

County Court money claim

For these claims, the court will:

- serve a notice requiring the defaulting party to comply within seven days; and
- if the party fails to do so, automatically strike out the party's statement of case.

All other claims

The court will make any order it considers to be appropriate, which could include:

- an order for directions;
- an order striking out the claim or the defence (in which case judgment will be entered); or
- listing the claim for a case management conference.

The court will also order the defaulting party to pay the costs.

12.4 Track allocation

Generally, the court will allocate cases in accordance with their financial value, although note that the rules are different for personal injury claims.

Which track?	Personal injury claims (non-RTA claims)	Personal injury claims (RTA claims)	Other claims
Small claims	Value for pain and suffering and loss of amenity is £1,500 or below	Value for pain, suffering and loss of amenity is £5,000 or below unless the claimant is a child, protected person or a pedestrian where the limit is £1,000 or below	Value is £10,000 or below
Fast track	Value is above £1,500 (for the pain and suffering element of personal injury claims) but below £25,000	Value is above £5,000 (or £1,000) (for the pain and suffering element of personal injury claims) but below £25,000	Value is above £10,000 but below £25,000
Multi-track	Value of the claim is above £25,000	Value of the claim is above £25,000	Value of the claim is above £25,000

However, the court may allocate a case to a higher track having regard to factors such as complexity, the value of any counterclaim, the amount of oral evidence and the importance of the case.

12.5 Case management directions

At the same time as the court allocates a case to a track it may also make case management directions.

In fast track cases, the court sends an order for directions to each party setting out the timetable of steps required to progress the claim to trial. These must be completed within a relatively short period of time and are known as standard directions.

However, in high-value multi-track cases the court is likely to convene a case management conference for the purpose of determining cost-proportionate directions.

12.5.1 Shorter trial and flexible trial schemes

The aim of the shorter and flexible trial schemes is to provide earlier trials for business related litigation, at a reasonable and proportionate cost. Also, they are intended to help change attitudes to litigation, with the parties recognising that comprehensive disclosure and a full, oral trial on all issues is often not necessary for justice to be achieved. This will lead to significant savings in the time and costs of litigation.

The **shorter trial** procedure offers commercial parties a streamlined procedure leading to judgment within a year of issuing proceedings. The procedure is intended for cases which can be fairly tried on the basis of limited disclosure and oral evidence. The maximum length of trial would be four days, including reading time.

The **flexible trial** scheme involves the adoption of more flexible case management procedures where the parties so agree, resulting in a more simplified and expedited procedure than the full trial procedure currently provided for under **CPR**.

12.6 Stay for settlement

One of the court's case management functions is to help the parties to settle the case (**CPR r1.4(2)(f)**), and another is to encourage and facilitate the use of ADR procedures if appropriate (**r1.4(2)(e)**). To comply with these objectives, the court may order a stay (postponement) of the proceedings for one month.

12.7 Non-compliance with directions: sanctions

Minor failures to keep precisely to the directions timetable in a case will not generally be a problem provided the parties co-operate and can still keep to certain key dates, such as for the case management conference and the trial. However:

- where a party has failed to comply with a direction given by the court, the other party may apply for an order to enforce compliance and/or for a sanction to be imposed;
- the court may order costs to be paid by the party in default.

To ensure compliance with the overriding objective:

- such a failure will not lead to a postponement of the trial unless the circumstances of the case are exceptional; but
- any such adjournment would be a last resort.

Other sanctions which the court may impose include depriving a party of the right to:

- raise or contest an issue; or
- rely on evidence to which the direction relates.

This highlights the need for thorough and careful case preparation and adherence to time limits.

In response, **CPR r3.9** enables parties to apply for relief from sanctions imposed by the court.

Whilst **CPR** expect the courts to adopt a robust and proactive approach to case management, quite how tough that approach should be has been the subject of much litigation.

Andrew Mitchell MP v News Group Newspapers Ltd [2013] concerned proceedings brought by Mr Mitchell for *The Sun*'s coverage of the "Plebgate" scandal. The Court of Appeal dismissed his appeal against the High Court decision that, because he had failed to file his costs budget on time, he could only recover court fees, regardless of how valid his case was or how much work his solicitors were required to do. This case sent shock waves through the legal profession and represented a significant shift in the way litigation is now conducted.

However, in more recent cases, judges have recognised that enforcing compliance with **CPR** is not an end in itself and that it is not part of the court's function to impose sanctions merely for punitive purposes.

This approach was reinforced in ***Viridor Waste Management Ltd v Veolia ES Ltd [2015]*** where a warning was issued against taking "unreasonable advantage" of late filing. Owing to an administrative error, the particulars of claim were filed one day late by way of second class post – a method not recognised by **CPR**. The defendant refused to consent to the claimant's application for an extension of time and applied to strike out the claim.

In deciding whether to grant relief from sanctions, the court must consider:

- the seriousness and significance of the breach;
- the reasons for the default; and
- all the circumstances of the case including the need to comply with rules, Practice Directions and orders but also for litigation to be conducted efficiently and at proportionate cost.

In this particular case, no delay was caused by the error and the course of the litigation was unaffected. To penalise the defendant for their unreasonable stance, costs were awarded to the claimant on an indemnity basis.

Adopting a common-sense approach is the key. If a minor or technical breach has no effect on the litigation, the party who takes issue may be penalised in costs if it loses. However, missing a deadline may still lead to serious financial consequences as the courts remain focused on ensuring the efficient conduct of litigation at a proportionate cost. It is a question of balancing fairness with procedural certainty.

12.8 Summary

(1) The court must further the overriding objective by actively managing cases and the court will take a robust and proactive approach to case management.

(2) To assist with this process, defended actions are assigned to one of three case management tracks. These are the **small claims track** for cases with a value not more than £10,000 (or £5,000/£1,000 for RTA PI claims), the **fast track** for cases exceeding of £10,000 (or £5,000/£1,000 for RTA PI claims) up to £25,000 and the **multi-track** for cases over £25,000.

(3) All parties must complete the **directions questionnaire**, which assists the court in deciding the appropriate track to which the case should be allocated. Allocation is governed by **Part 26**.

(4) The court usually gives **directions** at the track allocation stage. Directions in the small claims track are very limited; a set of standard directions (which can be adapted) is provided in **Part 28** for fast track cases; in multi-track cases, a case management conference may be convened to give directions.

(5) There are several sanctions that the court can impose for non-compliance with the directions timetable. It is difficult for parties to obtain relief from sanctions.

CHAPTER 13
Small Claims Track

13.1 Introduction

The small claims track is intended to provide a procedure suitable for the most straightforward types of case, such as consumer disputes, small accident claims, and some landlord and tenant cases.

The small claims track is governed by **CPR Part 27** and is the normal track for defended claims with a value not exceeding £10,000, except for certain personal injury cases.

13.2 Restrictions on complicated procedures

The idea of the small claims track is to provide a relatively inexpensive means of resolving disputes which have a limited financial value. Some of the more sophisticated procedures available for larger claims are therefore inappropriate for cases on the small claims track and do **not** apply. These include:

- most interim remedies;
- standard disclosure of documents (a more limited form of disclosure applies);
- most of the rules on experts; and
- **CPR Part 36** offers (because this would interfere with the no costs rule: see below).

13.3 Standard directions in the small claims track

When the court allocates a case to the small claims track, it will usually give what are described as **standard directions**.

These provide that:

- the parties must file and serve on the other side copies of the documents they intend to rely upon no later than 14 days before the hearing;
- the original documents must be brought to the hearing;
- notice must be given of the date and the length of the hearing; and
- the parties must inform the court if they settle the case by agreement.

13.3.1 Automatic referral to mediation

If the claim is allocated to the small claims track the court will automatically refer the case to mediation provided both parties agree. This increases the prospects of resolving the matter without the need for a trial, thus saving time and costs.

13.4 Special directions

A District Judge considering the court file at the allocation stage may decide that the case merits additional directions. For example, although the general rule in small claims track cases is that no expert evidence is allowed, if such evidence is regarded as necessary (for example, if the case involves technical matters such as a dispute over quality of workmanship in a case between a builder and their client), a **special direction** will be made.

Alternatively, the District Judge may list the case for a **preliminary hearing** to ensure that the parties understand what they must do to prepare the case, or if it appears from the documents the case should be struck out.

13.5 Determination without a hearing

If all the parties agree, a small claim can be determined on the papers without a hearing by the District Judge sitting in the County Court.

13.6 Hearing

A hearing fee is payable by the claimant which is dependent on the value of the claim. Final hearings in small claims track cases are usually dealt with by District Judges sitting in the County Court and are generally conducted in the judge's room rather than in one of the court rooms. Small claims hearings are informal and the strict rules of evidence do not apply.

The District Judge may proceed in any way that is considered fair. They may ask the witnesses questions before allowing the parties to do so, may refuse to allow cross-examination until all the witnesses have given evidence-in-chief and may impose limits on the scope of cross-examination.

After hearing the evidence and closing submissions on behalf of the parties, the District Judge generally gives an oral judgment there and then. The judgment is likely to be as short and simple as the nature of the case will allow.

13.7 Costs in the small claims track

Once a claim has been allocated to the small claims track, no costs will be ordered between the parties except:

- the fixed costs relating to issuing the claim;
- court fees;
- witnesses' expenses for travel, subsistence and loss of earnings up to (currently) £95 per day;
- experts' fees, up to £750 per expert;

- litigants in person conducting their own case may claim for legal work at the rate of £19 per hour.

The above restrictions apply in the vast majority of small claims cases.

13.8 Appeals and rehearings

Appeals in small claims track cases are dealt with in the same way as appeals in other tracks and are governed by **CPR Part 52**. Further consideration of appeals is beyond the scope of this manual.

13.9 Summary

(1) The small claims track is governed by **CPR Part 27**. It is designed to provide a cost-proportionate procedure for straightforward, low-value claims. Generally, the small claims upper limit is £10,000 except for personal injury claims.

(2) Some of the more sophisticated procedures that apply to the other two tracks do **not** apply to the small claims track. These include most interim remedies, rules on experts and **CPR Part 36** offers and payments. There is limited disclosure. Costs are ordered between the parties only in very limited circumstances.

(3) Small claims may be determined without a hearing if all the parties agree.

(4) Appeals, as for the other two tracks, are governed by **CPR Part 52**.

CHAPTER 14

Fast Track

14.1 Introduction

The fast track provides a streamlined procedure with cases being progressed to trial within a short timescale after the filing of defences. The fast track is governed by **CPR Part 28**. The timetable gives the parties enough time to undertake the work necessary to prepare the case for trial, but is sufficiently tight to discourage elaboration. Similarly, although the full range of interim remedies and orders are available in fast track cases, there is limited time for indulging in tactical procedural applications.

In this chapter we will cover:

- allocation;
- directions;
- time limits;
- pre-trial checklists; and
- costs.

14.2 Allocation to the fast track

The fast track is the normal track for cases falling into the £10,000.01 to £25,000 bracket; and most personal injury cases.

Cases are only suitable for the fast track if the trial can be dealt with in one day.

14.3 Directions

When it allocates a case to the fast track, the court will usually issue standard directions without a hearing. These are contained in **Part 28** and set out a timetable of the steps to be taken from this point through to trial. They also ensure that the issues are identified and the necessary evidence is prepared and disclosed.

Typically, the matters covered are:

- disclosure of documents;
- service of witness statements;
- expert evidence; and
- fixing a date for the trial, or a period (a "trial window") in which the trial is to take place.

Although the parties may agree different directions between themselves, these must be approved by the court. For example, the usual direction is for a single joint expert to be appointed, but the parties may wish to instruct an expert of their own. However, the court will not necessarily agree.

14.4 Time limits set out in the rules

Part 28 governs the standard directions and these are set out in the table below. Specific time limits, which run from the date of allocation unless otherwise stated, are also listed in **CPR**.

Standard directions

Step in the proceedings	Time limit
Disclosure of documents	4 weeks
Inspection of documents	7 days after disclosure

Step in the proceedings	Time limit
Exchange of witness statements	10 weeks
Exchange of experts' reports	14 weeks
Service of pre-trial checklists by court	20 weeks
Return of pre-trial checklists	22 weeks
Trial	30 weeks

14.5 Experts in fast track claims

Part 35 deals with experts.

In order to keep costs down and to reduce the length of fast track trials, the court will order the joint instruction of a single expert unless there is good reason for doing otherwise. In addition, the court will not usually direct an expert to attend the trial.

Normally, expert evidence should be prepared and be ready for exchange 14 weeks after the notice of allocation.

14.6 Pre-trial checklists (listing questionnaires)

Not more than eight weeks before the trial date the parties must (unless dispensed with by the court) return pre-trial checklists, which are also known as listing questionnaires, to the court. These forms are similar to directions questionnaires and are designed to check whether the case is ready for trial. In particular, the parties are asked to:

- confirm that all directions have been complied with;
- give details of and availability of the parties and witnesses;
- provide information about experts and the legal representation;
- consider the time estimate and other aspects of the trial to ensure a trial date may be set; and
- confirm that the relevant documents, an estimate of costs and the fee have been included.

A copy of the relevant form may be found at https://www.gov.uk/government/publications/form-n170-listing-questionnaire-pre-trial-checklist.

14.7 Varying the timetable

The parties may agree to vary the timetable but not the trial date or the date for returning pre-trial checklists.

If, for whatever reason, a party is not ready for trial it is possible to make an application to change the date, but this should be a last resort. Examples would include where there are significant problems with the evidence or, in personal injury cases, where the prognosis is uncertain.

14.8 Fast track costs

The power to award costs is limited. In the fast track:

- the normal practice is for fixed recoverable costs to apply in personal injury claims and, since 1 October 2023, non-personal injury claims.

The fixed costs vary depending on which "complexity band" the claim falls within (Bands 1, 2, 3 or 4 - 4 being the most complex).

Details of the fixed costs for the different stages and steps in a fast track trial are set out in Table 12 in **PD 45** - see https://www.justice.gov.uk/courts/procedure-rules/civil/rules/part45-fixed-costs/practice-direction-45-fixed-costs .

Note that fixed recoverable costs do **not** apply in housing claims relating to repossessions, disrepair and unlawful eviction. They also do not apply where the claimant is a "protected party" such as a person who has lost mental capacity.

There are separate tables in **PD 45** covering the fixed costs payable for the different stages under the RTA Protocol and the EL.PL Protocol - see **6.7**.

14.8.1 Summary assessment - cases which commenced before 1 October 2023

The normal rule for cases commenced prior to 1 October 2023 is that costs in non-personal injury fast track cases are dealt with by the judge by way of **summary assessment** at the end of the trial. To this end, each party is required to file and serve a statement of costs (form N260) at least two days before the trial. This form may be accessed at https://www.gov.uk/government/publications/form-n260-statement-of-costs-summary-assessment.

This provides full details of the work carried out by the law firm, including the time spent, on what tasks and by what level of fee-earner.

To assist judges in determining if the costs are reasonable, **guideline fee rates** are published for solicitors and other fee-earners covering the whole country. The guideline rates vary according to the grade of fee-earner. There are four grades: grade 1 applies to a solicitor with over eight years' post-qualification experience, whilst grade 4 applies to trainee solicitors and fee-earners of equivalent experience.

It is important to remember that in summarily assessing costs the court must place emphasis on the costs being proportionate (**CPR Part 44**).

There are also fixed trial costs for an advocate for preparing for and attending the trial of a fast track claim.

14.9 Summary

(1) The fast track provides a **streamlined procedure** with cases being progressed to trial within a short time (30 weeks) after allocation. It is the normal track for cases valued between £10,000.01 and £25,000 (including most personal injury cases) and is governed by **CPR Part 28**.

(2) The full range of interim remedies, procedures and orders is available in fast track cases.

(3) Directions are given on allocation; **Part 28** provides a list of standard directions, which may be adapted to the needs of individual cases. The parties must comply with the time limits in the timetable.

(4) **CPR Part 35** deals with experts; the court will usually direct that expert evidence be provided by a single, jointly instructed expert.

(5) **Pre-trial checklists** (**listing questionnaires**) are used to check that the directions have been complied with and whether the case is ready for trial.

(6) Since 1 October 2023, fixed recoverable costs will apply to most fast track cases in accordance with **PD 45**.

CHAPTER 15

Intermediate Track and Multi-track

15.1 Introduction

On 1 October 2023 a new intermediate track was introduced. It covers simpler cases valued above £25,000 up to £100,000. The multi-track, which, prior to 1 October 2023, covered all cases above £25,000, now covers cases above £100,000. Note, however, that certain more complex cases valued above £25,000 up to £100,000 continue to be allocated to the multi-track.

Claims which must be allocated to the multi-track

Under **r26.9** a claim must be allocated to the multi-track if it is:

- a mesothelioma or asbestos lung claim;

- a clinical negligence claim, unless breach of duty and causation have already been admitted and it would otherwise be allocated to the intermediate track; and
- a claim relating to harm or abuse of children or vulnerable adults.

The main rules dealing with the intermediate track are covered in **Part 28** and **PD 28**.

Cases on the multi-track range from simple contractual disputes to complex commercial cases involving difficult issues of fact and law with values of several million pounds. Case management on the multi-track is intended to reflect this. Straightforward cases should be given standard directions and the parties will be expected to comply with those directions without complicating or delaying matters. At the other end of the scale, the courts adopt a far more proactive approach, possibly with several directions hearings in the form of case management conferences and pre-trial reviews. The main rules for multi-track cases are in **CPR Part 29**.

Although there is flexibility to deal with each case in an appropriate way, **cost management** is an important feature and **Part 3** will be discussed at appropriate places in this chapter.

15.2 Directions in the intermediate track

Standard directions will normally apply in personal injury claims in the intermediate track.

In other claims, if directions have not already been agreed, directions will be set at the case management hearing.. Note, in particular **r28.14**:

- oral evidence will normally be limited to one expert per party;
- the trial estimate must not exceed three days;
- the total length of all the permitted witness statements and summaries must not exceed 30 pages; and
- any expert report must not exceed 20 pages.

15.3 Costs in the intermediate track

Fixed recoverable costs apply in the intermediate track in a similar way to the fast track (see 14.8). There are four complexity bands (1 to 4 in ascending order of complexity) (see **rr26.15** and 26.16) with associated grids of costs linked to the different stages of a claim - see Table 14 **PD 45** at https://www.justice.gov.uk/courts/procedure-rules/civil/rules/part45-fixed-costs/practice-direction-45-fixed-costs.

15.4 Directions on allocation

You may recall that on receipt of the completed directions questionnaire from each party, the court will also have:

- costs budgets on Precedent H forms (multi-track claims only) https://www.gov.uk/government/publications/form-precedent-h-and-r-costs-budget-precedent-h-and-budget-discussion-report-precedent-r;
- proposed directions based on standard directions available on the Ministry of Justice website https://www.justice.gov.uk/courts/procedure-rules/civil/standard-directions;
- costs estimates for proposed expert reports;
- a disclosure report.

From the information provided the court will seek to tailor-make directions which are suitable for that particular case. The court's concern will be to ensure that the issues between the parties are identified and that the evidence required for the trial is prepared and disclosed.

Similar steps will be taken in multi-track cases as to those in the fast track. However, because many multi-track cases are complex, it is recognised that the time required for each step may be considerably longer than that allowed in fast track claims. As a consequence, a case management conference will be held to ensure that appropriate directions are ordered, and these will be re-considered in a pre-trial review.

15.5 Case management conferences

A case management conference (CMC) will usually be held immediately after a case is allocated to the intermediate track or multi-track. CMCs are not simply directions hearings, but are intended to ensure that the real issues between the parties are identified.

The starting point will be to determine the directions – the timetable which takes the case all the way up to trial – and the parties must try to agree these. To assist, there is a "menu" of directions, including standard directions, which are provided on the Ministry of Justice's website and these may be adapted as required. Any agreed directions will be submitted to the court with the completed directions questionnaire within seven days of the CMC.

15.6 Attendance at case management conferences

If a party has a legal representative, someone familiar with the case must attend the CMC (**CPR Part 29**).

Normally, the person attending should be the fee-earner dealing with the file, or someone, possibly counsel, who is fully familiar with the case, the issues and the proposed evidence. They must:

- be able to deal with questions that are likely to arise at the hearing;
- have the authority to make concessions and agreements in relation to narrowing the issues, revising the costs budget and so on; and
- be capable of making representations on the matters reasonably to be expected to arise.

Where the inadequacy of the person attending (or their instructions) leads to the adjournment of the hearing, it will be normal for a wasted costs order to be made.

15.7 Issues to be dealt with at case management conferences

At a CMC the court will:

- make a thorough review of the steps the parties have taken to date in preparing the case for trial, including checking whether they have complied with any previous orders and directions;
- determine any aspects of the claim which can be agreed; and
- decide on the directions needed to progress the action in accordance with the overriding objective.

The court would also set a timetable by reference to calendar dates and times of day (e.g. that a step must be completed by "4.00 pm on 22 September 2019").

Sensible directions would cover:

- disclosure and inspection of documents;
- exchange of witness statements;
- expert evidence;
- date for pre-trial checklists and (if considered necessary) the fixing of a pre-trial review;
- arrangements for trial including trial bundles; and (possibly)
- that the parties consider using alternative dispute resolution.

The court may at any time make a "costs management order" where it:

- records the extent to which the budgets are agreed between the parties; and
- if necessary, revises the budget and records the court's approval.

15.7.1 Cost budgets

Case management and cost management are linked as the court, with input from the parties, will actively control the costs of the case (**CPR Part 3**). The parties are required to provide budgets, outlining their own costs, in the prescribed form (Precedent H). These will be submitted to the court for approval and updated from time to time. To ensure that costs are not incurred unnecessarily, the court will decide what steps should be taken in the proceedings and at what expense.

Timescales for filing and exchanging costs budgets

Unless the court orders otherwise, costs budgets (Precedent H) must be filed and exchanged:

- where the value of the claim is less than £50,000, with the directions questionnaires; or
- in any other case, not later than 21 days before the first case management conference.

Having done so, the parties should complete a budget discussion report (Precedent R) no later than seven days before the first case management conference setting out those areas which are agreed and those which are still in dispute.

Failing to file a costs budget

If a party fails to file a costs budget at all, they are treated as having filed a budget comprising court fees only, so that no solicitor's costs are permitted (**CPR Part 3**). You may recall that the claimant solicitors fell foul of this rule in ***Andrew Mitchell MP v News Group Newspapers Ltd [2013]*** and consequently had to forego nearly £50,000 in costs.

Filing an inaccurate costs budget

(1) Once a costs budget has been approved by the court, it is extremely difficult to persuade a court that it should be amended, unless there have been significant developments.

(2) As a consequence, it is vital that the costs budget reflects the true costs, because the parties will only be able to recover the amount of their budgets. This can cause real difficulties as litigation is inherently unpredictable. Because of these uncertainties, lawyers will carry out as much work as possible before issuing proceedings to ensure that the costs budget is as accurate as it can be. The effect is that much litigation is now "front loaded".

15.8 Case summary

As the matter proceeds towards a trial, the court will review the case and may order further directions. The judge may request a case summary to help them understand which issues are still "live". The case summary is, effectively, an updated case analysis.

The case summary should include a brief chronology of the claim, state the factual issues that are agreed and those in dispute, and the nature of the evidence needed to decide them. Responsibility for preparing the document rests with the claimant but, if possible, it should be agreed by the other parties.

15.9 Fixing the date for trial

The court will fix the trial date or the period in which the trial is to take place (a trial window) as soon as practicable.

15.10 Pre-trial checklists (listing questionnaires)

The pre-trial checklist is completed to ensure that all the directions have been complied with and the parties are ready to proceed to trial.

15.11 Pre-trial review

If a pre-trial review is listed, it is likely to take place about 8–10 weeks before trial, usually before the probable trial judge. The main purpose is to identify the issues to be tried and to set a timetable for the trial. In particular, time limits may be imposed for the questioning of witnesses and for speeches, to force advocates to focus their preparation and to produce better-managed trials.

15.12 Variation of case management timetable

The parties may agree in writing to vary the timetable provided that doing so does not make it necessary to vary the dates for any CMC, pre-trial review or checklists, or of the trial or trial period. In such cases any variation is only possible with the court's permission.

15.13 Overview

Set out on the next page is an overview of a personal injury multi-track case.

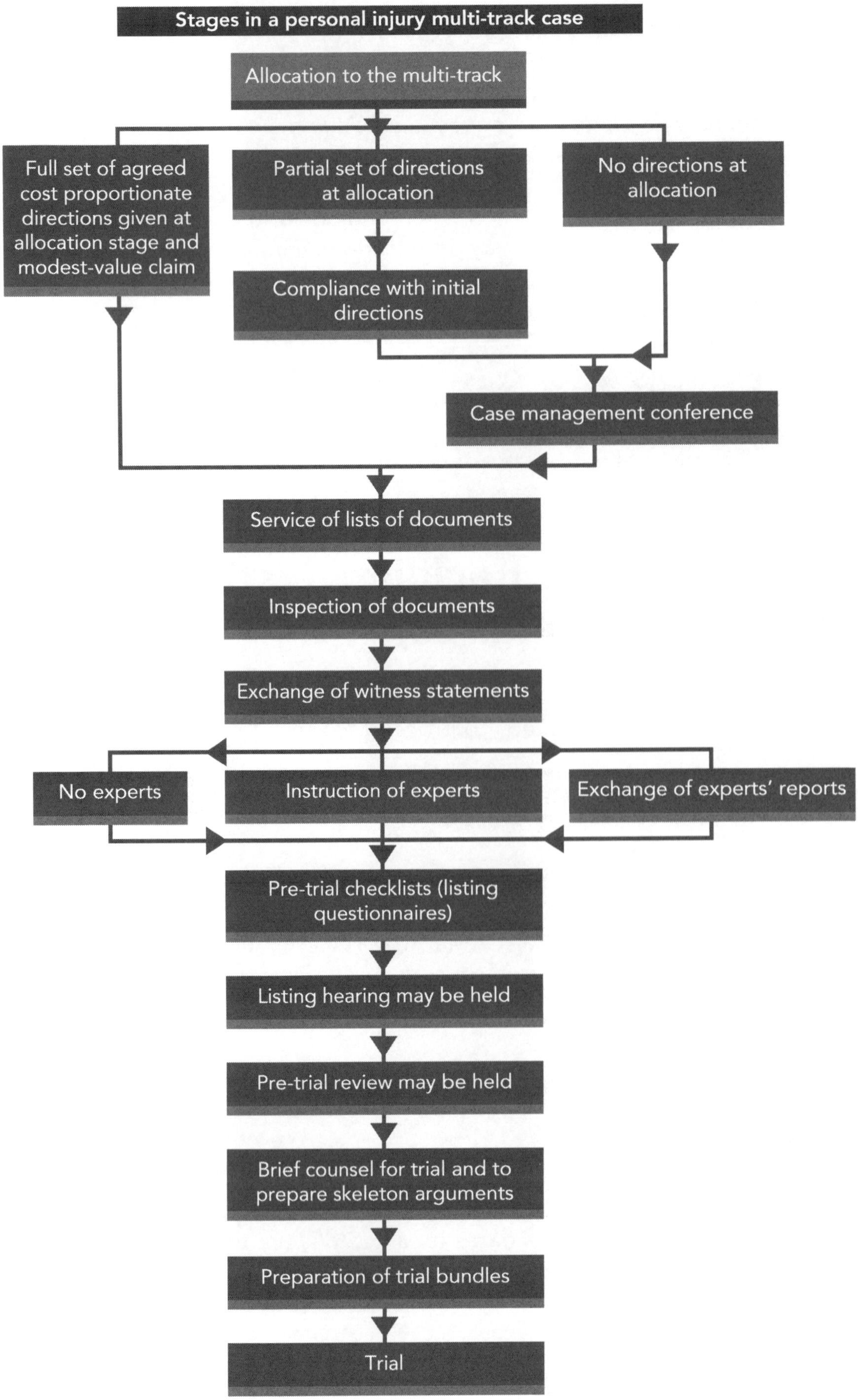
Stages in a personal injury multi-track case
Allocation to the multi-track
Full set of agreed cost proportionate directions given at allocation stage and modest-value claim
Partial set of directions at allocation
No directions at allocation
Compliance with initial directions
Case management conference
Service of lists of documents
Inspection of documents
Exchange of witness statements
No experts
Instruction of experts
Exchange of experts' reports
Pre-trial checklists (listing questionnaires)
Listing hearing may be held
Pre-trial review may be held
Brief counsel for trial and to prepare skeleton arguments
Preparation of trial bundles
Trial

15.14 Summary

(1) Most cases with a value greater than £25,000 up to £100,000 are now, since 1 October 2023, allocated to the intermediate track. There are some exceptions, such as mesothelioma cases, which are always allocated to the multi-track. Standard directions apply in the intermediate track and fixed recoverable costs apply in the intermediate track.

(2) The multi-track is used for all cases exceeding £100,000 and its procedures are designed to reflect the greater complexity and value of such cases. The multi-track is governed by **CPR Part 29**, and **Part 3** (costs management).

(3) On allocation, the court may give directions, or call a **case management conference** (CMC) to decide on appropriate directions and timescales. CMCs are also intended to ensure that the real issues between the parties are identified and, if possible, narrowed. The court must manage the case and the costs together to ensure that the proposed directions are proportionate to the costs to be incurred, and revise the budget if appropriate.

(4) The person having conduct of the case should attend the CMC and have the authority to deal with questions and make concessions.

(5) A **pre-trial review** may be conducted shortly before the trial to identify the issues to be tried and set a timetable for the trial.

CHAPTER 16

Disclosure

16.1 Introduction

Once the parties have filed and served a claim and defence, the case will proceed and directions will be issued by the court. Disclosure and inspection of documents is usually the next step which the parties are required to undertake.

The parties are obliged to disclose to each other all the documents in their possession that relate to the proceedings. Full disclosure is crucial to ensuring that justice is achieved between opposing parties in a dispute. The disclosure obligation includes documents that are unhelpful to the party giving disclosure and which they would prefer to keep secret. Many litigants find it hard to accept that they have to provide their opponents with the means to defeat them. However, it is a requirement of **CPR** with the aim being to allow a proper evaluation of the strengths and weaknesses of the case before trial, so that the parties can make informed decisions about whether to proceed. The client should receive some comfort from the fact that the opposing party is under an equal duty to disclose.

Lawyers are under a professional duty to advise their clients on the scope of their obligations regarding the disclosure of documents and cannot continue to act for clients who refuse to comply.

16.2 Stage when disclosure takes place

At the allocation stage or at a CMC, the court will give directions for the future progress of the case. Effectively, this is a timetable and it will include provision for disclosure and inspection of documents, with a specific day for compliance.

In cases to which pre-action protocols apply, some disclosure will effectively take place before proceedings are issued as claimants must support their claim and defendants are required to justify their denial.

16.3 What does disclosure mean?

Disclosure is defined in **CPR Part 31**, which states:

A party discloses a document by stating that the document exists or has existed.

16.4 What is a document?

A "document" for the purposes of disclosure is widely defined and means anything in which information of any description is recorded. This would include written documents such as letters, contracts and emails as well as information on video tapes, DVDs or computer disks and even photographs.

However, it also includes documents which you might not expect, such as the particulars of claim, the defence, attendance notes of conversations with the client and correspondence between solicitors.

This is because all of these contain *information* upon which the client will rely etc.

(1) The statements of case record information on liability and damages.

(2) Attendance notes will record discussions between the legal representative and the client on the dispute and thus will contain information in this regard.

16.5 Disclosure on each track

Small claims track

CPR Part 31 does not apply to the small claims track. However, the court will usually order that each party shall, at least 14 days before the date fixed for the final hearing, file and serve on their opponent copies of all documents on which they intend to rely at the hearing.

Fast track and intermediate track

The usual direction is for standard disclosure (see below).

Multi-track

In the multi-track, directions are tailored to take account of the range and complexity of the cases. To enable the court to do this effectively, the parties must complete a disclosure report outlining their requirements.

16.6 Standard disclosure

In most cases, the court will make an order for **standard disclosure**. This requires a party to disclose:

- the documents on which they rely;
- the documents which:
    - adversely affect their own case;
    - adversely affect another party's case; or
    - support another party's case.

Clients will be more than happy to provide documents which assist their case, but the definition includes those which are unfavourable too. The reason is to ensure that cases are dealt with fairly and accurately, and each party should be reassured that the same provisions apply to all.

Not all documents are included – it is only those which affect the "case". The relevant issues will be set out and defined in the statements of case, that is, the claim and the defence. The court is primarily interested in documents which assist in determining the disputed issues.

Example

Blooms Florists (Blooms) purchase a consignment of flowers for sale in the lead-up to Mother's Day. When the flowers arrive, they are wilted and cannot be sold. Blooms have to purchase alternative supplies at higher prices to catch the lucrative Mother's Day market.

The documents Blooms rely upon would include the contract, the delivery note, photographs of the flowers and the invoice for the alternative supplies.

There is an email from the manager of the shop asking a junior employee why the flowers were not immediately placed in water. Although this would adversely affect Blooms' case, and support their opponent's, this must also be disclosed as it is relevant to why the flowers wilted.

16.6.1 Control of documents

The party must disclose those documents:

- which they physically possess (e.g. the contract);
- they used to possess (e.g. the originals of letters sent out); or
- they had a right to possess or to inspect or take copies (e.g. medical records).

16.6.2 Form of disclosure

This is done by preparing a list of documents using a standard form (N265) which may be accessed at https://www.gov.uk/government/publications/form-n265-list-of-documents-standard-disclosure.

On receipt, the other side is entitled to inspect certain documents contained in the list; this will often take place by requesting photocopies.

The list is divided into three sections as follows:

- Part 1 identifies the actual documents which are in the party's possession and which they do not object to being inspected by the other party. These will be listed specifically to enable the opponent to decide if they wish to inspect them.

- Part 2 includes those documents for which the party is claiming privilege from inspection. These are described in general terms so that the contents are not apparent. The objections to privilege must be stated and the usual ground will be that the document is covered by legal professional privilege. The effect is that the opponent cannot inspect these documents.
- Part 3 lists those (non-privileged) documents the party once had, but no longer has, in their control. This may simply be the originals of letters, copies of which have already been disclosed in the first part of the list.

16.6.3 Continuing duty of disclosure

The duty of disclosure continues until the proceedings are concluded. This means that if, after disclosure has been carried out, a party finds additional documents they must notify the other party of their existence. This is usually done by filing (at court) and serving (on the other parties) an amended list of documents.

16.7 Duty to search

A party is required to make a **reasonable search** for such documents as fall within standard disclosure.

The factors relevant in deciding the reasonableness of a search include:

- the number of documents involved;
- the nature and complexity of the proceedings;
- the ease and expense of retrieval of any particular document; and
- the significance of any document likely to be located during the search.

A list of documents must contain a **disclosure statement** setting out the extent of the search that has been made and certifying that the party understands the duty to disclose and that, to the best of their knowledge, they have carried out that duty.

If a party has not searched for a category or class of document on the ground that to do so would be unreasonable, they must state this in their disclosure statement and identify the category or class of document affected.

A search may be limited in a number of ways.

(1) By time: How far back does the search go? If there are pre-contractual discussions, for example, check that the search would include these.

(2) By location: Has the party's home been searched if they work from there? What about branch offices and storage facilities?

(3) By category: Which files did the party search? What electronic devices were included in the search – not just computers but also mobile devices?

The use of technology has significantly increased the volume of documents and so it is not unreasonable for the search to be limited in some way, but you would need to check that the exclusion is not too wide.

16.8 Multi-track (except personal injury) disclosure requirements

In multi-track cases, except personal injury claims, standard disclosure is not the norm. The disclosure requirements reflect the increased complexity and variety of these cases and the court will tailor disclosure to suit the parties' needs. To ensure that the directions are appropriate, the parties will file and serve a disclosure report, verified by a statement of truth, at least 14 days before the first CMC. The disclosure report must:

- describe briefly any documents which may be relevant to the matters in issue;
- describe the location of the documents;
- describe how electronic documents are stored;
- estimate the broad range of costs which could be involved in giving standard disclosure including the cost of searching for and disclosing any electronically stored documents; and
- indicate the directions the party wishes the court to make in relation to disclosure.

CPR Part 31 provides the court with a list/menu of possible disclosure orders. The court will decide the appropriate order with regard to the overriding objective and the need to limit disclosure to what is necessary to deal with the case justly. The options include an order to:

- dispense with disclosure entirely;
- effect disclosure on an issue-by-issue basis;
- carry out standard disclosure; or
- any other appropriate order.

The court may also give directions as to how disclosure will be given and can make an order to include:

- what searches are to be undertaken;
- whether lists of documents are required;
- how and when the disclosure statement is to be given;
- what is required in relation to documents that no longer exist; and
- whether disclosure shall take place in stages.

Where electronic documents are to be disclosed, there are additional provisions which apply.

16.8.1 Disclosure of electronic documents

In addition to, for example, emails and databases, electronic documents also include documents which are stored on servers and back-up systems including those which have been "deleted".

To limit the work involved to a reasonable level, the parties must discuss disclosure of electronic documents before the first CMC. They may, if they wish, exchange an Electronic Documents Questionnaire in order to provide information to each other in relation to the scope, extent and most suitable format for disclosure of electronic documents in the proceedings. The questionnaire must be verified by a statement of truth which includes:

"[I understand] [The [claimant] [defendant] understands] that proceedings for contempt of court may be brought against anyone who makes, or causes to be made, a false statement in a document verified by a statement of truth without an honest belief in its truth."

If the parties cannot agree on the disclosure of electronic documents, the court will give written directions or order a separate hearing to deal with this aspect.

16.9 Privilege

Under the law of evidence, some categories of documents are privileged. Such documents must still be disclosed in the sense that they are identified in the list of documents, but the other parties cannot inspect them. Documents such as draft witness statements, attendance notes of meetings between the legal representative and the client and advice from counsel will all be privileged.

Unlike other documents which must be described sufficiently clearly for them to be identified specifically, these documents are usually "hidden" in a broad description which prevents the other parties guessing their contents.

Example

Continuing with the case study of Blooms, the contract between the parties would be described in Part 1 of the list of documents as:

Written contract dated 11 February 2022 between Blooms Florists and Greens Wholesalers Ltd.

In contrast, the privileged documents would be included in a general description in Part 2 as:

Correspondence, attendance notes, instructions to counsel and counsel's advice between the claimant and his lawyers. These were created for the purpose of giving or receiving advice and so are covered by legal advice privilege.

Privileged documents can be inspected if the party waives privilege. For example, a draft witness statement is privileged, but if the party wants to rely upon that witness's evidence, the statement must be sent to the opponent.

The main categories of privileged documents are as follows.

16.9.1 Documents covered by legal professional privilege

Legal professional privilege includes:

- legal advice privilege; and
- litigation privilege.

Legal advice privilege protects all types of communication made between a client and their lawyer for the purpose of legal advice.

Litigation privilege protects communications between either a client and a third party (such as an expert) or the client's lawyer and a third party. This type of privilege will apply only if the communication with the third party arises when litigation is pending (so proceedings have been issued) or contemplated (for example, when the client seeks advice from a lawyer). Thus, an expert's report that was commissioned when there was no possibility of litigation will not be covered by litigation privilege.

To qualify as privileged the sole or dominant (main) purpose of the document at the time it was created must be for use as evidence in litigation. Thus, a report on procedures in a factory will not be privileged if its purpose was to improve productivity.

The definitions of privilege will cover most or all of your correspondence with your client and file notes, draft witness statements, instructions to counsel, counsel's advices, drafts and letters of instruction to experts and their reports until you voluntarily disclose them.

Example

In ***Re the RBS Rights Issue Litigation [2016]*** the High Court rejected the bank's application for permission to withhold certain documents from disclosure on the grounds they were subject to legal advice privilege. These were records of interviews conducted by or on behalf of RBS with employees or ex-employees as part of its investigations.

The court confirmed that "client" for the purposes of legal advice privilege is narrowly defined and only applies to those employees who are authorised to seek and receive legal advice from the lawyer. This would usually only apply to a small number of persons at a relatively high level in the corporation, such as the board of directors. It does not extend to those who are merely authorised to provide information for the purpose of being placed before a lawyer. Although the legal advice eventually given would be privileged, the preparatory steps are not.

This is of particular relevance to corporate clients as it is clear and established that communications between an individual client and their lawyer are privileged. The consequence for such clients is that great care should be taken in a fact-gathering exercise, particularly where litigation privilege does not apply – because litigation has not started or is not in reasonable contemplation.

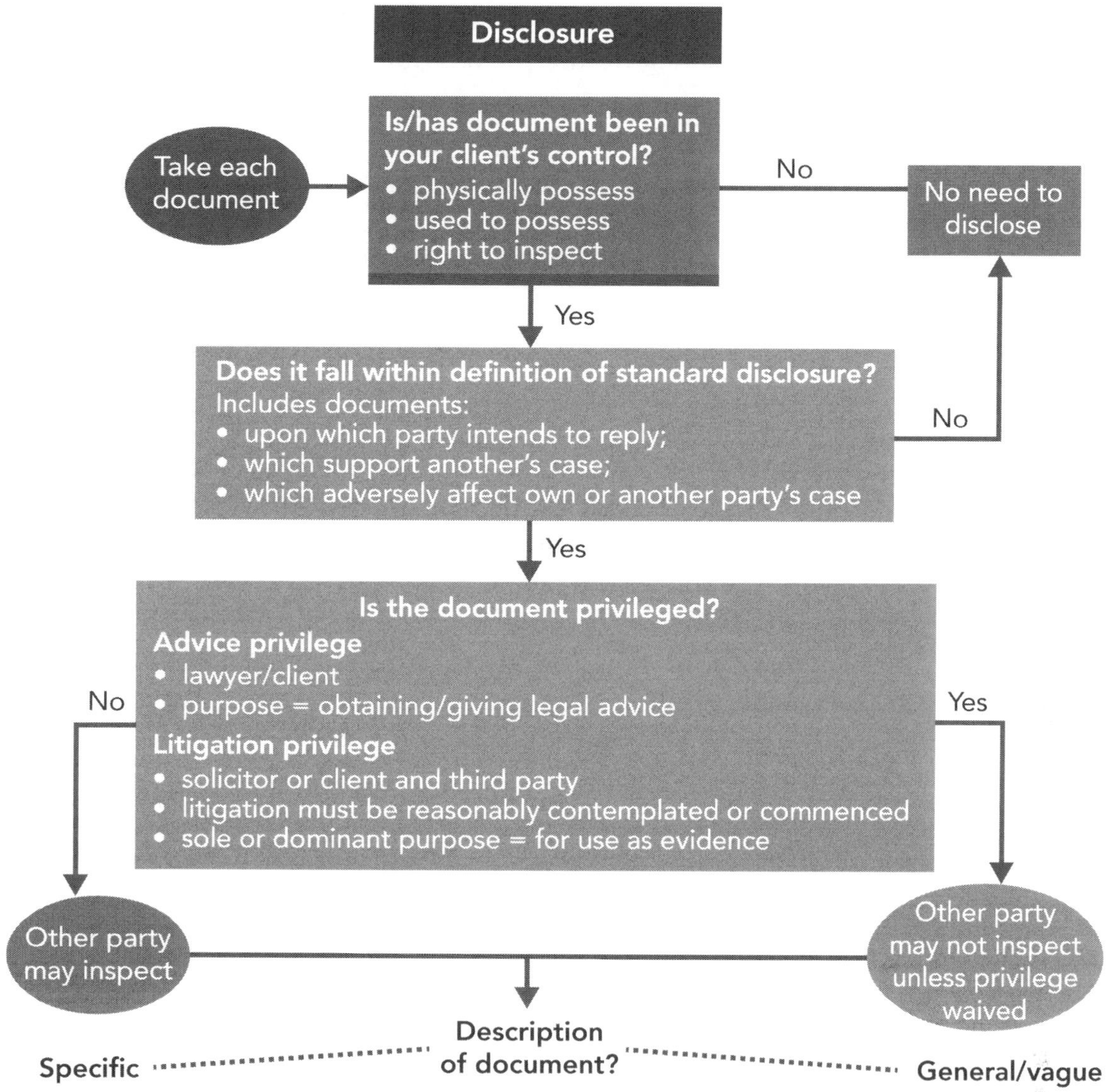

16.10 Inspection

Having received their opponent's list of documents, the party may give written notice of their wish to inspect. This request must be granted within seven days. However, rather than going to inspect the documents personally, a party may ask for copies of the documents, provided they agree to pay reasonable copying costs. Copies must be sent within seven days.

16.11 Specific disclosure

Once you have received your opponent's disclosure list, you should scrutinise it carefully to ensure that the duty of disclosure has been complied with. If you are dissatisfied with the disclosure provided and consider it inadequate, an application may be made for specific disclosure. This may be for specific documents or to broaden the search, perhaps to include the party's home or mobile devices.

16.12 Disclosure for the Business and Property Courts

In January 2019, a four-year pilot scheme commenced for disclosure in the Business and Property Courts only, although it is anticipated that the proposals will be introduced more widely thereafter. The reason behind the changes is the view that standard disclosure often produces large amounts of wholly irrelevant documents, leading to a considerable waste of time and costs. Further, whilst orders for standard disclosure may be appropriate for factually complex cases, there are many other cases which can be fairly and efficiently determined on the basis of more focused and limited disclosure. The issue has come to the fore primarily because of the huge amount of material which may be generated electronically. The requirements for the pilot are now set out in **PD 57AD**.

In summary, the key changes introduced by the Disclosure Pilot are as follows.

- Standard disclosure has been removed in its current form and replaced by **Model D**.
- The duties of the parties, and of their lawyers, in relation to disclosure are expressly set out. These include:
    - a duty to cooperate so as to promote the reliable, efficient and cost-effective conduct of disclosure; and
    - a wider duty to disclose adverse documents in all cases, irrespective of whether an order to do so is made.

16.12.1 Initial disclosure

"Initial Disclosure" will usually be given with the statements of case. These are key documents which are relied on by the disclosing party and are necessary for the opponent to understand the case against them. A search should not be required for Initial Disclosure, although one may be undertaken. It is not intended to be an onerous process (generally no more than 200 documents or 1,000 pages) and there are several exceptions where it can be dispensed with entirely. These may avoid the need for any further disclosure either in whole or in part.

16.12.2 Extended disclosure

After closure of the statements of case, it is compulsory for the parties to co-operate before the first CMC with a view to agreeing a proportionate and efficient approach to disclosure. In particular, the parties must meet, discuss and complete a joint **Disclosure Review Document** to:

- list the **issues for disclosure** in the case (those key issues in dispute which the court will need to determine);
- exchange proposals for "**Extended Disclosure**"; and
- share information about how documents are stored and how they might, if required, be searched and reviewed, including with the assistance of technology.

Further, in order to inform the court's decision on Extended Disclosure, the parties are under an express **Disclosure Duty** to engage before the CMC so that the court can be informed of:

- any joint view as to the Disclosure Model that should apply; and
- the estimated work and cost of using this Model.

At the CMC, the court should consider which of five "Extended Disclosure" models (**Models A to E**) is to apply. The models range from an order for disclosure of known adverse documents only on particular Issues for Disclosure, through to the widest form of disclosure, requiring the production of documents which may lead to a train of enquiry.

The court will be proactive in directing which is the appropriate Disclosure Model and should not accept without question the Model proposed by the parties. With a view to encouraging increased and more focused case management, the Practice Direction identifies a range of orders which the court may make to reduce the burden and cost of disclosure.

Further the parties can apply for a Disclosure Guidance Hearing to seek informal guidance from the court before or after a CMC to resolve any disputes between the parties in relation to this issue.

When considering what orders to make on disclosure, the test of reasonableness and proportionality is applied using criteria set out in the relevant Practice Direction.

In addition, the parties must give estimates of the likely costs of disclosure when filing the completed Disclosure Review Document in order that the question of proportionality may be considered.

16.13 Summary

(1) Standard disclosure by lists applies to fast track and personal injury multi-track cases. It is governed by **CPR Part 31**. Disclosure is made by serving a list of documents in standard form (form N265).

(2) The parties are obliged to disclose to each other all the documents in their possession that relate to the proceedings. An order for disclosure is for **standard disclosure** unless the court directs otherwise.

(3) A list of documents must contain a **disclosure statement**, which sets out the extent of the search, an understanding of the duty to disclose and that this has been carried out.

(4) Multi-track (non-personal injury) cases are subject to separate disclosure requirements including the filing and service of a **disclosure report**.

(5) The duty of disclosure continues throughout the case until proceedings are concluded.

(6) Some documents, such as correspondence with the client, counsel's opinion, etc. are covered by **legal professional privilege**. This means that, although there is a duty to disclose (i.e. include in the list) such documents, there is no obligation to allow the opponent to inspect (i.e. read) them.

(7) **Inspection** takes place seven days after disclosure.

(8) A party may apply for **specific disclosure** if they are dissatisfied with the disclosure given by their opponent.

CHAPTER 17

Witness and Expert Evidence

17.1 Introduction

CPR Part 32 deals with evidence. The court may control the evidence by giving directions on:

- the **issues** on which it requires evidence (i.e. liability or quantum or both);
- the **nature** of the evidence it requires to decide those issues, for example, expert evidence; and
- the **way** in which the evidence is to be placed before the court, either orally or by relying on the written statement.

These powers are exercised in accordance with the principles in the overriding objective. They may be used to save expense, to ensure that cases are dealt with proportionately and to ensure that the real issues are addressed at trial.

The matters dealt with in this chapter are principally aimed at fast track and multi-track cases. Generally, expert evidence is not allowed in small claims track cases, although, as with the other tracks, the court has a discretion to permit it, and there is no advance disclosure of witness statements.

17.2 Witness statements

Witness statements contain the evidence that a person would be allowed to give orally as a witness at trial. Full details of the requirements can be found in **Part 32**.

As with experts' reports, there are certain formalities which must be complied with. In particular:

- the statement must contain a formal heading with the title of the proceedings and the witness's details in the top right-hand corner of the first page;
- the opening paragraph should give details of the witness's occupation or description and, if relevant, the name of their employer, as well as if the employer is a party in the proceedings;
- the paragraphs of the statement should be numbered; and all numbers, including dates, should be expressed in figures (except months, for example, 11 December 2022 is acceptable, not 11.12.22);
- the statement must, if practicable, be in the witness's own words and it should be expressed in the first person;
- it is usually convenient to follow the chronological sequence of events;
- documents referred to in the statement should be formally exhibited;
- the statement must include a signed statement that the witness believes the facts it contains are true. False statements may be punished as contempt of court. The form of the statement of truth is now:

"I believe that the facts stated in this witness statement are true. I understand that proceedings for contempt of court may be brought against anyone who makes, or causes to be made, a false statement in a document verified by a statement of truth without an honest belief in its truth."

Unlike statements of case, a witness statement cannot be signed by a legal representative.

17.3 Directions for the exchange of witness statements

On allocation to the fast track or at the CMC for the multi-track, the court will make directions regarding when witness statements must be exchanged.

Normally, mutual exchange is required and it usually takes place 10 weeks after allocation and is, thus, a few weeks after disclosure and inspection. This is partly because the witnesses may need to comment on some of the documentation in their statements.

If a witness statement is not served within the time specified in directions, the witness may only be called with permission of the court.

17.4 Use of statements in court

Exchanged witness statements stand as the witness's evidence-in-chief unless the court otherwise orders.

Only if the court is satisfied there is a good reason will the witness be allowed to give additional oral evidence and this would be the exception rather than the rule.

17.5 Witness summons

Some witnesses are reluctant to attend trial or give evidence. They may be intimidated by the idea of coming to court, unwilling to get involved or simply unable to take time off from their employment. If so, their attendance can be compelled by a witness summons. A fee is payable and the applicant may also have to pay the witness's expenses in attending court. The address of the witness must be known and the service of the summons must take place not less than seven days before the witness is to attend court.

17.6 Experts

Experts play a substantial part in litigation and their use is governed by **CPR Part 35**.

Examples include:

- medical experts to deal with the nature of the claimant's injuries and prognosis in personal injury cases;

- expert accountancy evidence is required in many commercial and professional negligence cases to assess the loss suffered by the claimant;
- surveying and valuation evidence in disputes where property prices are in issue;
- architects or surveyors in cases involving defective building work as they are able to give evidence on issues such as the structure of the building.

The duty of an expert is to help the court on matters within their own expertise and this overrides any obligation to the person who instructed them.

17.7 Expert directions

Directions dealing with expert evidence will usually be made when the case is allocated to the fast track or multi-track, or at a CMC.

The primary rule is that no party may call an expert or put in evidence an expert's report without the court's permission. You may recall that the directions questionnaire (see **12.2**) requires parties to indicate the expert evidence they wish to rely on at trial and the estimated costs involved.

In deciding whether to grant permission, and if so to what extent, the court will seek to restrict expert evidence to that which is reasonably required to resolve the proceedings. The court can direct that the evidence be given by way of a written report rather than giving permission for the expert to be called to give evidence at trial. Additionally, the court can specify the issues to be covered by the expert evidence and the type of expert necessary.

17.8 Joint instruction of experts

Where both parties wish to submit expert evidence on a particular issue, **Part 35** provides that the court may direct that the evidence on that issue is to be given by one expert only. If agreement cannot be reached on who the expert is, the court will decide.

On the fast track, the court's general approach will be to give directions for a single joint expert unless there is good reason not to do so. Where an expert witness is jointly instructed they must send their report simultaneously to both parties' laywers, who share responsibility for the expert's fee in preparing the report.

In contrast, for multi-track cases, separate instruction of experts is more common and orders will be made following a CMC to give the parties an opportunity to submit their views on the matter.

Guidance for the Instruction of Experts in Civil Claims (2014) is available on the judiciary website: www.judiciary.gov.uk.

17.9 Written questions to experts

A party may put written questions to the expert for the purpose of clarifying the report.

The expert's answers to such questions are treated as part of the expert's report.

17.10 Without prejudice discussion and joint statement

The court may, at any stage, direct a discussion between the experts for the purpose of identifying the issues in dispute and, where possible, reaching agreement. Such a direction will normally also provide that, following the discussion, the experts must prepare a statement for the court showing:

- those issues on which they agree; and
- those on which they disagree, with a summary of their reasons.

17.11 Concurrent expert evidence

The court may direct that all experts from similar disciplines give their evidence concurrently. Known as "hot tubbing", it involves the judge hearing evidence on each issue from each expert. The judge may also ask questions before the parties do so, and will then summarise the experts' different positions on the issue.

17.12 Form of experts' reports

Under **Part 35**, an expert's report must:

- be addressed to the court;
- give details of:
  - — the expert's qualifications;

    - any literature or other materials the expert has relied on in making the report; and
    - any tests or experiments used for the report;

- where there is a range of opinion, summarise this and give reasons for the expert's own opinion;
- contain a statement:
    - setting out the substance of all material instructions; and
    - that the expert understands their duty to the court and has complied with it;
- include a summary of the conclusions reached.

An expert's report must be verified by a statement of truth in the form:

"I confirm that I have made clear which facts and matters referred to in this report are within my own knowledge and which are not. Those that are within my own knowledge I confirm to be true. The opinions I have expressed represent my true and complete professional opinions on the matters to which they refer.

I understand that proceedings for contempt of court may be brought against anyone who makes, or causes to be made, a false statement in a document verified by a statement of truth without an honest belief in its truth."

17.13 Summary of directions for experts in multi-track claims

In multi-track cases, both parties will usually be given permission to instruct their own expert.

(1) The court has the power to restrict evidence, for example, by directing that there be no expert evidence at all or limiting the number of expert witnesses each party may call or the issue on which they may report.

(2) The expert's report must be set out in a particular format to comply with **Part 35** and include their qualifications and details of how they reached their conclusions, amongst other requirements.

(3) Disclosure of the reports may be simultaneous or in sequence.

(4) Questions may be submitted by the other party to the expert and the answers will be treated as part of the report.

(5) There may be a discussion between the experts to try to narrow down the issues, after which a joint statement of the agreed issues and those in dispute (with reasons for the lack of agreement) will be filed.

(6) The judge will decide whether the expert may give oral evidence at trial or if they will rely upon the reports.

17.14 Summary

(1) Evidence is governed by **CPR Part 32**. The court has control of the evidence to be adduced in the course of proceedings. The court will give directions dealing with expert evidence and the exchange of witness statements.

(2) **Witness statements** contain the evidence that a person would be allowed to give orally as a witness at trial. The form the witness statement should take is found in **Part 32**.

(3) If a witness is reluctant to attend court, a witness summons can be obtained to compel attendance.

(4) Expert evidence is governed by **CPR Part 35**. The court may direct that evidence is to be given by a single jointly instructed expert and this is the norm in the fast track. However, it remains possible for each party to instruct their own expert and this is usual in the multi-track.

(5) An expert's primary duty is to the court and not to any of the parties.

(6) The form and content of the expert's report is provided for in **Part 35**.

(7) The court can require experts to prepare a joint statement and can also direct for concurrent expert evidence to be taken.

CHAPTER 18

Part 36 Offers

18.1 Introduction

Litigation is expensive and obviously the longer it takes, the more expensive it becomes, so it is in all parties' interests to settle the case early. Commercial clients, in particular, will be conscious not only of the costs, but also the management time involved in pursuing the case to trial.

CPR Part 36 is a very useful tactical tool designed to put pressure on the opponent to reach settlement and both claimants and defendants can take advantage of it. Indeed, although litigation should be conducted fairly, the aim is clearly to win for your client and **Part 36** is a way to "put the screws on" the opponent. Turning up the heat in this way will put pressure on the other party to settle, as the penalties imposed under **Part 36** will place the recipient in a real dilemma as to whether to accept or not. Risk-averse parties will be particularly susceptible to such a tactic.

Example

Ahmed Choudhry was injured in a road traffic accident and is claiming damages for personal injuries. Having obtained medical evidence it appears his claim is worth in the region of £28,000–£33,000. His lawyer may advise him to make a **Part 36** offer to accept £33,000 in settlement of his claim.

Alternatively, the defendant, Brian Hill (via the insurer) may make a **Part 36** offer to pay £28,000 to settle Ahmed's claim.

If either party rejects the other's offer, they run the risk of incurring significant additional legal costs in the event that the case proceeds to trial and they fail to achieve a better result than the offer.

Each party has the right to make offers to settle in whatever way they choose, but in order to benefit from the special provisions which apply to **Part 36**, the offer must comply with certain formalities.

18.2 How is a Part 36 offer made?

A **Part 36** offer must:

- be in writing;
- make clear that it is made pursuant to **Part 36**;
- specify a period of not less than 21 days within which the defendant will be liable for the claimant's costs if the offer is accepted;
- state whether it relates to the whole of the claim or to part of it;
- state whether it takes account of any counterclaim.

A **Part 36** offer may state that it is automatically withdrawn on a given date, but the advantages of **CPR Part 36** will be lost.

18.3 Acceptance

How is a Part 36 offer accepted?

The **Part 36** offer is accepted by serving a written notice, within 21 days, to the court and to the party making the offer.

What is the effect of acceptance?

The effect is that the defendant must pay to the claimant the sum stated in the offer plus the claimant's reasonable costs, up to the date of service of the notice of acceptance. If the parties cannot agree costs, a judge will determine the amount. The claim will then be over.

r36.5(5) provides clarity, particularly for litigants in person, that an offer to settle (a "**Part 36** offer") can include accruals of interest but, where it is silent on this point, the presumption will be that the offer is inclusive of all interest up to the date of acceptance.

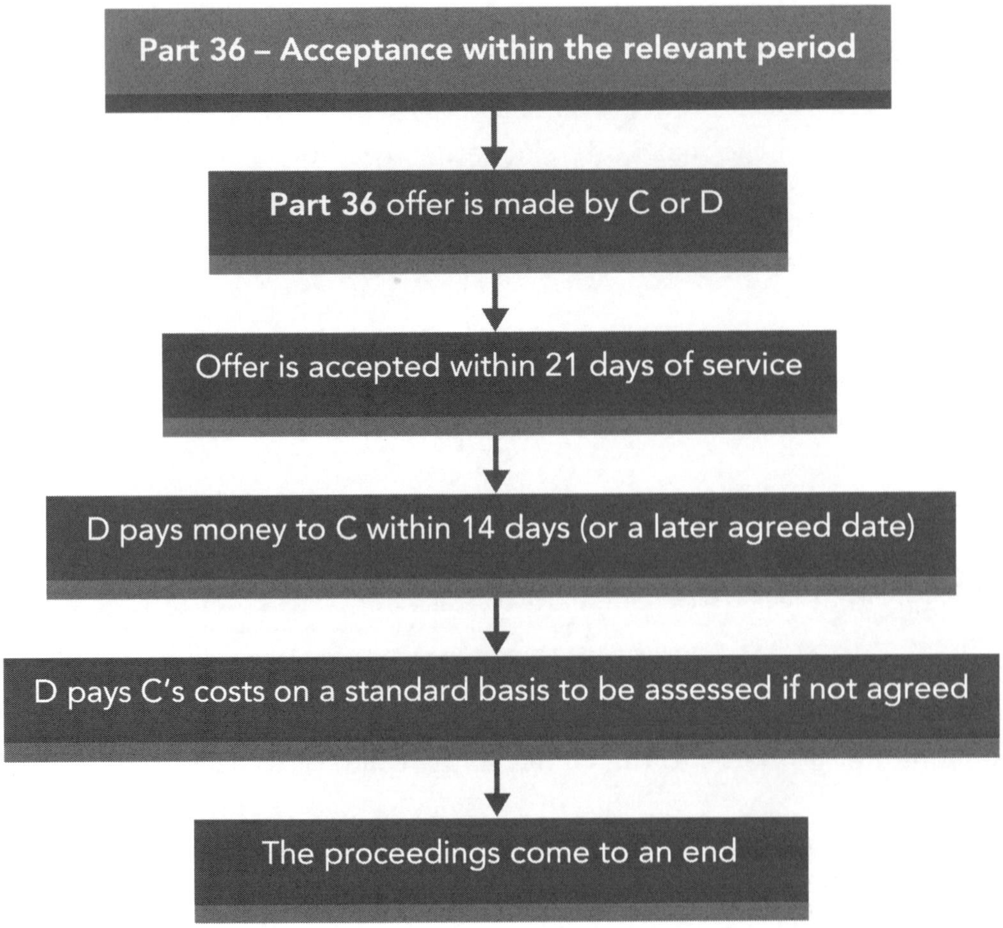

What if the offer is not accepted?

The case will continue. However, making the wrong decision can have a significant effect upon the outcome of the case. The reason is that, if a **Part 36** offer is refused, penalties will be imposed at the trial upon the party who gets it wrong. The justification for this is that, by continuing with the litigation, the party who unreasonably refused such an offer has caused additional costs and inconvenience, not just to the parties themselves but also to the court. The party who is "at fault" will effectively be penalised by the court for this error of judgment.

Note that the additional penalties will run from the date that the 21-day period for acceptance of the offer expired (Day 22).

Claimants who beat their own **Part 36** offer are entitled to more than just fixed costs. Effectively, **Part 36** takes precedence over **CPR Part 45** so that where claimants beat their own **Part 36** offer, they are entitled to costs assessed on an indemnity basis. This is another reason why defendants should consider carefully any **Part 36** offers being made by the claimants as the costs ordered are likely to be significantly higher than fixed costs.

Can the offer be accepted late?

Late acceptance is possible if the parties agree liability for costs or with permission of the court.

18.4 What are the consequences at trial of the claimant making a Part 36 offer?

Scenario

Polina Lazarz, a sole trader, instructs a law firm on 15 October 2020 in relation to a contract dispute. From that date, costs begin to run. Proceedings are issued on 3 May 2021. Polina makes a **Part 36** offer of £90,000 on 5 June 2021, giving 21 days in which to accept the offer. The defendant, Fiona McDonald, does not accept the offer.

The trial takes place on 21 February 2022, lasting three days.

There are three possible outcomes:

(1) Polina wins the case and is awarded £90,000 or more;

(2) Polina wins the case and is awarded less than £90,000;

(3) Polina loses the case.

Let us consider each of these in turn.

18.4.1 Outcome 1: The claimant wins at trial and equals or beats their own offer

In other words, the judgment is "at least as advantageous" as the **Part 36** offer. Should this occur, the defendant can expect to be penalised at trial because they have effectively wasted both costs and court time by turning down the offer. These sanctions will be imposed in every case, unless the court considers it unjust to do so, which will be the exception.

Percentage of damages

The first additional penalty imposed by **CPR** relates to the damages.

(1) For damages of up to £500,000, the defendant is required to pay an additional 10 per cent.

(2) If the figure awarded is between £500,000 and £1 m, 10 per cent of the first £500,000 is payable and 5 per cent of the amount awarded above that figure.

(3) The additional payment cannot exceed £75,000.

Interest on damages

From Day 22, the defendant may also be ordered to pay interest on the whole or part of any damages awarded, at a rate not exceeding 10 per cent above the Bank of England base rate. This is a higher rate than would be claimed under the **Senior Courts Act 1981** (**SCA 1981**) and the **County Courts Act 1984**.

Costs on indemnity basis

The defendant will also be ordered to pay the claimant's costs but, from Day 22, these will be on an indemnity basis. In **Chapter 20**, you will study the difference between costs being awarded on the standard basis and the indemnity basis. However, for the purposes of **CPR Part 36**, it is sufficient that you appreciate that if the defendant is ordered to pay costs on the indemnity basis, they will pay a higher percentage of those costs than on the standard basis.

Interest on costs

Finally, from Day 22, interest on those costs will be payable, at a maximum of 10 per cent above the base rate (although the norm is 4 per cent over base rate).

Summary

Without the Part 36 offer, the claimant would usually receive . . .	Part 36 imposes additional sanctions and the claimant will now receive . . .
Damages	Damages An additional percentage of the damages which varies in amount depending upon the level of damages awarded

Without the Part 36 offer, the claimant would usually receive . . .	Part 36 imposes additional sanctions and the claimant will now receive . . .
Interest on the damages as claimed in the particulars of claim	Interest on the damages as claimed in the particulars of claim Enhanced interest on the damages
Costs on the standard basis	Costs on the indemnity basis Enhanced interest on those costs

Scenario

Polina wins the case and is awarded £95,000. She has obtained a judgment against the defendant which is at least as advantageous to the claimant as the proposals contained in her **Part 36** offer (i.e. the judgment equals or beats the claimant's own offer). The court will, unless it considers it unjust to do so, order that Polina is entitled to:

- an additional 10 per cent of the amount awarded to her (i.e. the claimant's damages) up to a sum not exceeding £75,000 – here, Polina will receive an additional £9,500;
- interest on the damages awarded at a rate not exceeding 10 per cent above base rate starting with the date on which the relevant period expired – this would be higher than the 8 per cent claimed in the particulars of claim under **SCA 1981**;
- her costs on a standard basis from the date Polina instructed solicitors (15 October 2020) to the date on which the relevant period expired (Day 21 i.e. 26 June 2021) and thereafter, from Day 22 (27 June 2021) to the end of the trial on 24 February 2022 on an indemnity basis; and
- interest on those costs at a rate not exceeding 10 per cent above base rate.

The defendant, Fiona, is potentially very heavily penalised for not accepting the claimant's own offer. This puts tremendous pressure on a defendant to consider a claimant's offer. The earlier the claimant is in a position to make an offer, the more pressure is applied as the costs and interest will be higher the longer the period between when the offer was made and when the judgment is delivered; in particular, the costs of the trial are likely to be substantial. However, it is equally important that the claimant pitches the offer at the right level, so Polina's advisers must wait until they have enough information to assess the value of her claim properly.

18.4.2 Outcome 2: The claimant wins at trial but obtains a judgment which is less than their own Part 36 offer

You will now consider the second possible outcome if the case proceeds to trial. Here, the claimant has succeeded at the hearing, but the damages received are less than their own offer. In this situation, the defendant was correct to turn down the claimant's offer, which was too high, so no additional penalties will be imposed upon the defendant under **Part 36**. The usual orders will apply and the defendant will pay:

- the damages awarded by the judge;
- interest on those damages as claimed in the particulars of claim; and
- the claimant's costs on a standard basis.

Scenario

The general principle that the loser pays the winner's costs will apply. Fiona is therefore likely to be ordered to pay Polina's costs on a standard basis from the date she instructed lawyers to the end of the trial. Polina will not be penalised for having failed to obtain a judgment as high as her own offer as this would have the effect of discouraging claimants from making offers.

18.4.3 Outcome 3: The claimant loses at trial

The final outcome is that the claimant loses at trial. The claimant will obviously not receive any damages and will be ordered to pay the defendant's costs on a standard basis (as well as being responsible for their own).

Scenario

If Polina were to lose her case, the court is likely to order her to pay Fiona's costs; and Polina will also be liable for her own costs. The **Part 36** offer will have no effect.

It is apparent that the only scenario in which the claimant's **Part 36** offer has an effect is where the claimant wins the trial and obtains a judgment equal to or higher than the offer which they made. In this instance, the penalties for the defendant may be severe and you will need to advise your client accordingly.

18.5 What are the consequences at trial of the defendant making a Part 36 offer?

So far we have concentrated on what happens if the claimant makes a **Part 36** offer, but what about if the defendant does so?

Making a **Part 36** offer can be just as effective for a defendant as for a claimant and the main advantage is the certainty of the outcome; for example, in a road traffic accident, the defendant may dispute that they were liable, but also be aware that their witness may not be very convincing.

18.5.1 Why should a claimant accept a defendant's Part 36 offer?

The incentive for a claimant to accept a defendant's **Part 36** offer is that a claimant who rejects the offer but fails to beat it at trial will be penalised in costs. This is punitive, as a claimant who successfully recovers damages would not normally expect to pay any of the defendant's costs. Accordingly, the claimant, together with their legal advisers, must carefully consider the risks of rejecting the offer.

You will now consider the consequences of the defendant's **Part 36** offer at trial.

Scenario

Devinder Singh instructs solicitors on 27 September 2021 in relation to a contract dispute. From that date, costs begin to run. Proceedings are issued on 4 December 2021. The defendant, Ceri Jones, makes a **Part 36** offer of £40,000 on 7 April 2022, giving 21 days in which to accept the offer. Devinder does not accept the offer as he is advised that, if successful, he is likely to receive at least £46,000 in damages.

The trial takes place on 3 August 2022, lasting two days.

There are three possible outcomes:

(1) Devinder wins the case and is awarded more than £40,000;

(2) Devinder wins the case and is awarded £40,000 or less;

(3) Devinder loses the case.

18.5.2 Outcome 1: The claimant wins at trial and beats the defendant's Part 36 offer

In this instance, the claimant was correct not to accept the defendant's **Part 36** offer as the outcome of the trial established that it was too low. As a consequence, there are no additional penalties under **Part 36** and the usual orders will be made. The defendant will be ordered to pay damages to the claimant, together with their costs on the standard basis.

Scenario

Devinder wins the case and is awarded £43,000 at trial; he has beaten the defendant's offer. The rule that the loser pays the winner's costs will usually apply. Ceri will be ordered to pay Devinder's reasonable costs, to be assessed if not agreed. There are no adverse costs consequences on the defendant for the claimant beating the defendant's offer as the law does not penalise a party for seeking to settle a claim.

18.5.3 Outcome 2: The claimant wins at trial but fails to beat the defendant's Part 36 offer

A claimant can expect to be penalised at trial if they are awarded the same as, or less than, the defendant's **Part 36** offer, because costs have been incurred and the court's time has been wasted in pursuing the litigation unnecessarily. Although the claimant will be awarded damages together with interest in the usual way, penalties will be imposed in costs.

Ordinarily a claimant who is awarded damages at trial would expect the defendant to be ordered to pay their costs for the entire proceedings. However, in the scenario where the claimant fails to beat the defendant's **Part 36** offer, the court will usually order the defendant to pay the claimant's costs but only those incurred up until the expiry of the 21-day period for acceptance of the defendant's offer.

The consequence is that, even though the claimant has won, they will be liable for their own costs from Day 22, but, in addition, the claimant will also be ordered to pay the defendant's costs from the same date. The effect is that the claimant is paying two sets of costs from Day 22 until judgment and, if the offer was made early in the proceedings, these will be considerable, particularly as they may include the trial itself. All costs are payable on the standard basis.

Example

In November 1990, the Coronation Street star, William Roache, who played Ken Barlow, won his libel action against *The Sun* newspaper over an article in which they described him as "boring". Unfortunately for Mr Roache, he failed to beat the defendant's **Part 36** offer and legal costs swallowed up his £50,000 damages, but also left him with a six-figure costs bill to pay. He later unsuccessfully sued his solicitors for negligence.

Example

Another individual who fell foul of the **Part 36** provisions was Kwasi Afari Minta, the most severely injured survivor of the Kings Cross fire in 1987. He went to court in 1997 having turned down the £350,000 settlement offered by London Underground, but after being awarded just £110,427, he too was obliged to pay the legal costs of both parties, leaving him out of pocket.

Finally, the claimant will be ordered to pay interest on the defendant's costs from Day 22 until judgment.

This type of costs order is often referred to as a "split costs order", as the court splits the costs between both parties, with the point of the split occurring at the expiry of the 21-day relevant period.

Scenario

The judge decides in favour of Devinder but only awards damages totalling £38,000. Devinder has therefore failed to beat the defendant's offer.

The effect on costs will be as follows.

The defendant, Ceri, will pay Devinder's costs of £3,400 from 27 September 2021 (the date he instructed his lawyers) to 28 April 2022 (21 days after the date of Ceri's **Part 36** offer).

However, despite having won the case, from 29 April 2022 (Day 22) Devinder now becomes liable for Ceri's costs up to the end of the trial totalling £4,800. These will be payable on the standard basis together with interest. Devinder will also have to pay his own costs of £6,300 for that same period. Unless Devinder had the protection of an appropriate insurance policy, he will have to pay £11,100 in costs but will recover only £3,400 in costs from the defendant.

If he had accepted the offer of £40,000 within the relevant acceptance period (between 7 April and 28 April 2022), he would also have been entitled to his costs of £3,400 and would have avoided incurring the costs of pursuing the case to trial.

This illustrates why making a **Part 36** offer can be such a useful negotiating tool. If the offer had been pitched at the right level, it would have put tremendous pressure on Devinder to accept. For example, if Devinder's advisers had realistically hoped to be awarded in the region of £46,000 at trial, it is a big gamble to carry on with the proceedings rather than accepting the lower offer of £40,000.

18.5.4 Outcome 3: The claimant loses at trial

Let us consider the effect of the defendant's **Part 36** offer here.

Obviously, the claimant will not receive any damages and will be ordered to pay the defendant's costs on a standard basis up to the date of judgment. However, to penalise the claimant for having turned down the defendant's **Part 36** offer, interest (usually at 1–2 per cent above the base rate) will also be payable on those costs from Day 22 until the date of judgment.

Scenario

If Devinder were to lose his case, the court is likely to order him to pay Ceri's costs, to be assessed if not agreed, together with interest. Devinder will also be liable for his own costs.

18.6 Overview

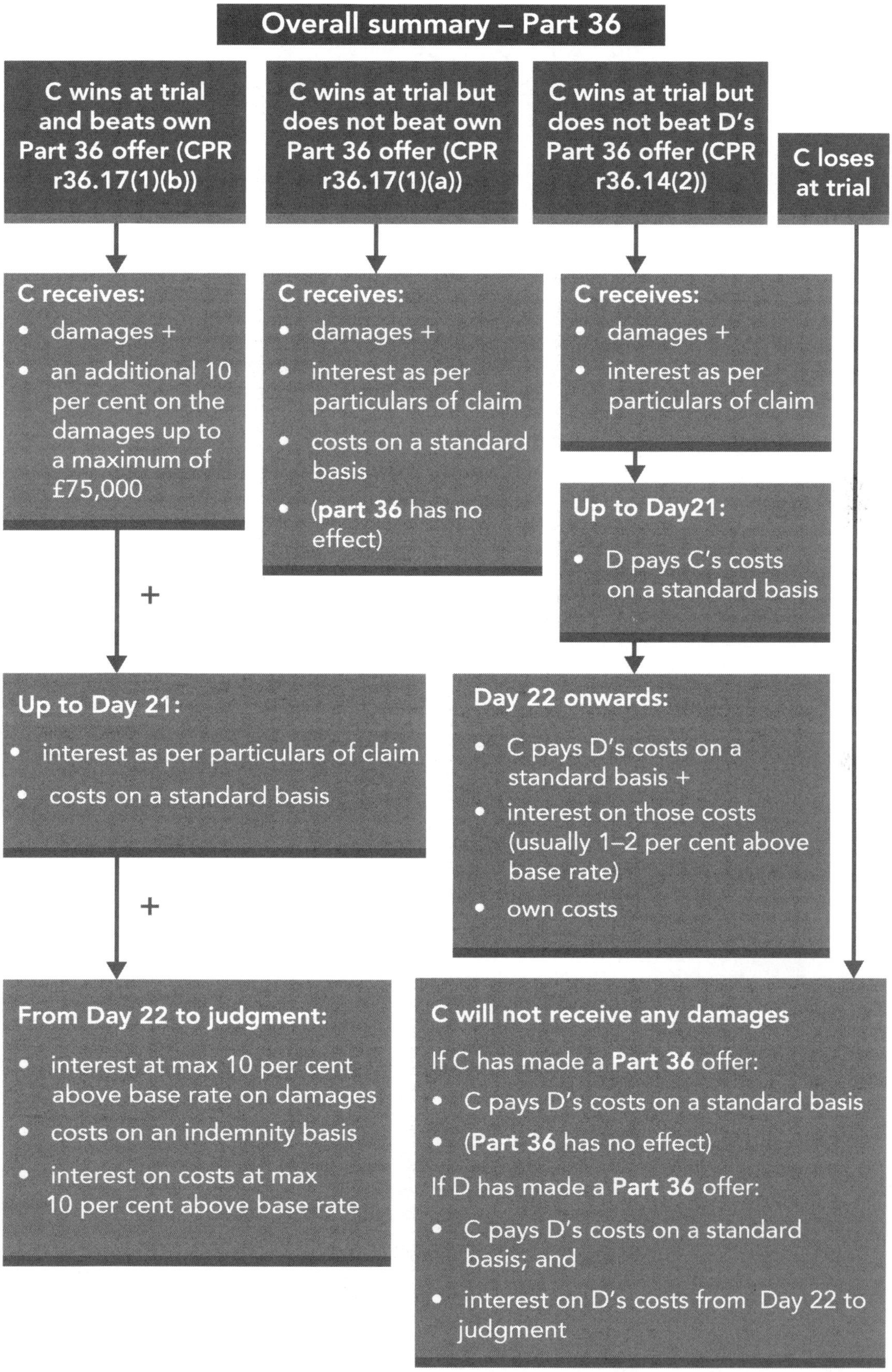

18.7 Deduction of benefits

In personal injury cases, if a claimant successfully sues a defendant and receives compensation, the Compensation Recovery Unit (CRU), which is part of the Department for Work and Pensions, will reclaim the value of any qualifying benefits that the claimant might have received as a result of their injury. The aim of this is to stop the claimant being compensated twice (once by the compensation and once by the benefits received).

The defendant will be required to inform the CRU of the judgment and the CRU will issue a certificate stating how much of any awarded compensation they will claim. The defendant will pay this amount to CRU.

Further information about the CRU is available at https://www.gov.uk/government/collections/cru.

When making a **Part 36** offer a defendant must state the amount of gross compensation, the name and amount of any benefit by which that gross amount is reduced and the net amount after deduction of the benefit.

18.8 Summary

(1) Both claimants and defendants can make **Part 36** offers.

(2) If a defendant's offer is accepted, that sum must be paid to the claimant within 14 days of acceptance. If it is not paid, the claimant can enter judgment.

(3) The form a **Part 36** offer should take is prescribed by the rules.

(4) The trial judge is not usually informed of any offer until the issues of liability and quantum have been decided.

(5) If a **Part 36** offer is accepted, proceedings are stayed.

(6) If a **Part 36** offer is not accepted, different costs consequences apply depending upon the outcome of the case.

(7) When considering the effect of **Part 36** in personal injury matters, the court will take into account that certain state benefits will be deducted from the damages.

CHAPTER 19

Trial and Appeal

19.1 Introduction

Success at trial depends, to a high degree, on the preparation beforehand. Judges will not be impressed if the paperwork is inadequate and arrangements for witnesses etc. break down.

At trial the responsibility for the case passes to the advocate, whether it be the chartered legal executive, the solicitor or the barrister. A set order of events is normally followed.

After trial and judgment it may be appropriate to consider an appeal.

19.2 Preparing for trial

To ensure that the trial runs smoothly, the documentation, witnesses and legal representation must all be prepared.

The attendance of witnesses

Most witnesses will attend willingly, and thus will only need to be told the date, time and location of the trial. However, if in any doubt, it is a sensible precaution to issue witness summonses to ensure their attendance.

Counsel

The barrister should be briefed an adequate time before the trial. If you have prepared full trial bundles, there will be little need to explain the background of the case in the brief (the instructions). Your impressions about the strengths and weaknesses of the witnesses may, however, be useful for counsel in preparing for their cross-examination.

Counsel often asks for a **conference** (meeting) prior to the trial. This has to be arranged and witnesses contacted.

Statements of costs

In fast track cases you will need to serve and file statements of costs two days before the trial.

19.3 Pre-trial checklists/questionnaires

The pre-trial checklist/questionnaire is an important step in the proceedings as it allows the judge to check that the parties have complied with all the directions and that the trial is ready to proceed.

The judge will review the questionnaires, make necessary directions for trial and decide if any pre-trial review is needed.

Pre-trial review

Pre-trial reviews are only usually held in multi-track cases to check that the parties will be fully prepared for trial. All the advocates representing the parties at trial should be present since the court will review the preparation done so far, identify the main issues in the case and set down the directions for trial, including a timetable.

19.4 Setting the trial date

When setting the trial date, the court may set either an actual date (the trial fixture) or a period of up to three weeks within which the trial will take place (the trial window). Although it is possible to change a trial date, in reality, judges are extremely reluctant to do so.

The trial is fixed at the allocation stage in fast track cases. In multi-track cases, the trial date/window is fixed "as soon as practicable" depending on the complexity of the case and the preparation required.

19.5 Trial

Trial bundle

The trial bundle is a file of all the relevant documents, fully indexed and paginated for ease of reference. It ensures that everyone at the trial is able to access them quickly when necessary; consequently, the core bundle should not usually exceed 250 pages to avoid crucial points being "buried".

Although the claimant is responsible for preparing the trial bundle, ideally, the contents should be agreed with the other parties. The court must receive the bundle between three and seven days before the trial. It should contain:

- the claim form and all statements of case;
- witness statements;
- expert reports;
- directions orders;
- any other necessary documents, such as the costs budgets in multi-track cases;
- a case summary or chronology if needed.

All copies of the trial bundle must be identical.

Order of events

(1) Claimant's counsel will begin with an opening speech, outlining the facts and summarising the legal principles.

(2) The claimant's witnesses will be called first. The examination-in-chief will simply involve the witness taking the oath, identifying their witness statement (which is already before the court) and confirming that it is true.

The witness will be cross-examined by the defendant's counsel and, if necessary, the witness can then be re-examined by the claimant's counsel.

(3) Defendant's counsel may then make an opening speech (although the judge may decide that this is not necessary), before calling the defendant's witnesses in turn. The procedure is as set out in (2) above.

(4) Defendant's counsel will make a closing speech.

(5) Claimant's counsel will make the final speech.

(6) The judge will deliver judgment.

(7) Other relevant applications will follow, for example, regarding costs and time to pay damages.

19.6 Judgment and appeal

Once judgment has been delivered, the judgment must be drawn up and sealed by the court.

In most cases, a party requires the court's permission to appeal. The request should be made at the trial or to the relevant Appeal Court, within 14 days.

The rules governing appeals are set out in **Part 52**.

19.7 Summary

(1) Preparation for trial includes ensuring the attendance of witnesses at trial, the preparation of trial bundles and instructing counsel.

(2) The court checks whether the case is ready for trial by obtaining pre-trial checklists/questionnaires from the parties and/or holding a pre-trial review if necessary.

(3) The trial date is usually a fixed date or window set by the court at the allocation stage.

(4) The trial bundle is prepared by the claimant/claimant's representative and contains all documents relevant to the trial.

(5) The order of events at trial is: claimant's counsel opens and presents the claimant's case (including witnesses); defendant's counsel then presents the defendant's case (including witnesses); claimant's counsel makes the final speech; the judge delivers judgment.

CHAPTER 20

Costs

20.1 Introduction

At the end of every interim hearing, and at the conclusion of the case, the court will consider the question of costs. It will have to decide who should pay for the application or the whole proceedings and on what basis. If the claimant succeeds, these will be added to the judgment debt; whereas if the claim fails, costs will be ordered to the defendant. The amount of the costs and the likelihood of success are crucial factors in a client's decision as to whether to proceed. The commercial realities of litigation cannot be ignored and costs will quickly eat into a settlement. It is, therefore, essential that clients are kept fully informed throughout the case so that informed decisions can be made.

Costs are a complex issue and it should be appreciated that this chapter contains only a brief outline of the main provisions.

20.2 Usual rule

The general rule is that the unsuccessful party pays the successful party's costs. This is encapsulated in the phrase that "costs follow the event". However, this is only the starting point and the court has discretion to make a different costs order if appropriate.

(1) Factors such as the conduct of the parties will be taken into account, in particular whether the parties followed any relevant pre-action protocols.

(2) In personal injury claims, the effect of QOCS (qualified one-way costs shifting) is that an unsuccessful claimant may not be responsible for the successful defendant's costs (see below for further details).

If possible, the parties, through their lawyers, should agree the amount payable for costs to avoid the need for further court action.

20.3 Proportionality

CPR r1.1 states that the court must deal with cases justly and at proportionate cost.

Under **CPR Part 44**, costs are proportionate if they bear a reasonable relationship to:

- the sums in issue;
- the value of any non-monetary relief;
- the complexity of the litigation;
- additional work generated by the conduct of the paying party;
- wider factors such as reputation or public importance.

Note also that:

- increasing provision for fixed costs in personal injury cases may effectively guarantee proportionate costs (and will also eliminate the need for summary assessment of these cases); and
- the introduction of costs budgets to multi-track cases also reflects the court's power to control costs throughout the litigation process and maintain focus on cost-proportionate litigation.

Under **CPR**, costs may be reduced if they are disproportionate to the sums in issue, even if reasonably and necessarily incurred.

Example

In ***BNM v MGN Limited [2016]*** the High Court judge reduced a bill, which had already been assessed as reasonable, by half on the grounds of proportionality.

In ***May and Another v Wavell Group plc and Another [2017]*** the court gave guidance on how to apply the new rules on proportionality. At first instance, the judge found that the claimant's reasonable costs were just under £100,000, but the figure was reduced to £35,000 on the basis of proportionality. On appeal, the judge found in favour of Brian May (formerly the guitarist from the rock group Queen) and his actor wife, Anita Dobson, and increased the costs to £75,000.

HHJ Dight stressed that the new proportionality test was not *"a blunt instrument"* to be used to reduce reasonable costs down to a *"rough and ready but proportionate amount"*. He pointed out that:

"The rules, difficult as they may be to apply in practice, require the specific factors in CPR 44.3(5) to be focused on and a determination made as to whether there is a reasonable relationship between them."

20.4 Qualified one-way costs shifting (QOCS) in personal injury claims

At present, QOCS only applies to personal injury claims. The effect of this provision is that the claimant will not be required to pay the defendant's costs if the claim fails, but the defendant must pay the claimant's costs in the usual way if the claim succeeds.

The advantage to claimants in personal injury cases is that they may proceed in the certain knowledge that they will not be liable for the defendant's costs (subject to certain exceptions referred to below). As a consequence, there is no need to take out after the event (ATE) insurance.

The effect is that insurers, who are usually the defendants in road traffic accident claims, can never recover their costs should they win. Whilst this may seem unfair, the theory behind QOCS is that any disadvantage is more than outweighed by defendants no longer having to pay ATE insurance premiums should they lose.

The effectiveness of QOCS in practice is unclear because the claimant may lose the protection in some limited situations, for example, where the claimant is found to be fundamentally dishonest (see **6.13**).

In these circumstances the defendant may succeed in obtaining a costs order against the claimant.

20.5 No or very limited costs recoverable (small claims track)

It should be remembered that in the small claims track, legal fees are not recoverable and the only costs likely to be ordered relate to the fixed costs of issue of proceedings, court fees, witnesses' expenses and experts' fees to a fixed limit.

20.6 Summary assessment of costs (fast track)

Summary assessment involves the court determining the amount payable by way of costs at the end of a hearing, usually on a relatively rough and ready basis.

The general rule is that the court will summarily (immediately) assess costs on conclusion of a fast track trial or hearing unless fixed costs apply. Two days before fast track trials, the parties are required to file and serve statements of costs itemising their costs of the proceedings - https://www.gov.uk/government/publications/form-n260-statement-of-costs-summary-assessment.

20.7 Detailed assessment (multi-track)

Unlike summary assessment, a detailed assessment is not generally conducted until after the conclusion of the proceedings. Detailed assessment:

- is carried out for multi-track cases;
- involves fully particularised bills of costs, formal written objections and responses often taking several months to complete.

The parties will usually be tied to their costs budget. For bills up to £75,000, the court will carry out a provisional assessment in the absence of the parties to try to resolve matters whilst also limiting costs.

Electronic bill of costs

All **Part 7** multi-track claims, unless subject to fixed costs or where the receiving party is a litigant in person, must be submitted by an electronic process. The electronic bill of costs makes the process quicker and easier by importing data from the law firm's time recording system.

The bill is in the form of a spreadsheet and is referred to as **Precedent S**. Its contents include a narrative, chronology, the charging rates, details of funding, summary of the costs claimed and a comparison with the last agreed or approved budget.

20.8 Bases of assessment

There are two bases of costs assessment: **standard** and **indemnity**.

The usual order is that the loser pays the winner's costs on the standard basis. An order for indemnity costs is less common and is usually imposed to penalise the defendant in some way. As the receiving party may only recover perhaps 60–70 per cent of its costs, even a successful party may have some costs liability to their own lawyer and you should warn your client of this.

On either basis, costs that were unreasonably incurred or are unreasonable in amount will not be allowed.

Standard basis

On the standard basis the court will only allow costs which are **proportionate** to the matters in issue and any doubt as to whether costs were reasonably incurred or reasonable and proportionate in amount are resolved in favour of the **paying** party.

Indemnity basis

On an assessment on the indemnity basis there is no reference to proportionality and any doubts are resolved in favour of the **receiving** party.

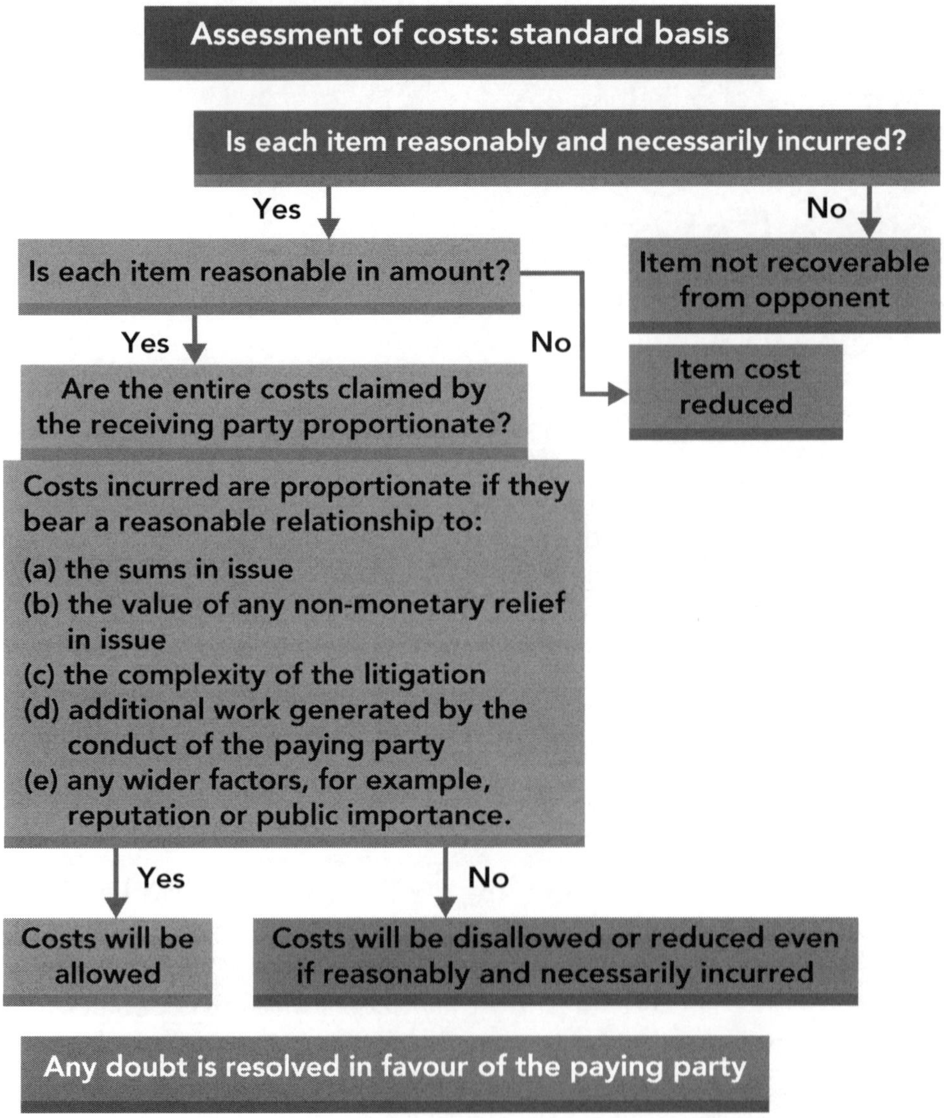
Assessment of costs: standard basis
Is each item reasonably and necessarily incurred?
Yes
No
Item not recoverable from opponent
Is each item reasonable in amount?
Yes
No
Item cost reduced
Are the entire costs claimed by the receiving party proportionate?
Costs incurred are proportionate if they bear a reasonable relationship to:
(a) the sums in issue
(b) the value of any non-monetary relief in issue
(c) the complexity of the litigation
(d) additional work generated by the conduct of the paying party
(e) any wider factors, for example, reputation or public importance.
Yes
No
Costs will be allowed
Costs will be disallowed or reduced even if reasonably and necessarily incurred
Any doubt is resolved in favour of the paying party

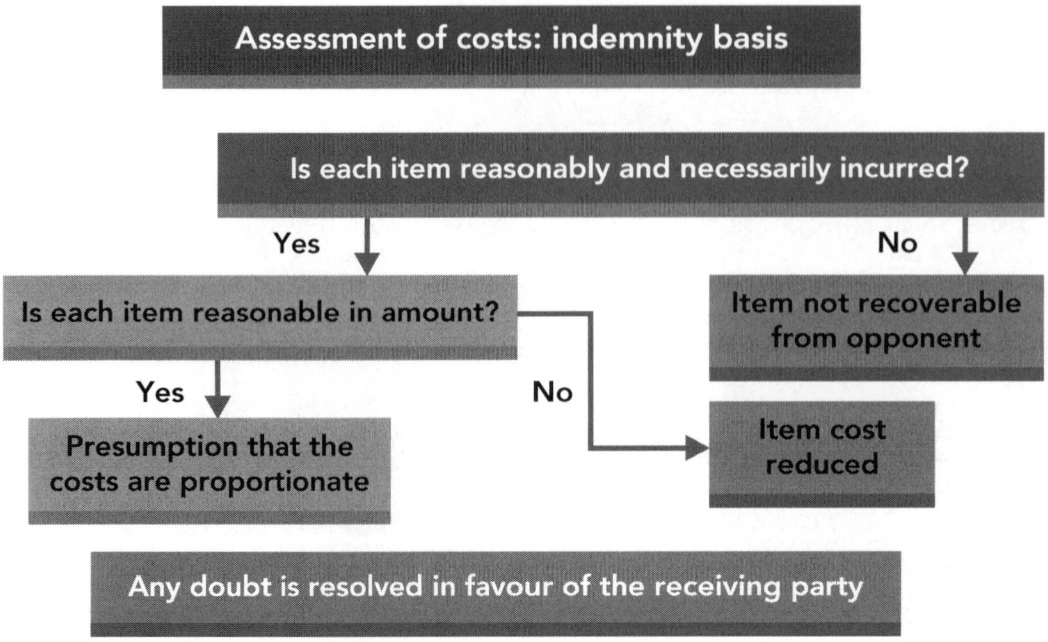
Assessment of costs: indemnity basis
Is each item reasonably and necessarily incurred?
Yes
No
Item not recoverable from opponent
Is each item reasonable in amount?
Yes
No
Item cost reduced
Presumption that the costs are proportionate
Any doubt is resolved in favour of the receiving party

20.9 Procedure on a detailed assessment

A detailed assessment must be commenced within three months of the relevant judgment or order giving the party the right to its costs (**CPR Part 47**).

The assessment is commenced by completing a Notice of Commencement of Assessment (form N252), which may be accessed at https://www.gov.uk/government/publications/form-n252-notice-of-commencement-of-assessment.

A fee must also be paid.

The following is a summary of the procedure for the assessment of costs.

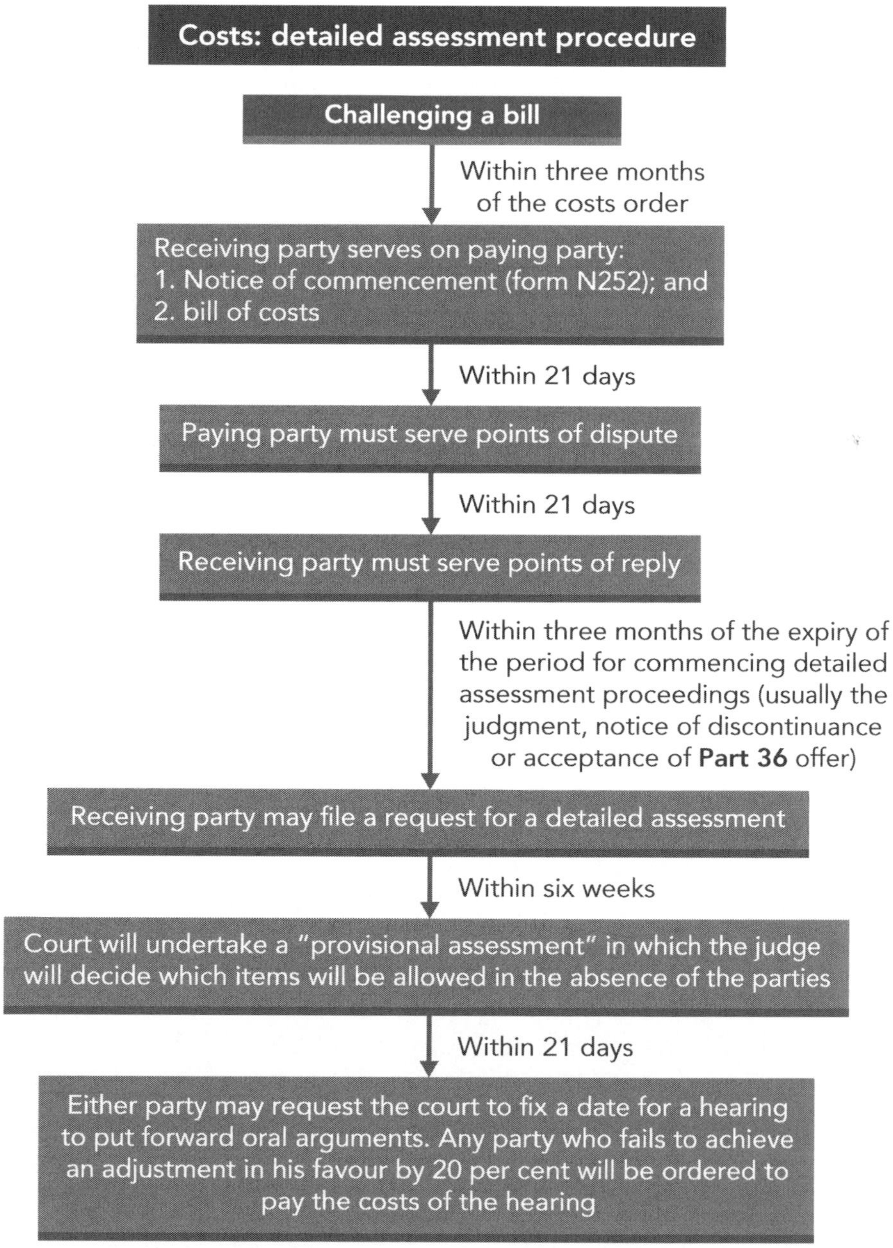

An example of a Request for Detailed Assessment Hearing (form N258) is accessible via the following link: https://www.gov.uk/government/publications/form-n258-request-for-provisional-general-detailed-assessment.

It is important to appreciate that it is open to the parties to avoid some or all of this by **agreeing costs**.

20.10 Fixed costs

For certain applications, such as judgments in default or on admissions and summary judgments, the amount of the costs is fixed by **CPR**. These are set at relatively low figures.

There are also specific fixed-costs provisions that apply in low-value road traffic accident claims under the RTA Protocol. In particular, fixed costs apply to claims which exit these protocols and subsequently conclude.

20.11 Summary

(1) The general rule on costs is that the loser pays the winner's costs, usually on the standard basis, but costs are always at the court's discretion. The court may make a different order, for example, if it wishes to show its disapproval of a party's conduct.

(2) Qualified one-way costs shifting (QOCS) applies to personal injury claims to protect losing claimants from liability for the defendant's costs.

(3) The **summary assessment of costs** is an approximate determination by the court of the amount of costs payable at the end of a hearing. It is used after the hearing of interim applications and after fast track trials.

(4) The **detailed assessment of costs** involves fully particularised bills of costs, formal objections and responses and may involve an assessment hearing.

(5) There are two bases of costs assessment – **standard** and **indemnity**. The standard basis is most commonly used and allows only for costs which are **proportionate**. Any doubts as to the reasonableness of incurring them or as to the amount are resolved in favour of the **paying** party. The indemnity basis does **not** refer to proportionality and any doubts are resolved in favour of the **receiving** party.

CHAPTER 21

Matters Arising After Judgment

21.1 Introduction

Judgments are not automatically enforced by the court and indeed, statistically, this is the most difficult part of the litigation process. This may be because the defendant genuinely does not have the means to pay, or simply that they are adept at hiding their money! If payment is not made within the time ordered, it is up to the claimant to take action and the creditor will need to decide which method they are going to use as a means of enforcing their judgment.

This chapter will consider:

- orders to obtain information;
- taking control of goods;
- attachment orders;
- third party debt orders;
- charging orders;
- bankruptcy/insolvency; and
- the debt respite scheme.

21.2 Order to obtain information

It may be necessary to acquire more information about the debtor's financial position in order to determine the best method of enforcement against them. The procedure is governed by **Part 71**.

In brief, the creditor's lawyer will apply for an order requiring the debtor to attend court to be questioned, on oath, about their finances.

(1) The questioning is usually carried out by a court officer, but the creditor may request a hearing before a judge if there are reasons to do so.

(2) If the debtor fails to attend, the judge may make a committal order against the debtor, suspended provided that the debtor complies with the order.

21.3 Taking control of goods

This method of enforcement is used when the amount involved may be recovered by seizing personal possessions of the judgment debtor of an equivalent value. This could mean their car or household items.

If the amount under the warrant is £5,000 or more, it must be enforced in the High Court (except for consumer credit proceedings); if it is under £600, it must be enforced in the County Court; if the value is between the two, either court is acceptable.

If payment of the debt is to be enforced in the County Court, this is done by **warrant of control**; and in the High Court by a **writ of control**, although the procedure is similar.

A summary of the financial restrictions on and relevant rules to control is provided in the following table.

Judgment sum	Relevant court to enforce judgment	Procedure to seize debtor's goods	Personnel
Under £600	County Court	Warrant of control	County Court enforcement agent (bailiff)
£5,000 or more	High Court (except for c onsumer credit proceedings)	Writ of control	High Court enforcement officer

Judgment sum	Relevant court to enforce judgment	Procedure to seize debtor's goods	Personnel
Between £600 and £5,000	Either court	The procedure appropriate to the court	The official appropriate to the court

The steps the lawyer must take are set out in **CPR Part 83** and summarised below.

(1) The creditor's lawyer will take to the court office a form of request for warrant of control together with the court fee.

(2) The court will then prepare a warrant of control which is passed to the **court enforcement agent** (also known as the **bailiff**) in the County Court or the **High Court enforcement officer** (**HCEO**) in the High Court. They are officers of the court and are empowered to carry out certain functions, including serving documents and seizing goods to satisfy judgments.

(3) The bailiff or HCEO will attend the premises where the debtor has goods and seize goods up to the amount owed and any costs so far incurred.

The bailiff or HCEO may remove the goods from the premises then and there, but normally will take control of them. This means they will allow the goods to remain on the premises for a few days to give the debtor a last chance to pay. Note that clothes, bedding, furniture and household equipment necessary for satisfying basic domestic needs as well as tools, books, vehicles and equipment necessary for the debtor for their personal use in their employment, business or vocation may not be seized.

The sale of the goods seized will take place at a public auction and will follow if the warrant is not paid shortly after controlled possession is taken. The amount required to pay the judgment, including costs and fees, will be deducted from the money raised at auction. Any surplus will be sent to the debtor. A creditor will hope that the threat alone of this method of enforcement may prompt the debtor to pay up as goods sold at auction are unlikely to achieve their true value.

21.4 Attachment of earnings

CPR Part 89 sets out the procedure for attachment of earnings orders (AEOs). If such an order is granted, the debtor's employer is required to pay to the County Court weekly or monthly instalments out of the earnings of the debtor.

The court will then send the money to the creditor.

All applications must be commenced in the County Court Money Claims Centre (CCMCC). The court will serve notice of the application and a reply form on the debtor for completion and return. This provides the court with details of the debtor's income and outgoings. On receipt of this questionnaire, a court officer will decide whether to make an AEO and will only refer the matter to a judge if there is insufficient information to do so.

Two assessments are made when determining how much the debtor should pay.

(1) The **normal deduction rate** is the periodical instalment that the court thinks it reasonable for the debtor to pay towards the judgment.

(2) The **protected earnings rate** is the amount that the court thinks is reasonable for the debtor to live on. The instalments will not reduce the debtor's income below the protected earnings rate.

Where an AEO is made as an administrative decision, both the creditor and the debtor have 14 days in which to apply to have the matter considered at a hearing. If such a request is made, the matter will be transferred to the debtor's local County Court hearing centre for full consideration.

21.5 Third party debt orders

Debtors may have debts owed to them from third persons such as banks at which they have an account in credit or from other debtors who are going to pay funds into their bank account. The existence of such debts may come to light as a result of an order to obtain information. The debt may be a trading debt or simply accounts with a building society or National Savings. The judgment creditor can apply to court to compel the payment of the debt to the judgment creditor rather than to the judgment debtor.

The procedure under **Part 72** is as follows.

(1) The creditor applies to court, without notice to the debtor, with written evidence describing the debt owed by the third party (e.g. a bank or building society) to the debtor.

(2) The court will then issue an **interim order**, which directs the third party not to pay the money owed to the debtor, but to attend court on a fixed date. This is served on the third party and the debtor.

(3) At the hearing, unless there is a good reason not to, the court makes a **final order**, requiring the third party to pay the sum to the judgment creditor.

Third party debt orders are appropriate if you are aware that there are funds in the debtor's bank account, but obtaining up-to-date information may be difficult.

21.6 Charging orders

These proceedings are governed by **CPR Part 73**. It is possible to apply for a charging order if the judgment debtor owns land.

The charging order, if made, will put the creditor in the position of a mortgagee, so this will not be an immediately effective method if there is negative or no equity in the land or property.

All applications for charging orders in the County Court must be made to the CCMCC. The creditor must apply with written evidence in support and a court officer will issue an interim charging order (ICO), based on the paperwork provided, as long as they are satisfied the debtor has an interest in the land. Although the court officer may transfer the matter directly to a judge, the majority of applications will be dealt with under the administrative process.

Thereafter, the procedure is as follows:

- the ICO must be served on the debtor within 21 days; and
- the debtor has 14 days to request that the decision be reviewed by a judge;
- the parties have 28 days from service of the ICO to object to the making of the final charging order (FCO);
- if an objection is received, the matter will be transferred to the debtor's home court (their local County Court hearing centre) for a hearing.

Success does not produce any immediate payment for the judgment creditor, although they can apply to the court as if they were a mortgagee for an order for sale, but this will clearly take some time.

21.7 Bankruptcy/insolvency

The creditor could consider issuing bankruptcy proceedings if the debtor is an individual or winding-up proceedings if the debtor is a company. Details of these procedures are outside the scope of this course.

21.8 Debt respite scheme

On 4 May 2021 a new debt respite scheme was introduced by the **Debt Respite Scheme (Breathing Space Moratorium and Mental Health Crisis Moratorium) (England and Wales) Regulations 2020 (2020/1311)**. The scheme provides a "breathing space" for individuals with problem debts to get advice and work with a debt advice provider to find an appropriate debt solution. There are two types of "breathing space":

(1) Standard breathing space

This is available to any client with problem debts and will give them protection from creditor action for up to 60 days. This protection includes pausing most enforcement claims as well as contact from creditors and will freeze most interest and charges.

(2) Mental health crisis breathing space

This is available to clients with problem debts who are receiving mental health crisis treatment as certified by an approved mental health professional. The period of protection is extended to the length of the mental health crisis (however long) plus 30 days.

In both types of breathing space the role of the debt advice provider is crucial. The debtor (or their nominated representative in the case of a mental health crisis breathing space) must engage with the debt advice provider.

Further detail about this scheme is available at https://www.gov.uk/government/publications/debt-respite-scheme-breathing-space-guidance/debt-respite-scheme-breathing-space-guidance-for-money-advisers.

21.9 Stay of execution

Generally, the courts are of the view that if a party has lost a case and is required to pay a debt to the other side, the winning party should not be deprived of this money or "the fruits of the litigation". However, if a losing party wants to stop the enforcement of the judgment, they may apply for a stay of execution. The judgment debtor must give evidence of means and show (in a witness statement) that they are unable to pay or it is not practical to enforce the order. If successful, the court will grant a stay of execution provided the judgment debtor pays off the debt in instalments.

21.10 Summary

(1) The procedure for an **order to obtain information** is provided under **CPR Part 71**. The procedure for a **third party debt** is provided under **Part 72**. The procedure for a **charging order** is provided under **Part 73**.

(2) Other methods of enforcement are **warrant of control** (County Court), referred to as a **writ of control** in the High Court, and **attachment of earnings** (County Court only).

(3) In certain circumstances, the judgment debtor may obtain a **stay of execution** if they apply to the court.

(4) Debtors may be protected by the debt respite scheme which allows a "breathing space" to enable debtors to deal with problem debts.

CHAPTER 22

Communication with Clients

22.1 Introduction

Communication skills are extremely important for all lawyers, including civil litigators. Most lawyers pride themselves on their communications skills, in both written and verbal form. It does not matter if you know the law; if you cannot communicate with clients, lawyers, judges and other professionals, you will not be successful. In this chapter we will discuss advising internal and external clients, before moving our focus to specific communication skills and methods.

22.2 Communication with internal and external clients

There are a number of different relationships that exist in the legal environment for the legal professional to learn to navigate.

The diagram on the next page illustrates this.

External	Internal
Consumer Client	Accounts Teams
Counsel Immigration	Human Resouces
Officers Mediators	Marketing
Cost Lawyers	New Business
Insurance Companies	Administration Teams
Local Government Bodies	Technical Support
	Project Management

Reflective question

Can you think of any other internal clients that exist within your own legal environment and how their role contributes to the overall service delivery?

22.2.1 Communicating with internal clients

There are benefits to internal client relationships including:

- a common goal, all parties in the relationship understand the ethos of the business and collaborate to achieve it;
- better understanding of internal process;
- greater opportunity for knowledge sharing;
- they may even be located closely together, enabling issues to be resolved quicker.

There are also pitfalls or barriers that affect internal relationships. These can develop out of familiarity, leading to the internal client becoming the least urgent client.

Internal methods of communication may take place in a team setting or take place using an internal intranet system. Internal communication will take the form of:

- telephone calls
- Teams/Zoom calls
- reports

- memos
- face to face
- email
- team briefings
- presentations

Internal client service standards

Client service standards within a business can differ significantly from external standards set by a regulator. Internal standards will be heavily influenced by the external standards as these are the overriding principles of the business, but the wording and service level will be specific to the department.

There may be complacency or a temptation to correspond with internal departments in a more casual or familiar manner, or a lawyer may not apply the department standards to avoid a challenging conversation. Email, letter or telephone correspondence may not meet a required standard. Face to face may be overly social or avoided altogether, creating the risk of missing business objectives or regulatory requirements. Remember that correspondence between departments must achieve the standards implemented by the business to improve client experience. Standards or charters will centre around response times or service level agreements for actions.

Examples of internal standards include the time that it takes for a cashier to transact a payment or how often supervision takes place between a senior fee earner and a trainee or the time it takes for a member of a business support team to respond with reports.

In whatever way the standards are implemented, they are all designed to support the business, to support the client and achieve external regulatory requirements. The standards set out the department goals and objectives and how success is measured.

22.2.2 Communicating with the external client

When communicating with the external client, high standards of communication must be met. Note the requirements of the **SRA Code of Conduct** and the **CILEX Code of Conduct**.

The **Data Protection Act 2018** (**DPA 2018**) has strict rules on how personal information disclosed by clients should be used and protected. It is important to note that all attendance notes should be factual and should not contain any opinion that the fee earner is not happy to advise the client. It should not be defamatory or unfair in any way. Under **DPA 2018** the client is entitled to make a Subject Access Request (SAR) at any time. In practice, however, an SAR often forms part of a complaint made. The client is entitled to view all information held on them.

When communicating, whether by email, post, telephone or face to face, the lawyer must use appropriate greetings and maintain professional conduct throughout. This includes remaining diplomatic, providing clear and succinct information and responding clearly and appropriately to questions.

When recording the event, the lawyer must make accurate notes, agree a plan for the next steps and ensure good factual attendance notes are made.

Appropriate methods depend on the type of communication taking place. External communication takes place by:

- letters
- email
- telephone
- direct mail
- portals
- video calling

In transactions within the client-lawyer relationship, both CILEX and the SRA set out specific rules to adhere to. The rules ensure the client has means of redress if they are unhappy and knows the level of service they can expect to receive, the level of competence the lawyer works within and is reassured that they will be treated fairly with their interests protected. Barriers that affect the relationship occur when client care rules are not met.

For example:

- the client is not regularly updated;
- the client is not advised of fees;
- there are unnecessary delays and no explanation provided;
- there is an inconsistent individual fee earner approach to service;
- there is a frequent change of fee earner;
- the client is not able to complain and expect a fair outcome;
- the fee earner becomes defensive and may be combative.

Other problems which may arise include:

- language barriers;
- client does not use email/telephone;
- poor interviewing skills;
- rushed or untimely interactions;
- technical failures;
- inappropriate use of legal jargon.

22.3 Communication skills

22.3.1 Verbal communication

Verbal communication is using spoken language to deliver a message. This can be carried out face-to-face in person, by talking using the telephone or through use of digital technology such as mobile video calling or Voice Over Internet Protocol (VOIP), for example, Microsoft Teams or Zoom.

When using verbal communication, tone of voice is important. Listeners will be influenced by a tone of voice which is:

- appropriate to the nature of the conversation;
- modulated so that there is gentle but obvious variation in tone;
- free from filler words, for example, "like", "you know" or "right?";
- controlled, so that the speaker does not end every sentence with a question mark.

Techniques for speaking effectively include:

- facing the person you are addressing and taking care about looking away for too long, as this will distract the listener;
- keeping your head up so that your voice can project;
- speaking clearly, taking time to enunciate each word;
- preventing your voice from dropping away at the end of a sentence by taking natural breaths;
- varying your speed according to the topic and the needs of your client;
- adjusting your tone.

22.3.2 Non-verbal communication

Non-verbal communication, which is sometimes referred to as body language, is the way that we send wordless messages through our body or voice. These signals may reinforce words that are being spoken or may be silent communicators of thoughts or feelings.

Non-verbal communication signals include:

- eye contact;
- head position;
- body posture;
- use of hands and arms (e.g. folding arms or pointing a finger);
- facial expression.

Facial expressions are particularly powerful and a high percentage of our interpretation of a person's thoughts and feelings can come from observing:

- mouth shape and position;
- eyebrow lifting or lowering;
- eye movements;
- chin height;
- head angle.

In addition to these physical elements, another facet of non-verbal communication relates to the way that spoken communications are delivered, including:

- pitch of voice;
- emotions within the voice;
- speed of speech;
- emphasis which the speaker gives to certain words, which implies importance.

These features are commonly known as "paralanguage", which is a way of describing the influence that these factors have on the way that a speaker's words are interpreted by the listener.

What is body language?

The following YouTube video explores the impact of body language:

Make Body Language Your Superpower – Stanford Graduate School of Business https://www.youtube.com/watch?v=cFLjudWTuGQ

22.3.3 Listening skills

In the meeting room with a client in front of you, your natural instinct may well be to talk, start asking questions and tell the client what they need to know. There are a number of dangers which are easy to fall into:

- the client will become frustrated if they are not given the opportunity to tell their story;
- the client may find it harder to explain the problem if there is not enough space left in the conversation;
- you may make inaccurate assumptions about the issue which are based on what you have said rather than what the client has said.

It is important that listening is active. When we demonstrate a concentrated form of attention, we will show the speaker that we are doing this by providing a range of non-verbal signals.

Although signals vary from person to person, indicators of deep/active listening can include:

- making little "mmm" sounds;
- slow head nods;
- placing our head on one side;
- making prolonged eye contact;
- smiling or matching the speaker's facial expression;
- leaning forward;
- keeping our hands and body still.

In addition to these non-verbal behaviours, active listening will also involve:

- clarifying key points using checking questions to ensure that you have understood;
- summarising by neutrally reflecting some of the key points that have been heard.

It is also important to know when to be silent. The ability to listen silently and without interrupting may not always feel natural, although it is a skill that can be learnt. Silence can also be useful as a way of encouraging a client to provide more information. This involves listening to an answer and then leaving a silence as though you were expecting more. Be aware that overuse of silence may appear aggressive, so all things in moderation.

A useful way of remembering some of the key skills of listening, is LISTEN:

Let the person finish before interrupting.

Inquire using checking questions.

Summarise.

Test your understanding.

Evaluate the "whole" message.

Neutralise inner feelings.

Active listening

This resource discusses the benefits of active listening and how to be an active listener:

Active Listening: Techniques, Benefits, Examples
https://www.verywellmind.com/what-is-active-listening-3024343

22.4 Client interviews

A common situation where you will be speaking to a client is in the client interview. The client interview is an opportunity for the client to meet their lawyer and decide if they wish to place the case in their hands, an opportunity to ask questions and to receive advice. For the lawyer, an interview is an opportunity to receive information, ask questions and engage the client. First interviews are extremely important and can set the tone for the whole of the client-lawyer relationship.

22.4.1 Preparing for the interview

The interview should be in private and the client should not be able to be overheard by others nearby. The interview should not be interrupted by the telephone or others entering the room. It should last a sufficient length of time to take instructions properly, give considered advice and to give the client the lawyer's full attention.

The lawyer should prepare for the interview too. For the first interview, it is important not to pre-judge what the client's problem may be – it often takes time for a client to disclose their problem, particularly in more sensitive cases. In later meetings, you are likely to have an agenda and will know what the discussion is to be about, but always be prepared for the client to disclose new problems or to have fresh concerns.

You should ensure that your office or interview room is prepared for the interview by making sure that you have a ready supply of:

- pens and paper;
- funding forms;
- court forms in case of a need to make an urgent application;
- standard forms, for example, file checklists;
- business cards.

If the meeting is taking place online, make sure that you are confident using the software, including sharing screens. It is good practice to use an anonymous background, rather than a view of your room, and to encourage the client to do the same, particularly if there are children in the house.

If your client consents, it is also helpful, particularly with complicated discussions, to record the interview. Note, however, the importance of obtaining consent from the client and ensuring the requirements of the **General Data Protection Regulation** (**GDPR**) are complied with.

22.4.2 The start of the meeting

Welcome your client. This early stage is often described as "meet, seat and greet" in that the client is met by the lawyer and taken to the interview room, offered a seat and formal introductions are made. It is extremely important to be friendly and informal and to put the client at ease.

Your non-verbal communication will be important here.

(1) Have you made eye contact with the client? Did you smile and appear friendly?

(2) Be confident (even if you don't feel it) but remain approachable, sympathetic and friendly.

(3) Speak naturally and sincerely – this becomes easier with practice. Avoid the temptation to play the "role" of a lawyer.

(4) Avoid the situation where you are behind a desk and the client is facing you. A better, more natural arrangement is to sit around a table.

22.4.3 Asking for information

The next phase of the interview is to gain information from the client. In an ideal world, the client would tell their lawyer everything they needed to know and have all the documents relevant to the case.

Clients are often distressed when they come to the first interview or are nervous, disorganised or in a hurry. There are a number of strategies for eliciting information.

It is important that you communicate effectively with the client and use language that your client fully understands and that you feel comfortable using. One tip for gauging your client's comprehension of language is by inviting them to explain why they have come to see you, in their own terms. Listening carefully to their response, and mirroring their use of language throughout the interview, will maximise the effectiveness of your communication with the client.

Some clients will talk all day and some will take some prompting. Aim to establish a free-flowing conversation rather than starting to ask questions immediately.

If a client is slow to open up the conversation:

- use open questions: "why, who, where, how, when" in a question will produce a more expansive answer than a question that can be answered with a "yes" or "no";
- summarise your client's instructions and ask them to add any further information;
- invite the client to talk about a particular topic: "Is there anything else you would like to add?", "Please tell me about . . . ", "Please go on";
- be an active listener.

There are some off-putting interview styles for clients. Avoid asking multiple questions, for example, "What time did the accident happen? Where were you standing? Did anyone witness this?" as the client will not know which to answer and may become confused. Leading questions are inadvisable as they will not necessarily bring out the truth but rather what the client thinks that the lawyer wishes to hear, for example, "After the assault, did you feel too frightened to go home?" or "You wouldn't want to return home after that, would you?"

Don't be afraid of silence. A client may need time to think or, if they are distressed, to collect themself. Avoid the temptation to jump in with questions or comments and allow a short period of silence.

Try to avoid closed questions at the beginning of the interview. A closed question will only elicit a "yes" or "no" answer or a short response. Closed questions can be used later in the interview to clarify points with the client, for example, "Was it Mr Smith or Ms Grey who helped you to your feet?" or "In which hospital did you receive emergency treatment?"

One commonly used questioning technique is "funnelling". The idea of "funnelling" is to ask the client an open question to start the discussion and, as the client tells their story, listen carefully. Once the basic story has been obtained, the interviewer can ask questions which set the story in context and use "why, who, where, how, when" in order to do so. Once the context is clear, the interviewer can ask questions to probe exactly how the events unfolded and clarify any unclear points using "how" and "why" as a starting point. Finally, closed questions can be used to clarify or check any final details. This funnelling process can be repeated to cover a number of topics if necessary.

Many firms use checklists to ensure that all relevant information is covered in interview. Checklists are a very useful tool but should not dominate the interview; clients will not appreciate a "tick box" approach to their case and interviewers must avoid this temptation.

22.5 Legal writing skills

Writing is one of the main ways in which a business communicates with its clients and the popularity of email has meant that many of us are relying more on this as a method of communication.

There are multiple reasons for placing information into text, which include:

- to meet legal requirements;
- as a permanent record;
- to provide a client with information they can review at a later date;

- to clarify an issue;
- to explain a complex piece of information clearly

Legal writing touches upon the professionalism of a lawyer and poor legal writing reflects badly on professionalism. Law firms also expect a high standard of written communication from their employees.

Good legal writing comprises a number of elements:

- correct grammar, spelling and punctuation;
- clarity of expression and explanation;
- a concise and succinct style;
- the correct tone for the purpose of the communication and its intended audience;
- a clear, logical structure.

Writing skills

These links show a variety of resources that will assist you in developing your writing skills, including grammar, spelling and punctuation:

How to Improve Writing Skills in 15 Easy Steps
https://www.grammarly.com/blog/

Write Compelling Documents: Legal Writing Tips
https://www.clio.com/blog/legal-writing-tips-for-lawyers/

Advice and Worksheets on Improving Writing and Editing Skills
https://www.bbc.co.uk/teach/skillswise/writing/z73747h

22.5.1 Using precedents

It is common for law firms to use precedent documents. A precedent is a template created by someone else that can be adapted to fit the situation you have before you, instead of you having to draft the entire document. (This should not be confused with case law precedent, whereby courts follow the decisions in previous cases!) Precedents may have been written from someone within your firm, or it may have been purchased from a legal publisher.

The benefits of using precedent documents is that it saves you time and will include the standard clauses/phrases that should go into that type of document. For some documents there may be statutory or other requirements as to the form of the document, and you can be reasonably confident that an often used precedent document will include these. However, it is only a starting point. You must make sure that the document meets your client's needs. You will lose the benefits of the precedent document if the document you draft is incomprehensive and poorly drafted.

22.5.2 Attendance notes

Following client interviews and meetings, it is important that you keep a record of what the client said and what the lawyer advised and agreed to do.

If there is no attendance note or it is inaccurate or incomplete, the following unhappy consequences may arise.

(1) You may have the embarrassing task of phoning the client to ask about some details which you need.

(2) Your client may have asked for something to be done which you do not realise has not been done until it is too late.

(3) You may spend time carrying out work which the client did not agree to. You may then not be able to charge for your time.

(4) You and your firm may be subject to a claim for professional negligence because you cannot prove that you gave the client appropriate advice.

(5) You (or a more senior colleague) may manage to retrieve the situation with the client but your relationship continues to be difficult and there are future disputes, especially when your bill is submitted.

22.5.2.1 Taking notes

(1) **Sitting in on someone else's client interview or meeting**

You may be asked to sit in on another fee-earner's interview or meeting. Here, you have a chance to meet the client and enable the fee-earner to concentrate on managing the interview. The advantage of this is, of course, that you are able to focus on recording what was said without having to pose the questions to the client or give advice. You may have the following difficulties to overcome:

- the fee-earner or the client may talk too fast for you to keep up;

- you may not have enough knowledge of the area of legal practice at this stage to understand all the implications of the fee-earner's advice and the point of their questions. This makes it harder to identify what is important information;
- the client may be very sociable and want to involve you in the conversation.

There are a number of things you can do to deal with these problems:

- you have to develop the speed at which you take notes. Remember, the notes have to be readable by one person only – you. If you are struggling to keep up, the fee-earner should slow the discussion down;
- it is always useful to discuss with the interviewer beforehand who the client is and what the fee-earner understands will be discussed;
- during the interview, try and take your cue from the fee-earner if the client starts to involve you in the conversation. You should always be polite and friendly but do not start giving advice yourself and let the fee-earner steer the conversation back to what is relevant. The client should have no doubt that the fee-earner is in charge;
- as soon as possible after the interview discuss your impressions with the fee-earner and ask any questions;
- add any notes which the fee-earner has made themself to your own before you start to draft the attendance note.

(2) **Taking notes as you carry out the interview yourself**

If you have planned the interview carefully, you will expect to be able to discuss the facts and issues in a logical and straightforward way. The interview will progress smoothly at an even pace and taking notes will be easy. Unfortunately, even the best interviewer will sometimes face difficulties keeping to their plan.

There are several key things to do in these circumstances:

- write down relevant information as soon as it is given. If you have time, draw arrows linking the information to other associated details;
- if you are not sure whether something is relevant or not, write it down anyway;
- try not to let the note taking distract the client – ensure that you maintain eye contact and empathy;
- do not be afraid to stop and ask the client to clarify details – remember to make sure you spell names and addresses correctly. For example, if the name given is "Carol Stephens" it could be spelled "Carole Stevens" or even "Karel Stephens";

- take particular care that you record what your advice is and what has been agreed will be done next by you and the client.

(3) **Using a checklist**

Your firm may well have standard checklists which you are expected to use in certain types of interview. Even if it does not, individual fee-earners are likely to have their own versions. The advantages of checklists are:

- they enable you to ensure that all the standard information is covered in the interview and recorded;
- they give you a clear framework for the interview;
- a completed checklist will be very helpful as you prepare a detailed attendance note.

Using checklists also carries some risks.

(a) Mechanically working your way through a checklist risks alienating the client who may not understand the significance of your questions or who may be burning to get to the heart of their problems.

(b) Some questions on a checklist may be clearly irrelevant for this particular client by the time you reach them.

(c) Do not ask questions following a checklist if you cannot explain why the information may be helpful for this client.

(d) Clients always like to feel that their circumstances are unique or at least sufficiently distinctive to be treated individually. Reading out checklist questions without making an effort to make the discussion personal risks making the client feel you are simply processing them rather than listening to their story. Clients who feel cherished are more likely to pay their bills!

(e) The wording of questions on a checklist may use vocabulary which is too complex or, sometimes, too unsophisticated for the particular client in front of you. If you are unprepared to paraphrase or vary a question, you risk confusing some clients and patronising others.

22.5.2.2 Draft the attendance note

Do not delay! As soon as possible after the interview, you should draft or dictate your attendance note. If you wait, you will forget what you heard. Even the most detailed notes are best supplemented by your own memory. You will usually find that preparing the attendance note will be easier and quicker if you can prepare it soon afterwards.

Read through your notes (and those of any other fee-earner who was in the meeting) and try to identify a logical pattern. If you have used a well-drafted checklist in the interview, you may find this to be fairly easy. In a more wide-ranging interview pieces of information which are associated may have been recorded in different parts of your notes. It is often helpful to mark up the notes linking the information, for example, by using arrows.

Organise the material. Where the interview was wide ranging, try numbering the paragraphs of your notes in a logical order. As you do this, start thinking which bit of information will most logically be needed first. For instance, after an interview taking instructions to make a claim following a road traffic accident, a key task will be to set out the events in the particulars of claim. Try and record the events in your attendance note in chronological order, even if the client's account "jumps around" the story during the interview.

Use **headings and paragraphs**. If you prepare an attendance note which is simply a stream of recollections (an easy trap to fall into if you are dictating it for someone else to type), the attendance note will be hard to read and confusing. Headings and paragraphs will make it easier to organise the material.

Exclude what is **irrelevant or contradictory**. When interviewing a personal injury client you may, for example, find that the initial categorical statement of the client about the circumstances of the accident "I was never told I had to keep the guard up on the welding machine" upon further questioning turns into "Well I suppose the foreman did show me how to use the machine with the guard and tell me always to do so when I started six years ago, but none of my mates bother now – it just slows things up". Recording both statements in the attendance note will not be helpful and may simply confuse things later on – only record the later statement.

Take extra care in recording precisely the **legal advice** given during the interview. If this is omitted or inaccurately recorded, your firm may subsequently face a completely unfair professional negligence claim with no effective defence. Where the client has to make a difficult decision, for example, whether or not to accept a **Part 36** offer, it is crucial that your advice, including the costs consequences, is very clearly described.

Follow your firm's **conventions** when drafting your attendance note. For example, fee-earners may be referred to normally by their initials in attendance notes. Remember that other fee-earners, including the partners, may well read your attendance notes and will expect them to follow the firm's normal style.

Be precise in describing what is said about **legal costs**. If a quote or estimate is given, ensure that you state whether or not it includes VAT. It is important to record any provisos or qualification to the advice on costs, for example, particularly where a conditional fee agreement or damages-based agreement has been discussed.

Spell out clearly the **next steps** to be taken by you and by the client including any statements as to when they will be carried out. This information will be vital when you next review the file.

Record the time you spent on the interview and attendance note. This will always be useful if your bill is challenged subsequently.

22.5.3 Matter creation forms

These important forms must be completed as soon as the initial instructions have been received. Some of the information may have been supplied on a pre-interview checklist. The attendance note for the initial meeting may also record some of this information. The forms will vary in design according to your firm's procedures but will require you to complete accurately names, addresses, phone numbers, email addresses, etc. This information may well be used to set up the client's entry on the firm's computerised database. It is vital to record the details accurately taking particular care with numbers and the name and address of the client.

Please note the following important points.

(1) **Names of client** – include all of the client's names and make sure they are spelled correctly. This is important for the purpose of preventing money laundering.

(2) **Preferred contact method** – clients may have expressed a preference for a particular contact number to be used or not used. They will be upset if their instructions are not followed.

(3) **Case type** – this is usually as simple as, for example, "personal injury claim", "debt recovery" etc. Some forms will give a list of standard categories and you will be required to tick the relevant box.

(4) **ID type** – this refers to the passport etc. which needs to be shown to the firm for money laundering purposes (see **4.2**). If the documentation has not been presented at the initial interview, the form must clearly indicate this fact by using "not yet presented" or the wording preferred within your firm. This highlights the fact that the client must still prove their identity before the firm can proceed with the case.

(5) **Names of opponent(s) or other parties to the transaction**, for example, the person from whom your client is buying a house – include full names. Simply referring to "Mr Smith" will not enable you to check accurately on your firm's database whether or not the opponent is already a client. This is important because there would then be a risk of a conflict of interest not being identified at the beginning of the transaction.

(6) **Mode of address for letters** – this means what should follow "Dear" at the beginning of the actual letter. This is an important convention to get right because it helps to set the tone of the rest of the letter.

(7) **Mode of address for envelopes** – this simply means how the client's name is referred to on address labels, for example, "Ms K Leung", "Dr G Williams", "Mrs N Feng". The client's name should be referred to in the same way at the top of addresses in letters.

(8) **Marketing info** – do not forget to include any information you may have on why a new client has come to the firm. If someone has been referred to you by another client or contact (such as an accountant), a partner might wish to thank him personally. Sometimes, new clients come to a firm in response to a particular advertising campaign – recording this sort of information accurately and consistently helps the firm to judge whether or not the advertising was financially worthwhile.

22.5.4 Client care letters

The **CILEX Code of Conduct Principle 5** (specifically **5.7-5.11**) requires you to provide certain information to your client. Firms have developed the use of an introductory letter known as a "client care letter" as a way of providing required information.

The client care letter must include the name, status and contact details of the person:

- dealing with the "case"; and
- supervising the case.

The letter must provide clear information about the:

- key facts the client has told you about their case;
- legal advice you gave the client at your meeting and any additional advice now available;
- timescales and next steps you will take;
- actions the client needs to take;
- likely outcome of the case estimated costs, VAT and payments to third parties, including court fees and expert fees, (disbursements);
- the firm's complaints procedure including the client's right to refer a complaint to the Legal Ombudsman or CILEX Regulation where appropriate;
- the firm's standard terms and conditions.

Two copies of the firm's standard terms and conditions will usually be sent with the client care letter. The client will be asked to sign one copy and return it to the firm.

22.5.4.1 Style of client care letter

Note the following specific issues to be covered in client care letters.

(1) **Starting the letter**

The client care letter is the first letter your client receives from you. It is your opportunity to build on your friendly, but business-like, meeting with them.

Write in the first person, using "I" rather than "we".

You can help you client engage with the content of your letter by making it:

- easy and
- attractive

(2) **Explain the letter's purpose**

Give the letter a short heading in bold type.

Make your letter personal to your client. For a litigation client use a heading of "Your personal injury claim" rather than "Jones v Cartwright Cars Ltd".

Start your letter by explaining why you are writing.

(3) **Keep it concise**

Long letters are hard to read, so try not to repeat information.

Include information that the client will find important in the first part of the letter.

Some parts of the letter will need more detail than others. When you summarise the client's case, you do not need every detail. Concentrate on the legally significant parts.

When you confirm your legal advice, make sure you are clear about issues which are often misunderstood by clients.

If you realised that the client struggled to understand some aspects of your advice during the interview, take particular care to explain it again as simply as possible.

Clear costs information is important. Clearly set out the costs estimate, VAT, and costs payable to third parties (disbursements). Explain when the client must pay these.

(4) **Use plain English**

For example, rather than "endeavour" use "try".

Avoid legal language, or if there is no suitable alternative, explain the legal term.

Use everyday phrases rather than ones that are wordy or sound pompous.

(5) **Make it easy to read**

The following ways of writing help clients read and engage with your letter:

- short sentences, as these are easier to read;
- avoid dense bodies of text, so important information does not get lost;
- numbered headings help a client work their way through the letter;
- use short paragraphs to organise information making it easier to read;
- font size 12 and above is more inviting and helps people with visual impairments;
- make information stand out using:
  - highlighting
  - bullet points tables.

(6) **Enclosures**

Lengthy but important information which must be given to the client can be sign-posted in the letter and then enclosed separately. This makes the letter shorter and as a result the client is more likely to read the letter through to the end.

Many firms will use this approach for details of their complaints procedure and terms and conditions.

(7) **Closing**

Always try and end the letter on a friendly note and ask the client to contact you if they are unclear about anything.

Sign "Yours sincerely" and add your name.

It is good practice to enclose a duplicate copy of the letter and to ask the client to sign and return it to you. You need to make sure you follow your firm's policy on this.

22.5.5 Other letters to your client

Apply the same high writing standards whenever you write to your client during the transaction. Keep your writing clear and precise. Remember, if you are vague or unclear, the client will soon be phoning or emailing you.

Do not forget the importance of your final letter wrapping up the transaction. If you are reporting back on a court hearing, make sure you are very clear in summarising the result to the client. You will need to enclose your final invoice. Some firms will also enclose a client feedback form with this letter. Such information can be very valuable for the managers and partners in the firm and it is important that you follow your firm's policy.

22.5.6 Other routine letters

Again, keep these letters as succinct and precise as possible. It is important to remain polite even when writing to the opponent's lawyers. Even if the parties in a court case dislike each other, you must retain a measure of detachment in your correspondence with other lawyers and remain polite. Use "we" and "Yours faithfully" in letters to other lawyers and organisations.

Always be courteous when writing to a member of the public who is not a client. Even if you have to explain that you cannot help him, for example, because of a professional ethics issue, you should keep in mind that the recipient of your letter is a potential future client. You should write this sort of letter using "I" and "Yours sincerely".

Remember the importance of including accurate references when writing to organisations, including insurance companies, and firms of lawyers. This will help ensure that the letter reaches the right person as quickly as possible and does not hang around in a post room without a home. Again, make sure you use your firm's standard system for references. Those who receive your letters will copy that reference on to their replies.

22.5.7 Communicating by email

There are a number of golden rules for business emails:

- use an appropriate title which will be meaningful to the recipient;
- start the email with "Dear . . .";

- avoid using abbreviated text language;
- be very careful about using humour – remember emails can easily be forwarded to unexpected recipients;
- unless the message is very short, it may be appropriate to attach a longer Word letter;
- remember the courtesies of thanking the recipient etc.;
- use paragraphs and bullets and ensure that the content is logically set out;
- consider whether you need to copy in your principal or any other colleagues;
- read and apply your firm's email protocols (if any) – you may be expected to include the file number in the title;
- close the email with "Regards" and your first name (not simply an initial), followed by your email standard signature (full name, job title and phone number).

There is a temptation when writing an email for the more relaxed style of writing to induce less precision. This can be dangerous when you are communicating vital practical information. If, for example, you are giving directions to a particular court, it is vital that the client will be able to find it easily. Giving the accurate postcode and a link to the Google map may need to be supplemented by some practical advice that, for example, there is no parking at the court and the public car park across the road is usually full up by 9.00 am. It is, of course, particularly important that your client gets to the court hearing on time.

22.6 Other methods of communication

22.6.1 Communicating by telephone

There are some key points when communicating by telephone.

- Do not take a call from a client if you are in the middle of a meeting or otherwise engaged.
- If you are phoning a client who is overseas, remember to check the time difference first.
- Work on developing your skills at expressing emotions such as warmth, sympathy, firmness and confidence using your voice alone.
- If the issues are complex or distressing for the client, consider arranging a meeting instead.
- If there are a number of points which you want to discuss, prepare a short list beforehand so that you can work your way through them methodically.

- When leaving messages, do not breach your duty of confidentiality or simply cause embarrassment to the client if someone else hears the message first. Mentioning that you are phoning from Williams & Khan lawyers may give rise to embarrassing questions to the client as to why they are instructing a lawyer.

Conference calls

Sometimes, you may need to make a conference call with several colleagues using the loudspeaker function on your phone. Make sure the person(s) at the other end knows that they are now on the loudspeaker. This type of call is best done in a quiet room to help the person(s) at the other end to distinguish what is being said by whom. Make sure that everyone introduces themselves verbally at the beginning of the call, ensuring that they are close enough to the phone to be audible. Remember that only one person should be speaking at a time. At the end of the call, do ensure that the loudspeaker function is turned off.

22.6.2 Videoconferencing

A video-conference is something of a hybrid between a face-to-face meeting and a telephone call. Increasingly, firms are referring to it on their websites as a method of communicating, particularly with overseas clients. As well as providing a chance for clients who are thousands of miles away to see you and your colleagues during the discussions, the technology enables, through split screens, documents to be reviewed and amended electronically.

It is important to plan the video-conference ahead of time, ensuring that you are clear how to use the technology. You will need to dress as smartly as you would for a face-to-face interview and ensure that all mobile phones are switched off.

During the video-conference, all participants should introduce themselves at the beginning and ensure that they are visible on the screen. They should avoid moving around and only speak one at a time. It can be helpful for participants who are not speaking to use the "Mute" button to minimise background noise. Where there are a number of participants, it may be appropriate for participants who are not speaking to be on "mute" but to use the "hand up" icon to signify that they want to speak.

22.6.3 Communicating via your firm's website

Some firms have a section of their website on which their clients can access information about progress on their cases by using a password. They are able to see how much time has been spent and how much the case is costing. This sort of system is likely to be linked to a case management system and is particularly appropriate for firms which carry out a large number of standard transactions, for example, debt recovery claims.

You must, of course, ensure that you update the case management system promptly as you progress each case – clients will expect the website to be accurate.

22.6.4 Text messages

Most people have a mobile phone and text messaging is an easy way for them to keep up to date on information. While traditionally lawyers have shied away from such informal methods of communication, it is increasingly being expected by clients. Many other sectors use text messages on a regular basis, to remind people about appointments or provides updates on their situation. In addition to your firm's phone systems, it may be that your firm's CRM system includes automated responses or allows fee earners to send texts to clients, for example to remind them of court appointments. Whatever the method used, make sure that you comply with any internal rules.

Activity

If you are working within a law firm, do some research into the different methods of communication used within your firm. If some methods mentioned in this chapter are not used in your firm, do some further research into those methods and think about the benefits and risks associated with these methods.

If you are not currently working within a law firm, or your firm already uses all of these methods, choose a couple of communication methods to do further research into and think about the benefits and risks associated with these methods.

22.7 Summary

(1) You must comply with internal and external service standards to ensure that the client receives the best standard of care.

(2) Be aware of the importance of developing both your verbal and non-verbal communication skills.

(3) Make sure that your listening is active.

(4) Prepare for interviews in advance and use a combination of open and closed questions to draw out information from your client.

(5) 'Funnelling' may assist you in obtaining information from your client.

(6) Be careful with spelling, grammar and punctation in your written correspondence.

(7) Attendance notes should be written to capture key information from the client.

(8) Client care letters must be sent to clients at the beginning of the matter and be easy for the client to read and understand.

APPENDIX – CONTENTS

Claim Form

In the County Court Money Claims Centre (1)	
Fee Account no.	
Help with Fees - Ref no. (if applicable)	H W F – –
	For court use only
Claim no.	2(a)
Issue date	2(b)

You may be able to issue your claim online which may save time and money. Go to www.moneyclaim.gov.uk to find out more.

Claimant(s) name(s) and address(es) including postcode

Filbert Engineering Limited (3)
85 York Road
Leicester
LE24 6GM

SEAL

Defendant(s) name and address(es) including postcode

City Exports Limited
Registered Office, 2 Lowther Terrace, Nottingham NG1 8TN

Brief details of claim

(4)

Price of goods sold and delivered

Value

(5)

Defendant's name and address for service including postcode

City Exports Limited
Registered Office, 2 Lowther Terrace, Nottingham NG1 8TN (7)

	£
Amount claimed	52,709.45 (8(a))
Court fee	8(b)
Legal representative's costs	8(c)
Total amount	8(d)

For further details of the courts www.gov.uk/find-court-tribunal.
When corresponding with the Court, please address forms or letters to the Manager and always quote the claim number.

N1 Claim form (CPR Part 7) (06.22)

Notes

(8(a)) Amount shown is the £50,400 claimed plus interest due to issue date.

(8(b)) Court fee depends on value of claim.

(8(c)) The legal representative's costs are fixed amounts (found in standardised tables – details are outside the scope of this course).

Claim no.	

You must indicate your preferred County Court Hearing Centre for hearings here (see notes for guidance)

Leicester County Court Hearing Centre (6)

Do you believe you, or a witness who will give evidence on your behalf, are vulnerable in any way which the court needs to consider?

☐ Yes. Please explain in what way you or the witness are vulnerable and what steps, support or adjustments you wish the court and the judge to consider.

☑ No

Does, or will, your claim include any issues under the Human Rights Act 1998? (9)

☐ Yes

☑ No

Claim no.	

Particulars of Claim (10)

☑ attached

☐ to follow

1. By a contract contained in or evidenced by the Defendant's Order dated 6 January 2020 the Claimant agreed to sell and deliver six machine tools to the Defendant for the sum of £42,000 plus VAT. A copy of the contract is attached.
2. Despite the Claimant delivering the machine tools to the Defendant and rendering an invoice number G3456 dated 13 March 2020 the Defendant has failed to pay all or any part of the price of the machines.

PARTICULARS

Price of the machine tools £42,000
VAT at 20% £8,400
Total £50,400

3. The Claimant is entitled to interest at the rate of 8% per annum pursuant to a contract between the Claimant and the Defendant dated 6 January 2020, on the sum of £50,400 from 13 March 2020 to 8 October 2020 inclusive amounting to £2,309.45 and continuing from 9 October 2020 to judgment or earlier payment at the daily rate of £11.05.

AND the Claimant claims: (11)

1 The sum of £50,400
2 Interest on the sum of £50,400 pursuant to the contract from 13 March 2020 to 8 October 2020,
amounting to £2,309.45.
3. Interest from 9 October 2020 at a daily rate of £11.05.

Statement of truth (12)

Note: you are reminded that a copy of this claim form must be served on all other parties.

I understand that proceedings for contempt of court may be brought against a person who makes, or causes to be made, a false statement in a document verified by a statement of truth without an honest belief in its truth.

☐ **I believe** that the facts stated in this claim form and any attached sheets are true.

☑ **The claimant** believes that the facts stated in this claim form and any attached sheets are true. **I am authorised** by the claimant to sign this statement.

Signature

Claire Smith

☑ Claimant

☐ Litigation friend (where claimant is a child or protected party)

☐ Claimant's legal representative (as defined by CPR 2.3(1))

Date

Day Month Year

Full name

Claire Smith

Name of claimant's legal representative's firm

Root Anderson & Co

If signing on behalf of firm or company give position or office held

Director

Claimant's or claimant's legal representative's address to which documents should be sent.

Building and street (13)

6 Castle Hill

Second line of address

Town or city

Newark

County (optional)

Nottinghamshire

Postcode

N	G	2	4	2	A	E

If applicable

Phone number

DX number

Your Ref.

Email

Find out how HM Courts and Tribunals Service uses personal information you give them when you fill in a form: https://www.gov.uk/government/organisations/hm-courts-and-tribunals-service/about/personal-information-charter

IN THE COUNTY COURT MONEY CLAIMS CENTRE (1)

(2) Claim No. 52Q 24368

BETWEEN

FILBERT ENGINEERING LIMITED

Claimant

-and- (3)

CITY EXPORTS LIMITED

Defendant

DEFENCE (4)

1. Paragraph 1 is admitted. (5)

2. Paragraph 2 is admitted. The tools that were provided, however, did not correspond to the sample that was shown to the Defendants on 22 December 2019, prior to entering into the contract. This is in breach of s15 Sale of Goods Act 1979. Despite requesting that the Claimant replace the tools with those that match the agreed specification, the Claimant has not done so. (6)

3. Paragraph 3 is denied for the reasons outlined in Paragraph 2. (7)

Statement of Truth (8)

I believe that the facts stated in this defence are true. I understand that proceedings for contempt may be brought against anyone who makes, or causes to be made, a false statement in a document verified by a statement of truth without an honest belief in its truth.

Signed: (to be inserted)
Name: (to be inserted) Position/office held: (to be inserted)
Dated: (to be inserted)

INDEX